PRAY TODAY'S GOSPEL

Reflections on the Day's Good News

(for Personal, Family, and Homiletic use)

by

Rev. Bernard C. Mischke, O.S.C.

and

Rev. Fritz Mischke, O.S.C.

ALBA · HOUSE 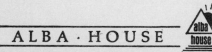 NEW · YORK

SOCIETY OF ST. PAUL, 2187 VICTORY BLVD., STATEN ISLAND, NEW YORK 10314

1

Library of Congress Cataloging in Publication Data

Mischke, Bernard C.
   Pray Today's Gospel.

   1. Devotional calenders——Catholic Church.
I. Mischke, Fritz, joint author. II. Title.
BX2170.C55M57   242'.2   80-14186
ISBN 0-8189-0403-8

Nihil Obstat:
Ernest Martello, O.S.C.
Censor Deputatus

Imprimi Potest:
Daniel Davidson, O.S.C.
Provincial

Nihil Obstat:
David A. Dillon, S.T.D.
Censor Liborum

Imprimatur:
†John R. Roach, D.D.
Archbishop of St. Paul and Minneapolis
August 15, 1979

The Nihil Obstat and Imprimatur are
a declaration that a book or pamphlet is considered
to be free from doctrinal or moral error. It it is not implied
that those who have granted the Nihil Obstat and
Imprimatur agree with the contents,
opinions or statements expressed.

Designed, printed and bound in the United States of
America by the Fathers and Brothers of the
Society of St. Paul, 2187 Victory Boulevard,
Staten Island, New York 10314, as part of their
communications apostolate.

1 2 3 4 5 6 7 8 9 (Current Printing: first digit).

INTRODUCTION

"Pray Today's Gospel" offers a reflection on each passage of the Gospels as it appears in the new Catholic Lectionary for each weekday of the year. The Good News of Jesus, as it comes to us in each of the readings, deserves to be reflected upon. It is important that we listen carefully to what the Lord is telling us in each reading.

We suggest that you begin by reading the day's Gospel passage from your Bible. The particular Gospel, chapter and verses are given herein for each weekday. Then after reading and reflecting on the passage, you may find our day's meditation helpful. We try to apply the Gospel to our daily Christian living.

Preachers of the Word may find our reflections useful in giving the daily homily on the Gospel. But all of us, all who want to be disciples of Jesus, need to meditate on these Gospel passages over and over.

The Word of Jesus in the Good News also calls for a response on our part. That's why we call this volume "Pray Today's Gospel." To "pray the Gospel" is to communicate with God, to respond to our Savior by thinking over His message in our hearts and applying it to the way we live. Thus we come to know Jesus, to experience Him, and to love Him for what He is, giving Him the first place in our life.

Frequently in this book we offer the beginning of a prayer of response to the Gospel reading and meditation. It is important to note that our "prayer response" is only a beginning. Sometimes it is a response from a Psalm or liturgical prayer-poem of the Church. We need to respond to the saving action of Jesus as individuals and as members of the Christian community. The response is not so much in words as in the inner movements of the heart. The words are but the signs of the deeper reality.

It is our prayer that all our readers will benefit greatly from this volume. May it deepen your knowledge and appreciation of the Gospel message, so that you may experience ever more the Person of Jesus and the joy of the Good News He brings us.

A note about the arrangement of this book. After the Advent and Christmas seasons, the weeks of the year are used until the beginning of Lent, Ash Wednesday. (These weeks are found after the Lenten and Easter seasons.)

After the Easter season (which ends with Pentecost) you resume the weeks of the year. This varies from year to year, but the weeks continue where they were interrupted by the Lenten and Easter seasons. A Catholic calendar will indicate for you on Sundays which week of the year is current.

Fr. Bernard and Fr. Fritz

TABLE OF CONTENTS

LENT AND EASTER

WEEKS OF THE YEAR

Reflections on the Day's Good News

PRAY TODAY'S GOSPEL
Reflections on the Day's Good News

TRUST ME

The pagan officer tells Jesus, "I am not worthy to have you under my roof. Just give an order and my boy will get better."

Jesus says, "I assure you, I have never found this much faith in Israel."

Faith, or trust, means really leaving things in the hands of the person you trust. The officer does just that. Rather than pressuring Jesus to come down to his house to "see what you can do for my boy," he at once places full confidence in Jesus: "Just give an order, and my boy will get well."

Jesus recognizes real faith here, and He recommends it to us:

1) Don't get up tight and worried when you pray. You are not the healer: I am, says Jesus. Be like this trusting Roman officer who knows what I need; just give an order and his prayer is heard.

2) Don't feel the Lord's reputation is at stake if all your requests are not heard at once. The officer says, "For I, too, am a man subject to authority." That authority has the power and the wisdom to make his own decisions. Is not the Lord the Final Authority? Can you not trust Him completely then?

3) You are called to trust in the Lord all the way, no matter what seems to be happening. And what happens if you hesitate—and hold back your trust? Your life will be full of troubles, most of which will never happen. You will spend your days in anxiety and worry, and you will leave this world in fear and dread.

But your trusting faith is the wellspring of happiness, the secret of the victorious life, the cornerstone of the triumphant spirit. "Trust me," says Jesus, as he said to the believing officer. "Go home, and what you believe in, what you trust in, will be done for you."

> **Send out Your faithful truth and light,**
> **and lead me to Your dwelling place,**
> **Up to your lofty mountain's height,**
> **where I may see You face to face.**
> **In God my strength I place my hope,**
> **and thank His name forevermore!**
> **For in His presence I shall live,**
> **my God, whose greatness I adore! (Ps 43).**

4

WHY LIVE?

First Week of Advent, Tuesday   **Luke 10:21-24**

Jesus says, "I praise you, Father." How often do we stop to think that a life which does not praise God is a life wasted? No tragedy can be so great as a life empty of God. Really, if we are Christians at all, what does it matter whether we are rich or poor, healthy or sick, remembered or forgotten, exalted or humiliated—so long as our actions are praising God?

The famous musician, Bruno Walter, had conducted the New York Philharmonic Symphony Orchestra in an afternoon of Anton Bruckner's music. At intermission time he was asked by interviewers, "Which do you think is the best of Bruckner's musical compositions?"

Bruno Walter answered, "His *Te Deum*, of course."

"What is the greatness you feel or see in Bruckner's *Te Deum*?" they asked.

"It is so Catholic," he answered.

Somewhat puzzled, they asked, "What do you mean?"

"Well," said the great conductor, "It *belongs* in the Church: it is Bruckner's whole life. It is sincere praise of God; it was his whole effort, like the birds singing in the morning. All he ever wanted to do with his music was praise God."

Such music indeed is "Catholic" and "belongs in the Church." If Bruno Walter's statement is right, then here is a musician who has caught the spirit of Jesus when He praises the Father "full of joy in the Holy Spirit."

> Lord, I sing with grateful voice,
> Your great deeds are my delight!
> Lord, I love your dwelling place,
> Bathed in pure and perfect light!
> Save my life from blood and strife,
> Keep me safe from sinner's sight (Ps 26).

MAKE ROOM

First Week of Advent, Wednesday   **Is 25:6-10; Mt 15:29-37**

Isaiah is the prophet of Advent because his vision of the Lord's coming is truly inspired. Speaking of the banquet which the Lord will prepare for all peoples, he foresees that the Lord will destroy "the web that is woven over all nations, he will destroy death forever. The Lord God will wipe away the tears from all faces."

See the remarkable pledge of fulfillment given by Jesus in the Gospel. Here on a mountainside (Isaiah's mountain of the Lord), the cripples, the deformed, the blind and the mute are brought to Jesus, and He cures them all. The Lord has come to wipe away the tears, to restore lost souls, to heal our weaknesses.

Now Jesus sees before him a vast crowd with no food. They must indeed be hungry, for in Mark's Gospel we are told they have been with Him three days, and there is good reason for Jesus to say, "they may collapse on the way." Their food has been the Lord's own words, His saving message. It must indeed have been inspiring, to keep them three days. Has any sermon in our time kept a crowd that long?

This crowd has learned somehow that "no one who waits for the Lord will be disappointed." Jesus rewards them with a multiplication of loaves and fishes that more than satisfies them all, for seven baskets of leftovers are filled. Without realizing it, perhaps, these people have learned to make room for their redemption. They have given Jesus an opportunity to act on their behalf. They have made themselves poor, hungry, for Him, and He has not disappointed them.

What opportunity do we give the Lord? Will we so block His way with Christmas parties, expensive gifts, and elaborate externals, that He will again find no room among us? How sweet and pretty are the ornaments of Christmas—as we have fashioned them, not as Jesus brought them. He brought His poverty, and kept it so all His life: the Gospels will not let us forget. He emptied Himself, from manger to cross, and how we try to cover it up! Just what meaning will Christmas have for us? Will there be any Christ left in it?

Jesus, let me see my poverty, so that I can be open to receive your riches.

SOLID FOOTINGS

First Week of Advent, Thursday   **Matthew 7:21, 24-27**

Jesus says, "Anyone who hears these words of mine and obeys them is like a wise man who built his house on rock. The rain poured down, the rivers flooded over, and the wind blew hard against that house. But it did not fall, because it was built on rock." Then Jesus contrasts it with the foolish man who built his house in the lowlands where the rain came and the river flooded and washed it away.

In today's terms, Jesus is speaking of building on high ground, safe from destroying floods. So if you want to build for permanence, for success that stands the winds of the world and the corruption of time, you need solid footings. Or else your structure caves in. Here are four solid footings on the high ground, Jesus, so that His word will not be washed out of our hearts by the world's flood of garbage.

1) Personal Prayer, our life-line to God. In the Gospels we see Jesus regularly "recharging his power" by going off alone to pray. Prayer is the union of two loves: my love with God's love. No matter what important jobs I have, the most important time of my day is that personal time I spend with the Lord.

2) That leads us to our second footing: Faith—absolute trust in Jesus. Trust is real: it shows that our love for God is real. How often are we called upon to express our love by giving up our life for it—as Jesus did? But we *are* often called upon to trust in the Lord. If we truly know Him by experience of Him, we can trust Him.

3) Daily Bible reading: the mind and heart of God is there. The Bible is God's love letter to you and me. God's Word is alive and active. He speaks to us: and how much we need to listen! After your prayer-time or Bible-reading time, write down the thoughts that come to you. You'll be surprised to see what you are gaining—what the Lord is teaching you.

4) Community sharing: no one is an island. A community is a network of committed relationships, in which we help one another to live in the Lord. If it isn't there, the Lord may be calling you to get it started. We need that energy-field of faith, from which we can draw daily power.

Jesus says, "Where two or three are gathered together in My Name, I am there in their midst" (Mt 18:20).

HE DARED TO BE DIFFERENT

First Week of Advent, Friday **Matthew 9:27-31**

Jesus works great signs, but keeps saying, "See that no one knows of this." How different from the "saviors" of our day! To save the world! "What an operation," says the ambitious man of the hour. "Why, he'll have to organize, gather lots of money, rally huge armies, hire a raft of officials and secretaries, contact all the important people; orchestras, megaphones, slogans, rousing speeches and big promises—all to stir up the public sentiment." After all, what had every king before Christ done to "win the world?" Wealth, military might, bloody wars of conquest, absolute power—these were essentials!

But Christ the King dared to be different. "See to it that no one hears of this!" The kingdom of God comes quietly—and only to those who of their own accord open the door to Him! He dared to defy the "apostles" of this world. "Blessed are the poor," he said. Not blessed are the power-hungry conquerors, but "Blessed are the meek, for *they* shall possess the land." Not, blessed are they who succeed by promising and deceiving and betraying and enslaving people, but "Blessed are those who suffer persecution for justice's sake for theirs is the kingdom of heaven."

Surely You could have chosen power, position, wealth and influence, Lord. You could have impressed the millions with your might; You could have turned the very sun and stars out of their courses, so that a cry of fear and amazement would have swept over the earth. But You lived a simple life of prayer and work and love and sacrifice in hidden simplicity.

This is the striking fact of Christmas: Christ the King shocking the world, awaking the world at last to true greatness.

> "As I am your Father and your Friend,
> Now have I become your Brother too!
> Love we one another to the end:
> Give yourself, as I gave all for you."

THE TOUCH OF JESUS

First Week of Advent, Saturday **Matthew 9:35-10:1, 6-8**

Jesus told his disciples, "As you go, make this announcement: 'The reign of God is at hand! Cure the sick, raise the dead, heal the leprous, expel demons."

Each one of us needs direct human contact with the power and the love of God. We are human, and we need to see things happen and feel them happen: we need to experience God! To take care of this need, Jesus already in His public life began sending out disciples to bring His personal touch, his healing to the people (cf. Lk 10:1, 9).

To continue taking care of this need, Jesus established a Church with apostles and disciples to go out and bring this intimate touch of His loving forgiveness and healing to anyone who wanted it.

From Pentecost Day on, these men did so, and with great success and power, as we can read in chapter after chapter of the Acts of the Apostles.

This special personal contact of Jesus with you and me we call the Sacraments. They are channels through which God's powerful life flows into us. You and I need to hear the forgiving words of Jesus, we need to feel the touch of His powerful love, we need to see the Bread of Life which He promised us, we need to know at this moment we are truly meeting Jesus face to face.

When Jesus said, "I am with you always, even to the end of the world," He meant to say more than merely, "I hope you all come to hear about me." Rather He meant, "I will remain with you as a personal friend and close companion, as your Father and Brother, as your nearest one to be with you in all your needs, to be present to you in a way that you can truly meet me face to face, that you will touch me and hear me and see me, that you will feel the touch of my healing and the embrace of my love."

Born for us of purest Virgin, our companion Christ could be;
Word of God came down to teach us, lived among such men as we,
Met at final Paschal Supper with His chosen company.
There the Word made Flesh was given: banquet of the promised Bread!

Cup of wine He blessed and told them: "Take My Blood, which
shall be shed."
So with us He lives forever: man with Bread of Life is fed ("Pange
Lingua").

HE WANTS US HEALED

Second Week of Advent, Monday   **Luke 5:17-26**

Luke says, "Jesus was teaching, and the Power of the Lord made
Him heal." Jesus wants all His people to live a happy, joyous life.
Therefore He wants us healed of anything that saddens or depresses
us, obstacles that make it impossible to love. He wants us to live a
victorious Christian life, right in the devil's back yard! Jesus holds
this power out to us, but often we don't receive it, because we don't
even believe it's there! We don't really expect to receive good things or
great things from God, and so we don't receive them. We close the
door on the greatest and most powerful doctor, Jesus, the eternal
healer.

What we need is a conviction, a trust, a confidence that Jesus lives
right now, right here, with all the same power to heal that He had in
the Gospels. If we really had that full, expectant faith, if we really put
our life in His hands, as Matthew, Zacheus, and their converted
sinner-friends did, Jesus could work just as powerfully in each of us.
He could really change us, He could make the dullest life sparkle, He
can change the worst sinner into the happiest Christian saint. He can
make the saddest person joyful and the sickest person healthy, as He
has done thousands of times.

But our trouble is, we don't really believe that. We don't think
God loves us personally enough to do that for us as individuals. But
we're wrong. He does! Yet, until we *know* He does, and are fully
convinced of His personal love for us, we are not ready to receive His
powerful gifts.

> Come, Holy Spirit, open our eyes and our minds to the
> great potential in God's love for each of us. Jesus

quoted in reference to Himself what You had inspired
Isaiah to write of Him:
"The spirit of the Lord upon me rests,
Because the Lord, my God, anointed me,
He sent me with glad tidings for the poor,
With strength to bring the captive liberty,
With sympathy to heal the broken heart,
Announce a year of favor and award,
Proclaim the loving kindness of the Lord" (Is 61:1-3).

THE QUALITY OF MERCY

Second Week of Advent, Tuesday   **Matthew 18:12-14**

This parable's description of God's mercy has overwhelming
power and beauty. The theme of divine mercy is like a Shakespearean
song that pictures mercy so high above the supreme power of kings as
to be truly divine. God, who has nothing and no one to fear is richest
in mercy, and thus it is in him totally unselfish, totally free, totally
beautiful.

The quality of mercy is not strain'd;
It droppeth as the gentle rain from heaven
Upon the place beneath; it is twice blest;
It blesseth him that gives, and him that takes:
'Tis mightiest in the mightiest: it becomes
The throned monarch better than his crown;
His sceptre shows the force of temporal power,
The attribute to awe and majesty,
Wherein doth sit the dread and fear of kings;
But mercy is above this sceptred sway;
It is enthroned in the hearts of kings,
It is an attribute to God himself;
And earthly power doth then show likest God's
When mercy seasons justice. Therefore, Jew,
Though justice be thy plea, consider this—

That in the course of justice, none of us
Should see salvation: we do pray for mercy;
And that same prayer doth teach us all to render
The deeds of mercy (*Merchant of Venice*, Act IV).

In man, mercy is greater than power. In God, it is all one. Yet if it is humanly possible to speak of a greater in God, it must seem that His mercy is more striking than His power, or even that His mercy *is* His greatest power. His power would never have created me, were it not for His infinite mercy. Had anyone rebelled against me with half the ingratitude I have toward God, I would long ago have used my power against the culprit. It surely seems that God's mercy holds back His power.

Lord, I deserve so little, You so much; I have so little mercy, You have so much. Why is that, Lord? How true that mercy is mightiest in the mightiest!

COFFEE BREAK

Second Week of Advent, Wed.   **Is 40:25-31; Mt 11:28-30**

Today's readings sound like a call for Mid-Advent Coffee Break. Isaiah sees that the Lord "gives strength to the fainting." He finds that "hope in the Lord" is what renews strength. Jesus in the Gospel invites us to come to Him if we are weary and find life burdensome, and He will refresh us.

Coffee break: we look forward to it, we appreciate it, we need it. We thrive on that occasional rest from work, the refreshment that restores us and makes our work better. Can we ever be too busy to stop for spiritual refreshment? Jesus says, "Slow down and listen a while," and your soul will find rest.

We place too much emphasis on merely "doing things," rushing from job to job, from promotion to promotion. Or, if we are more charitable, we are absorbed with the rush to solve social problems. This may be good, if it does not become subject to "overkill." The best of work, if it leaves no time for spiritual refreshment, for prayer and silent reflection, will eventually become sterile.

Dedication needs a sense of direction. The finest works of charity, the best in Christian action cannot survive without the spiritual coffee-break. We are never beyond the need for divine direction on this earth. It is altogether too easy to lose your way, as too many sad personal histories can tell.

It is wisest to stop regularly, to take out those refreshing minutes with Christ, who promised that we would learn from Him, and that He would bring peace to our souls.

"The Lord said to his people: Stand at the crossroads and look. Ask for the ancient paths, and where the best road is. Walk in it, and there you will find rest for your souls" (Jr 6:16).

NO ONE IS GREATER

Second Week of Advent, Thursday   **Matthew 11:11-15**

The Gospels tell us a good deal about John the Baptist. He is a saint who received that honor from Christ Himself. For Jesus said, "Of all men born, there is none greater than John the Baptist." John was a man of strong character and austere penance. Jesus said, "What did you go out in the desert to see? A man in soft garments? A reed shaken by the wind?"

John was a man worthy of his important mission. He was a man in every way suited for his task of preparing the way for the Lord. He was the first prophet Israel had seen for a long time, and thousands went out in the desert to hear him. He spoke with power and magnetism. He spoke boldly of repentance and return to God, and he was himself an inspiring example of penance and devotion to God.

John introduced a symbolic rite of cleansing. Baptism, which stirred his followers to a desire for moral purification. John's teaching was impressive: he had a way of going straight to essentials. He preached plainly a change of heart, a spiritual reform in men's hearts, so that they could make room for the coming of the great Redeemer. To his listeners he gave concrete examples: soldiers, be content with your pay and honest with one another; tax-collectors, be just and incorruptible—you need not quit your job if you are honest in it; to all his listeners: charity—he who has two coats, give one to a man who has none at all; he who has food, share with the needy. John's teachings were full of common sense and practical wisdom.

John's language was firm and severe, and yet it revealed a man of profound humility. Even Herod could not help respecting him, though John sternly rebuked Herod for his murders and adultery.

Among all his excellent qualitites, what impresses us most about John the Baptist is his deep humility. His success never went to his head; he clearly realized the limits of his mission: he was preparing the way for Someone else. Someone greater. "He must increase, I must decrease," John said with deep sincerity.

Dear Lord, are we so clear and so honest about our mission in life?

PLEASE EVERYBODY?

Second Week of Advent, Friday   **Matthew 11:16-19**

Have you ever wanted to be a great acrobat, fabulous magician and a miracle worker? Did you give up that dream as impractical or impossible? But why did you give it up? Don't you know that if you want to be a good Christian or a good pagan, and at the same time be one of the crowd, please everybody, and be constantly popular, why, you'll have to be all those things: an acrobat, magician, and miracle worker!

You'll have to be able to stand on your head and your feet and your hands, all at the same time. You'll have to be able to say yes and no to everything and everyone at the same time. You'll have to blow hot and cold and lukewarm at one and the same time, so as to please everybody from every point of view.

We piped you a tune, but you did not dance!
We sang you a dirge, but you did not wail!

In this humorous and satiric Gospel passage, the Lord offers "consolation" to anyone who tries to please God and "the crowd" at the same time. To those who want God and riches at the same time, to those who want God's approval but can never say no to the "gang," Jesus says with a smile, "No acrobat has ever done it." In fact, you must have noticed that the Son of God Himself never succeeded in performing that contradiction.

It has been said often enough, there is one sure rule for failure: try pleasing everyone.

It's a lot less frustrating to get our priorities in order. Try putting God first, and notice the back-breaking gymnastics you can avoid, notice the two-faced double-talk you can do without, notice the solid back-bone that begins to form, right where you need it.

Jesus, let me put my house in order by seeking Your Will, first and last. You are the only audience I need to please. I can trust Your Will for me, since Your Love for me is complete and unlimited.

CHRISTMAS SPIRIT

Second Week of Advent, Saturday   **Matthew 17:10-13**

Jesus tells his disciples how the people and their leaders failed to recognize John the Baptist or the Son of God Himself. Isn't that the way we also spend our season of reform—not recognizing the Lord? The Roman martyrs, those persecuted Christians of the catacombs, knew more of the true Christmas spirit than our modern tinsel-hangers and gift wrappers, who might more honestly be celebrating the "birth of big business" than the Birth of Jesus. Those heroic Roman Christians inscribed their Christmas message in the catacombs, where it remains today for us to read: "If you would understand the spirit of the birthday of Christ the Lord, you must give in the spirit of Christ the Lord." He gave everything; He gave His very self. There is the secret of happiness, of freedom, of Christmas.

If you do not give but only take, selfishly wrapped up in yourself, you will wither and dry; you cannot grow by feeding on yourself; rather, you will become smaller and smaller. God gave us this universe to grow in, to expand ourselves by giving to others.

This was the conquest of the Christians in the catacombs: they were feared and hated, but they gave love. They were unjustly persecuted, but they brought the gift of conversion and redemption. They were happy, because they had found life; so they grew, expanded, and conquered the world, not by the sword but by the tree of life, the Cross. They truly knew the joy of Christmas, because they "gave in the spirit of Christ the Lord."

> **Glory for ages to come**
> **To Christ whose friendship we crave:**
> **Lord of the worlds has become**
> **Child of the poor in a cave!**
> **Smallest of small He will save,**
> **He among kings the one King,**
> **Came down to live as our slave!**
> **To His example we cling:**
> **Born for us, servant and king!**

A QUESTION OF AUTHORITY

Third Week of Advent, Monday   **Matthew 21:23-27**

The Pharisees had already shown their hatred of Jesus openly, and sought a way to capture Him and have Him executed. They were held back only by fear; Jesus was as yet too popular with the people; they would have to discredit Him first, or else catch Him secretly and have Him done away with before the public found out about it.

Meanwhile Jesus taught openly in the temple and on the streets still striving to make the people understand that He was truly the promised Redeemer and Son of God. One morning in the temple court the Pharisees openly attacked Jesus by demanding that He tell them where He got His authority. Jesus promised to tell them, if they would answer *His* question: "Where did John the Baptist get his authority?"

This the Pharisees were too cowardly to answer; Jesus had cornered them. If they said that John's authority was from God, Jesus would answer, "Then why did you refuse to believe him?" If they said it was not from God, the people would stone them for slandering John. So they said, "We don't know."

Jesus was not satisfied with this hypocritical answer. If they were cowards, He was not. He pursued the question of His authority by telling them a story which unveiled their sin. The owner of a vineyard had sent messengers to his employees, demanding that they pay him what they owed from the revenue of his vineyard. When the evil servants killed his messengers, he sent his own son, saying to himself, "Surely, they will respect my own son." But he soon received the shocking news that the workers had killed his son, too. What was he to do?

The Pharisees, many of whom owned their own vineyards and demanded revenues aplenty, did not hesitate to say that these workers should be executed, and the vineyard should be rented to others who would pay their debts on time.

"You are right," said Jesus. "I tell you, then, that the kingdom of God will be taken away from you, and given to a people who yield the revenues that belong to it" (Mt 21:33-46).

What of us, Lord? You know well enough how their

faults are our faults, and how much like their false standards ours are, and what poor builders of the kingdom of God we have become!

TALK OR ACT?

Third Week of Advent, Tuesday   **Matthew 21:28-32**

What is Jesus talking about in this parable? About playing games with God, making head trips, talking faith, hope and love, but living mistrust, depression and resentment. Saying, "Lord, I trust in You for everything," but actually doing my own "thing," making my own decisions and then "twisting God's arm" to make Him see it all my way—where does such a life lead me? Not to His Kingdom, says Jesus.

There is so much "Sunday morning Christianity," a mentality that gives one hour to God (supposedly) and keeps all the other 167 hours of the week for self. How can this be following Jesus, who demands that we die to sin and self and build our life on God's Will alone? "Not everyone who says to me 'Lord, Lord' will enter my kingdom, but only those who do my Father's will."

At the end of today's Gospel, Jesus says there is no entering the Kingdom of God unless we "repent and believe." We repent when we make a firm decision to abandon all sin and begin to act on that decision. We believe when we accept Jesus as the total Lord of all life. To the degree that we do really repent and believe, to the degree that we truly release more and more areas of our life to Jesus, we are like the son who actually did the Father's will.

Otherwise we are like the son who says, "Yes, Father," and does nothing about it. That person's faith is only in the head, and produces no fruit.

> **Break forth in joy and gladness,**
> **Rejoice, faint heart of sadness!**
> **Lord God, forgive my sin,**
> **Create new life within.**

Your presence keep before me,
A steadfast spirit grant me;
A willing heart be mine —
Of sorrow true the sign!
Your justice be my teaching,
My thoughts Your mercies reaching,
My heart, O God, I raise,
My soul must sing Your praise! (Ps 51).

GO AND REPORT

Third Week of Advent, Wednesday   Luke 7:18-23

"Go and report to John what you have seen and heard. The blind recover their sight, cripples walk, lepers are cured, the deaf hear, dead men are raised to life." Thus Jesus describes Himself to those who ask for John, "Are you 'He who is to come' or do we look for someone else?" Jesus is the Great Healer, the one whose presence and whose touch brings healing to those who ask Him.

Jesus in the Bread of Life is still the great Sacrament of Healing. He himself promised to heal us in His sacramental presence, the Bread of Life. "If anyone eats this bread, he will live forever. The bread that I will give him is my flesh, given for the life of the world. Whoever eats my flesh and drinks my blood has eternal life" (Jn 6:51, 54).

As Jesus healed people wherever He went, so He gave us the great Sacrament of Healing, to strengthen our spiritual, mental, emotional and physical health. The Church has always taught this, but we so easily forget. The very words of the Church that we say before receiving the Bread of Life are, "Lord, I am not worthy to receive you, but only say the word and I *shall be healed*."

The Saints understood very well the healing power of Jesus in the Eucharist. St. Teresa of Avila, sixteenth century foundress of the Reformed Carmelites, writes very openly about it. She tells her readers how many healings she herself has experienced from the Eucharist. And she explains: "Now if, when Christ was in the world, the sick were healed by merely touching His garments, how can we doubt that He will heal us when He is within us, if we have faith? The Lord does not pay cheaply for His lodging, if we show Him true hospitality!"

Lord Jesus, if I really welcome You in the Bread of Life, and place no obstacles in your way—to paraphrase Your words, offer You no stumbling block—how powerfully You will work in my life!

ONLY ONE BOAST

Third Week of Advent, Thursday   Luke 7:24-30

What is it that makes the Bible so unique a book? What sets God's people apart from all others? What is the distinctive thought of Hebrew literature? Precisely that it does not boast of Hebrew heroes. Other nations boasted of their patriots and kings and the victories they won. But Israel's literature is rather a long, sorrowful confession of the nation's guilt, of its spiritual weakness and senseless ingratitude, of a nation chosen and favored, but sad in its failure to measure up.

The sacred writers produced the most exalted hymns of praise, but all praise was kept for God. He alone had saved them, He alone had given them strength in battle, He alone had blessed their fields and vines, He alone brought them wisdom and purpose. This is the joyous cry of the martyrs and all the saints from Abraham to our own day, "The pagans praise themselves and their great deeds. But our glory is in the Lord our God; He alone is our pride."

All this may seem little more than a gymnastic with words. Far from it! Let anyone dare to *live* this difference, and what a change it will make in his life! Yes, merely to boast in God instead of one's self! What a new person it would make, what a changed attitude! St. Paul's own conversion and his new life as an apostle will illustrate what results this great Biblical secret is able to produce.

How well Jesus Himself put it: He praised John the Baptist in this way: "There is no man born of woman greater than John. Yet the least born into the kingdom of God is greater than he."

> **Jesus, which of us has anything to boast about—except what we have received from you? The truly great among us understand this, so with your saints we boast only about You, Lord, the most generous Giver.**

CHRISTMAS FOR LIFE

Third Week of Advent, Friday   **John 5:33-36**

When St. John the Baptist prepared his people for the coming of Christ, he spoke to them of justice and charity and the fear of God. He did not speak of buying the best gift and the latest in decorations. Whatever we buy, if Christ doesn't really live in us, there is no real Christmas; it is only an empty memorial and a wasted opportunity.

We become so lost in the external trimmings and so exhausted running from store to store to find bigger and bolder gifts that the real Christ is gone out of our Christmas. We would then be more honest to wish each other a "Merry Merchandise."

But if we have grasped the great truth of St. Paul that Christmas means putting on the mind and heart of Christ, then every Christmas is a real birth of Christ for us, and brings us ever closer to the ideal of Christian love and joy. Then our whole life becomes a perpetual Christmas, as our sins and vices die away, and beauty and strength of character grow and bloom.

If your friends and neighbors can see Christ acting through you and living in you, then you are Christian. When life is over, we will see that all else was useless. If Christ was truly born in you and remained in you, you have become a living Christmas for all eternity.

We were born into this world that we might grow into the perfection of our nature: that perfect person is Christ. In the goodness of Christ and by the example of Christ, we will find peace and joy, and only there. Peace on earth is for men of good will, men who seek God's will, for in His will is our peace.

Make your peace with God, then, and may that peace bear fruit. Begin to know Christ better and better, so that you may truly think and act like him.

Jesus, the very works that You performed testified that the Father had sent you. Do the works that I perform testify that You have sent me, too?

FEAR NOT, JOSEPH

December 18   **Matthew 1:18-24**

Which of the Saints has memories to compare with the glorious and intimate family stories that St. Joseph could tell us about Jesus? Jesus the little boy, Jesus the teenager, Jesus the young man, Jesus the strong, hard-working, obedient young carpenter. St. Joseph can walk up to the most glamorous and brilliant of Saints, look each of them in the eye and say, "You became famous because you gave your life over to the work of Jesus, the Savior of the world. But do you remember who trained that boy into manhood? Do you remember whose assistant Jesus was in the humble carpenter's trade? Do you remember who was Christ's teacher? Who answered all that bright little boy's questions?"

Yes, St. Joseph can listen to all the great theological discussions of the great saintly bishops and teachers of history, and say to them, "But *I* was the religion teacher of Jesus, your Lord and your God. Mary and I were His home and His family, His school and His instructors. What do you think of the job *we* did on our one and only child?" When it comes to fond memories of a happy and holy and significant life on earth, nobody has memories like St. Joseph!

Looking at all those colorful and flashy saints, with their glittering uniforms, Joseph can say, "Just paint me in dusty brown, in shabby work clothes, with my saw and hammer, on a floor of sawdust and shavings. No razzle-dazzle, no fanfare, no gilded robes or symbols."

But Joseph would have one request for that painting: one that would outscore the whole galaxy of heaven's saints. He would ask, "Just one request for my portrait, please! Would you mind putting my wife and my little boy on the painting? I just can't tell you about my life apart from those two I loved so dearly: my family—Mary and Jesus!"

The dawn of day calls forth the sun: all sleeping life has stirred,
And in the house of Nazareth a hammer's sound is heard.
The carpenter a skillful man, his helping hand a Boy:
See Joseph and the Son of God make honest work their joy.

TRUST HIM

December 19   **Luke 1:5-25**

The Angel Gabriel comes to Zechariah to announce the coming birth of a son, and is met with some anxiety, because Zechariah and Elizabeth are advanced in age. When that same angel announces the good news of a son to Mary, she is also surprised, because she is a virgin by choice.

However, there is a contrast here. Zechariah will remain mute till the birth of his son, says the angel, "because you have not trusted my words."

Mary receives no such reprimand. On the contrary, she is praised by Elizabeth: "Blessed is she who trusted that the Lord's words to her would be fulfilled."

From the very beginning of his "Good News," Luke tells us how we are to respond to that wonderful message of God's love: trust completely in the Lord.

How real is our trust in God? How convinced are we of His love for us in all circumstances? Do we have to wait until God's promise is fulfilled before we thank Him for it, as Zechariah did? He does come to faith and a spirit of joyful thanksgiving, but it seems he has to wait and see what the Lord will do.

Mary, the perfect daughter, the model Christian, needs no such proof. Her trust in the Lord is unquestioning. She praises God her Savior before the fact, since her faith in God's infinite love is constant and total.

> O Lord, my cup and my apportioned lot,
> My future days are safe within Your care;
> Prepared and measured is my earthly plot,
> I hold Your promise as a treasure rare.
> I praise the Lord, my guide, who counsels me,
> My heart will trust You in the dead of night;
> I will not fear, for You encircle me,
> Before my eyes You live in fullest light (Ps 16).

GOD'S CHOSEN ONE

December 20   **Luke 1:26-38**

Many of us think we have a right to be made happy, as though it were everyone else's duty to brighten our day by doing exactly what our feelings desire.

If anything is clear to us in Holy Scripture, it is this: those whom God loved best were surrounded by sorrows and trials and even great tragedies. And yet they were deeply happy; they spoke and sang of their joys. They praised God and thanked Him for the very things that many of us would complain about bitterly.

Mary, the Mother of Jesus, led a life of unglamorous poverty. God had promised her His grace; she would be the Mother of the world's Redeemer, but this would bring her no personal wealth or earthly favors, no assurance of the world's honors and attentions. Indeed, when she brought her child to the temple, the old man Simeon prophesied that her soul would be pierced by the sword of suffering.

When the angel's joyful news came to her, "You shall bear a son, and he shall save his people from their sins," Mary accepted willingly, saying that she was the servant of God. But she spent no time congratulating herself on making demands of God or neighbor.

Rather, she thought of others. Her cousin Elizabeth was with child in her advanced years. So Mary made the long trip and spent three months in the service of Elizabeth and Zechariah. Like Mary, those of us who will ever experience true joy must find it within ourselves. No one else can give it to you—but if you really want it, it is available from God, who promised it to those who search for it.

> I praise the Lord with joy eternally,
> My heart I lift to God like clouds above:
> For with salvation's robe He vested me,
> He wrapped me in the mantle of His love!
> A bride bedecked with jewels, God I praise!
> The earth brings forth its fruit at His command.
> As garden grows and thrives through sunlit days,
> So God makes justice flourish from His hand. (Is 61:10-11)

VIRGIN AND MOTHER

December 21   **Luke 1:39-45**

Deep within every good woman is a desire for the qualities of both a virgin and a mother. She wants a meaningful purity, both physically and spiritually: a purity of mind, heart, and will. She desires to be a mother, that is, to give life. A mother gives life physically, but even more, spiritually, by giving life its value, by giving meaning and purpose and encouragement to others.

These two images or ideals, virgin and mother, are not contradictory but complimentary in the character of woman. They manifest the two tendencies of the human personality: self-containment—holding oneself faithful to one, and self-abandonment—giving oneself away for many others. Both of these qualities taken together make up the ideal of woman.

God realized this ideal perfectly in one person: His mother, Mary. She was both virgin and mother in every sense, physical as well as spiritual. God calls every woman to be spiritually both virgin and a mother, regardless of her state of life: married, single, or religious.

See these beautiful feminine virtues in both Mary and Elizabeth as they meet. See how they have held themselves open to God. How joyfully they have accepted the opportunities of their life. How they have treasured God's inspirations in the silence of their own hearts, and how they have given of their best to others.

How beautiful is a woman who combines these precious qualities! Happy is she who keeps safe her gift of wisdom and sanity, her trust, her ability to understand and to sympathize. She is then ready to respect others, to support them, to have compassion. She has the ingenuity to bring everything to its most useful, fruitful, lovely and precious purpose.

> **"Blessed are you, Mary, for you trusted that the Lord's words to you would be fulfilled."**

THE FIRST CHRISTIAN

December 22   **Luke 1:46-56**

The first and best of Christians is Mary, the Mother of Christ. She was the first to receive God's call to redemption in His Son, and her response to that call was joyous and complete and lifelong. She is the Christian model of wholehearted response to God's word. That is why we ask her help in answering the call to life in Christ. It is because of her willing reply that now we, too, are privileged to be invited to share the riches of God.

Mary replied to God with joy: she sang her praise and thanksgiving. "My soul proclaims the greatness of the Lord; my spirit finds joy in God my Savior." We ask to share in her optimism, the joy of all who are confident in Christ.

Mary was the first Christian to receive Christ. No one has known and loved the Savior as she has. Her role is to lead us to the same love; her example inspires us to the same eagerness to listen and obey and love. When a grateful listener praised the mother who had borne and nursed the Messiah, Jesus replied, "Rather, blessed are those who hear the word of God and keep it." These words increased tenfold the praise that had been given to Mary. For of all people who ever heard or would hear the word of God and keep it, Mary was the greatest.

Mary was the first great Christian teacher. In Hebrew life the parents were the principal teachers. Hence Mary and Joseph were the teachers from which Jesus received His human wisdom and learning. When Mary said "Yes" to God's plan, she agreed to become both the Mother and the Teacher of Jesus Christ our Savior. Thus the importance of her place in our salvation.

"Blessed are you among women, Mary, and blessed is the fruit of your womb, Jesus."

Hail to Mary, guiding star! Gate of heaven, full of grace! Virgin Mother of the Lord, come to save our fallen race. How beautiful she is to see, where grace and love is stored: Delight and joy you bring to me, great Mother of the Lord!

JOY AND PRAISE

December 23   **Luke 1:57-66**

In this passage from the first chapter of Luke's Gospel we find a theme that keeps appearing again and again throughout the writing of St. Luke. "Rejoiced" and "praised God" are the theme words here. Note the response of Elizabeth's neighbors and relatives to the birth of her son: "Hearing that the Lord had extended His mercy to her, they rejoiced with her."

Luke has already told us how Elizabeth praised Mary for trusting in the Lord. Now Elizabeth shows her own trust in God's word by saying, contrary to friends and relatives, "The boy shall be called John."

Luke told us that Zechariah had been struck dumb because he had not trusted in the Lord's message. But now Zechariah obeys the

Lord's word without hesitation. All the relatives and neighbors say, "Name the son after his father." This surely would have been a source of pride to the father, it would have been traditional, and it would have pleased the relatives!

But Zechariah obeys the angel's command, "You shall name him John." This response to God's word loosens the father's tongue, and he, too, begins "to speak in praise of God."

What Luke is teaching us here is this: if we are God's people, we accept God's word, and we rejoice in the wisdom of God's plan. Luke thus connects obedience and trust in the Lord with rejoicing and praising God. They are the right response to God in our lives!

Luke shows us this: Elizabeth, Zechariah, Mary and Joseph, the shepherds, Simeon and Anna—and later, John the Baptist and Jesus: these are the poor of the Lord, the holy ones who are empty of pride and self-will; they have opened the way for God to work in their lives. God in turn fills them with the Holy Spirit, who inspires them to rejoice and praise God for the wonderful things He does! This teaching runs throughout Luke's Gospel, so that his is called the Gospel of joy and praise!

Lord, let this message of Luke speak powerfully to our lives, as You intended!

PREPARE THE WAY

December 24   **Luke 1:67-79**

"You, child, shall be called prophet of the most High; you shall go before the Lord to prepare a straight path for him."

Zechariah speaks of his son, and we cannot help thinking of that fiery young man who later lived in a rocky wasteland, browned by exposure to sun and weather, a man lean and strong and muscular, wearing a rough camel-skin. "He went over all the country around the Jordan, announcing a baptism of repentance for the forgiveness of sins, as it is written in the prophet Isaiah: the voice of one crying in the wilderness: prepare the way of the Lord, straighten out his paths.

Every valley shall be filled, and every mountain and hill shall be lowered, the crooked shall be made straight, the rough paths made smooth, and all mankind shall see the saving power of God" (Lk 3:3-6).

Roads were cleared and widened for the arrival of the great king. Indeed the great king arrived! But were the people prepared for that king? St. Gregory the Great observes that the Lord's own country could not have been less prepared for its reckoning. Materially, while the Roman empire had one ruler, tiny Palestine had four! Spiritually, they had no part with him. "He came to His own, and His own did not receive Him." They gave him no welcome.

Blessed are those whose hearts are prepared to receive their God—those who make straight the way of God into their lives.

Lord, when You come to me in the Sacrament of Yourself, You will be stumbling over missing floorboards in my soul, but You will see the house under repair. And I know that *You* will have to do the repair work, filling the holes, and cleaning out the filth and dirt. But if I may be so informal, I remember that You were a carpenter, and that all these centuries You have come to Your people and have swept out and remodelled houses in the most appalling condition!

WHERE IS JESUS?

Feast of Christmas   **December 25**

"Before the Lord's presence let the whole earth bow in reverence," the psalmist sings. "Tell the nations, the Lord is King, he has put the world in order, nevermore to be thrown into confusion" (Ps 96).

"He has put the world in order," by shocking us all in the manner of His coming. The world expected a dazzling spectacle, exterior pomp and might, because it forgot that the true power lay in the love of God.

"He has put the world in order," by despising materialistic

From Jesus to you . . .

By Father John Reedy

Christmas columns are hard to do.

Everything seems to have been said — so many times that even our most sincere and personal messages slide into familiar formulas about the joy of Christmas . . . happiness for you and yours . . . at Christmas and throughout the year.

So, I tried to imagine what Jesus might write if he were sitting at this typewriter, addressing his thoughts not to a "mass audience," but directly to you, to the faith which should be at the center of all your Christmas celebration.

He might write:

My brother . . . my sister:
I know that for you these days are hectic, full of pressure to complete all the details on time. There's frustration in wanting to express your love in gifts for those who are closest to you . . . and finding yourself again expressing that love in gifts of clothing or household items which don't really say what you want them to say.

I understand the strange mixture of happiness — at all the sounds and sights of a festive season — and strained nerves and irritation at having too much to do in too little time.

And I also understand the slight sense of guilt which lies deep in your heart as you feel that you should be giving more time and thought to the real, religious meaning of Christmas. But there never seems enough time; there's always something else that needs to be done.

I don't want you to feel guilty about this — especially at this time. I want you to enjoy the happiness of your family gathering, the warmth of friendships remembered.

Our God, our Father wanted you to know that he understands and accepts all these human emotions, efforts, frustrations. His sign of that understanding and acceptance was my own coming to be one with all your human experiences.

But most of all I hope you will be able to experience some of that profound joy and relief that should fill your life as you grasp the truth I came to reveal.

You know the joy, the sense of worth that comes from recognizing that another human being — a man, woman or child — really loves you. My coming was to give you that same joy, that same sense of worth, at a much more profound level. I came to offer the evidence of how deeply the God of the universe loves and cares for you.

Our Father's love for each of us is mysterious. At times it is very hard for you to believe that the creator of the sun and the stars loves you personally — when He allows your life to be marked with pain and suffering, especially when he allows you to fail, to sin.

And your world today also makes it difficult for you to recognize the Father's love. You see a world scarred with poverty, with violence, with economic problems, especially with fear of weapons that can destroy all the lives He loves.

But our Father's love is mysterious. You can't recognize it by seeing everyone enjoying a land of milk and honey, by seeing the lion and the lamb lying down together. You must accept it through faith.

It was this faith I came to give. This was my gift to each of you on that First Christmas. It was my gift to you in my teaching and healing. It was the same gift I offered as I hung on the cross, and especially when I rose from the tomb on Easter morning.

If you are able to accept me as God among you, as the beloved son of the Creator, you should be able to realize that the Father's mysterious love was with me in spite of all the failure and suffering which was present in my life.

Suffering, failure, sin — none of these obstacles of human life can ultimately overcome the love of the Father on whom our faith rests.

This is the real cause for your rejoicing as you celebrate Christmas. Enjoy all the good things of your human celebration, but don't fail to recognize the real reason why the angels sang and the universe rejoiced at my coming.

externals, by emptying Himself and becoming an infant, born like an outcast, working as a son of the poorest, living like a vagabond. For in such a life there was nothing to spoil the purity of His selfless love, of His total dedication to "setting the world in order."

He made Christmas an intimate, family feast because He made Himself so small. We awaited the crash of cymbals and the blast of trumpets, the thunder of His armies and the cry of His judgment—and He surprised us. Heavenly messengers are sent to tell us, "You will not find Your Savior in the palaces of kings, you will not find Him courting Caesar's favors, nor in long conference with the dictators of this world; you will find Him among His beloved poor, sharing their meager meals, sweating in the carpenter shop to serve them, walking their dusty roads to heal them and to teach them."

Here is the secret of His mysterious coming: "He gave Himself for us." If in our ignorance we failed to distinguish what in this world is truly important, and what is small and mean and unprofitable and even dangerous and destructive, we now have no more excuse. We have the clear example of Jesus Christ, perfect man, Son of God, who also insisted that His pattern of life was to be ours.

> **Where is the Child who is born for us?**
> **Where are you, Jesus, where can you be found?**
>
> **In the caves of the poor, with the tears of the lonely,**
> **With the outcast who seeks a new home do you share?**
> **In the working man's shop, on the streets with the crowd,**
> **On the last painful way of the cross, are you there?**
>
> **Lord, as we discover you,**
> **Heal our hearts, our lives renew.**
> **Come, Lord Jesus, come and stay:**
> **Come, our Light, and lead the way!**

STEPHEN, THE FIRST MARTYR

December 26   **Matthew 10:17-22**

Jesus predicts persecution for His followers: "Brother will hand over brother to death; children will turn against parents and have them put to death. You will be hated by all on account of me. But whoever holds out till the end will escape death." Jesus means that the faithful ones will escape eternal death, since He has already predicted bodily death for many of His witnesses.

St. Stephen was one such witness who understood the spirit of Jesus to the full. Christ-like giving—Christmas giving—meant for him the gift of his very life. At first sight it seemed he received no earthly gift in return. His persecutors stopped their ears so as not to hear his final testimony to God's love.

But once Stephen has offered that greatest Christmas gift—"Lord Jesus, receive my spirit"—the power of God is at work. How Stephen must have jumped with joy in heaven when he saw the Lord's return gift on earth, a gift he hadn't expected, a gift worth all he had given, a gift worth his blood! One of the radical young men that stood by cheering and holding coats when Stephen was stoned to death was a young Pharisee named Saul. He had been so filled with hate at what Stephen said, that he took it as a cue for a long rampage of Christian arrests. Saul became such a famous persecutor that when he came down the street, all Christians automatically locked their doors.

And now see what the Lord has given Stephen in return for his life: the life of a converted Saul, a Paul who becomes the world's greatest missionary for Jesus.

You see, we never know who our friends are, or who our friends in the future may be.

> To Your strong hands my spirit, O Savior, I commend:
> O risen Lord, reclaim me, Your promised counsel send;
> Lord of glory, I'll seek You to the end.
> I'll build upon Your promise, my light in darkest night,
> A comrade to befriend me, a guide to set me right:
> Lead me safely forever in your sight.
> I revel in Your mercy: You heard my heartfelt prayer,
> You helped me in my troubles, You healed my dark despair:
> In my anguish, I felt Your tender care (Ps 31).

JOHN THE APOSTLE

December 27   **John 20:2-8**

In the fourth Gospel John is called "the disciple whom Jesus loved." He is also a disciple who loved Jesus deeply. This we can easily see when reading his Gospel and the intimate personal portrait of Jesus that he gives us. Who has grasped the Lord's message of love better than John?

Jesus often chose John, with Peter and James, to be with Him on very special occasions. These three alone went in with Jesus when He raised the little daughter of Jairus back to life. They were alone with Jesus at His transfiguration, and they were closest to the Lord in the Garden of Gethsemane. Of all the disciples, John alone stood with Mary beneath the cross of Jesus.

John, with Peter, was first of the apostles to witness the empty tomb on Easter morning. Early that Sunday morning Mary Magdalen found the tomb empty and ran off to tell Peter and John. The graphic recollection of John the eyewitness is beautiful. He describes the empty tomb and the remaining burial cloths in detail. "He saw and believed." But then he adds, "As yet they did not understand the scripture that Jesus had to rise from the dead," because the Holy Spirit had not yet come to teach the disciples. It was the Spirit that taught them the true meaning of the Lord's resurrection.

This confirms what John tells us Jesus said at the Last Supper, "I have much to tell you, but you cannot bear it now. But when the Holy Spirit comes, He will teach you all truth" (Jn 16:12-13)).

Even John, the beloved disciple, the one closest to Jesus, does not seem to have expected the resurrection of Jesus. But now, seeing the empty tomb, he comes to believe. How earthly were the thoughts of these first Christians—as are ours! They surely needed the power of the Holy Spirit! How feeble is man without God, how earthbound and unable to understand! We are truly poor before God. Without the gift of faith—His totally free gift—we cannot understand.

With the disciples we pray, "Lord, increase our faith!"

THE HOLY INNOCENTS, MARTYRS

December 28   **Matthew 2:13-18**

We've all been embarrassed sometimes by failing to recognize someone. It happened once to a state inspector at a small school. He had a temper, and when he heard a lot of noise in the next classroom, he went in, grabbed one of the older boys who seemed to be doing most of the talking, dragged him into the hall, stood him in the corner and said, "Now shut up and don't move!" A few minutes later a smaller boy caught up with the inspector at the end of the hall and said, "Please, sir, may we have our teacher back?"

Herod was guilty of more than one mistake in identity. He killed the infant boys of Bethlehem, feeling sure he would catch up with the boy Jesus. He missed, not figuring on that angel who knew all along when the ax would fall, and not figuring on Joseph who was willing to listen to the advice of angels, even when it meant a journey full of dangers.

Herod was guilty of a greater mistake in identity. He judged the newborn King by his own standards. As if Christ the King would give *him* competition! Why, they were persons of two different worlds! A true king is not fair game for a faker, and the kingship of Jesus was worlds away from the sham glitter of Herod.

If Jesus had taken advantage of His high position in a worldly way, we might at times be bold enough to say, "He didn't suffer what we suffer; it was never hard for Him."

But there's His poverty in the little shanties of Bethlehem and Nazareth. There's His humiliation at depending on others in His public life for food, money, and shelter. There's His exile in Egypt and His greater exile among His own people, who don't appreciate Him, who are full of envy and hatred. There are the religious leaders, who should have been His chief supporters, and who instead try to catch Him making a mistake, so they can discredit Him and eventually have Him put out of the way.

> Jesus, why did You take so little comfort in this world? Was it because of the tremendous witness it gave to Your teaching and to Your martyrdom and resurrection?

THE LIVING TEMPLE

December 29   **Luke 2:22-35**

The Presentation of Jesus in the temple occurred forty days after His birth. The Son of God entered His own temple, the visible house of His Father on earth. The prophet Isaiah had seen a great vision of the Lord God, high and holy, filling the temple with His divine presence. Now God-made-man, Christ the divine Son, fills the temple with His presence, both divine and human. This mystery signifies not only the mission of Christ, to be totally dedicated to his Father, but also that Jesus Himself is the great temple of God.

Jesus comes to the temple, the house of sacrifice, the place of worship where offerings of all kinds are brought to God. Christ's life shall be a continual temple service: the service of the New Law, climaxed on the Cross and in the Bread of the Eucharist.

The mystery of Jesus' presentation has the meaning of total dedication in our lives. Jesus comes to fulfill what God's design has established for Him. We come to our Christian temple, the Church, with the same spirit of dedication. We are to come with the same reverent love and worship; we are to come and fulfill God's divine plan for our own calling in life.

And so we pray with the Spirit-filled old man, Simeon:

> **"This child divides the nations**
> **And fickle hearts unfold,**
> **As Child and Mother suffer**
> **The sword of soul foretold.**
> **Dismiss your servant, Master;**
> **Your light has come to birth,**
> **Salvation's promise triumphs**
> **Across the darkened earth."**

ALL BEAUTY WITHIN

December 30   **Luke 2:36-40**

"The child grew in size and strength." Who would have thought it, as they met a quiet, sun-browned, dark-haired boy on the dusty streets of a miserable small town, that this was He? Who would have guessed it, as He wandered through the marketplace to buy a few provisions for His parents and Himself, as He traded, dressed in the clothes of the poor, that this was He? Who would have imagined, as they passed His father's workshop, and saw Him, a strong young teenager, sweating and straining with a few crude tools, that this was He?

If passers-by had stopped to look closely, or if they had known for what they were looking, they might well have been amazed at the lad's attractive qualities. Had they been searching for it, they would have been impressed by the mystery, the unassuming greatness of this family. There was an air of quiet dignity and perfect composure about them that might have fascinated the more appreciative and truly pious Jews, but here at Nazareth it could go on quite undetected.

After all, wasn't it a Galilean proverb that "nothing good had ever come out of Nazareth"? Joseph and Mary and her Son were hard-working people, who had managed to stay out of trouble (so far), unlike Nazareth's zealots, swindlers, beggars, small-time scribes and meddlesome Pharisees. But it was not likely that in such a common family there was One to whom God had said, "From birth, princely state shall be yours; you are my son, born like dew before the day-star rises."

> How truly hidden is the God of Israel;
> O Savior, are You not a God of mystery?
> Disgrace benights all who in anger turn away,
> In shame they carve new images to wrest them free.
> While Israel is saved forever in the Lord,
> Through ageless time His faithful ways are her reward.
> Thus says the Lord, creator of the universe,
> He who designed and forged all nature's subtle plan,
> No wasteland did He make the living, breathing earth,
> Who says, "I am the Lord who heightens heaven's span,

I do not speak from man-made corners of the earth,
Nor do I vainly bring my promises to birth" (Is 45:15-18).

YOUR LIGHT

December 31   **John 1:1-18**

In the very first chapter of his Gospel, John says of Jesus: "Whatever came to be in Him, found life, life for the light of men. That light shines on in darkness, a darkness that did not overcome it."

Then the Gospel refers to John the Baptist as "a witness to testify to the light." And this Light, John says, "the real Light, which gives Light to every person, was coming into the world."

So a Christian is a person who can say in all truth and honesty, "Jesus, You are the Light of my life." That's not just a nice thing to say. It has to be the truth! How can Jesus be the Light of your life, day by day? Take a few examples:

He is your Light when you mend a quarrel with someone. For He said, "Before you bring your gift to the altar, go first and be reconciled to your brother." He is your Light when you share a joy or happiness with another person. St. Paul says, "Remember that the Lord Jesus said it is better to give than to receive." He is your Light when you gladden the heart of a child by a kindness or by encouragement, for He said, "Bring the little children to me, and do not forbid them; the kingdom of heaven is for such as these." He is the Light of your life when you take the time to keep a promise, for He Himself is the Promised One, He is God's Promise, perfectly and completely fulfilled.

Jesus is the Light of your life when you really listen to others and sincerely try to understand them, for He knows from bitter experience what it means to be misunderstood and not listened to by your own people.

Jesus is the Light of your life when you express your gratitude for the goodness others show you. For it was Jesus who said with feeling, "Were not the ten lepers made clean? Where are the other nine? Has no one returned to praise God but one stranger?"

Jesus is the Light of your life when you take time to pray, for He spent whole nights in prayer. He is your Light when you praise God for whatever happens to you, because He prayed in His agony, "Father, not my will, but Your Will be done." And it was He who prayed that His joy and His peace might be yours.

MOTHER OF GOD

January 1   **Luke 2:16-21**

An old priest who had spent much of his life reading and writing books about the Blessed Virgin Mary said, "When you have called Mary the *Mother of God*, what else is there to say?"

During Advent and Christmas time, we read the Gospels that tell us about Mary—the little they seem to tell us. But what the Gospels tell us about Mary is powerful, and really speaks to our life. Everything they say about Mary seems to converge on one fact: Mary had an unshakeable trust in God. Her faith never wavered. Trust means "leaving everything in the hands of God." That's not as easy as it sounds, because we have such a strong desire to plan our own life.

Yet a prayer is no more than just verbalizing, if we don't have genuine trust in God. The Lord is the one who makes all the final decisions. How many times has a disappointment in prayer really turned out to be a great blessing!

If Mary, the Mother of God, would not have had an unfailing trust in God, her life would surely have been full of disappointments. There was much suffering in her life, because things looked so bleak for her Son, Jesus. But, as the Gospel says, "Mary treasured all these things and reflected on them in her heart." She treasured whatever happened, because she saw everything as part of a loving God's plan for her life and for the life of Jesus. This she expressed in her great hymn of faith and praise:

My soul praises God my Savior, joy in Him exalts my heart,
For the Lord my God regarded His poor maiden's humble part.
Henceforth all shall call me blessed, for the Lord has honored me;

To all ages lasts His mercy, meant for souls of piety.
Lo, the proud like wind He scatters: they shall fear His mighty arm;
From their thrones the great ones tumble, but the humble fear no harm.
With good things He fills the hungry, leaves the rich in poverty,
Grants to Israel His mercy, promised through eternity (Lk 1:46-55).

A BAG OF SNAKES

January 2   John 1:19-28

The attitude taken by John the Baptist is not a popular one in our time. He wants no credit for himself. He says he is not the Messiah, nor Elijah, nor any great Prophet. He confesses to only one purpose: he must prepare the way for someone else, someone so much greater than himself, that he is not worthy to unfasten the strap of that person's sandals.

Such humility, such willingness to take the back seat, such simplicity is not popular. And yet, everyone dislikes the opposite, pride, when he sees it in others. We don't want to see someone else "acting as if he's almighty." We're unaccountably drawn to do those same proud things ourselves. We act like the monkeys in Darwin's famous experiment. He showed a bunch of monkeys a bag full of snakes. They threw up their arms and shrieked and ran away, but they couldn't resist. They kept coming back to look at the snakes, kept shrieking and running away, and coming back for more. Now pride— self-importance—is a real bag of snakes, more harmful than the snakes. Yet we shriek at the snakes when someone else is involved, but keep coming back for more ourselves.

John the Baptist was wiser than most of us. He resisted the enticing temptation to be more admired than the one to come, to keep his own followers for himself, to see to his own ego. "What a thankless job," we think, "to risk your own life and spend your energy and give up your admirers to someone else who is to take your place."

But John understood his vocation fully: he was to lead others to Christ, not to glory in himself.

Really, this is the vocation of every one of us. To lead others to Christ, not to take the credit ourselves when we have accomplished something good. Does this seem too much for God to expect of us? Yet in fact, it's the only way in which we can find true self-fulfillment, the only way our good works will have a lasting effect, the only way our love can be real and convincing.

Jesus, make me real by letting me know You, and letting me know myself. For then the bag of snakes will offer little temptation.

LAMB OF GOD

January 3   John 1:29-34

When John the Baptist saw Jesus coming toward him, he said, "Here is the Lamb of God, who takes away the sins of the world." John spoke in the Aramaic language, the modern Hebrew of his time. The word for lamb was "thalya," which also meant servant. Thus the Lamb of God meant also the Servant of God.

Isaiah wrote, "He is like a lamb led to the slaughter." In other words, Jesus the Lamb is perfectly obedient to the Father. Isaiah also calls Him "the suffering Lamb" and therefore "the suffering Servant."

Jesus takes away the sins of the world by suffering, by letting the evils of sin hurt him. He lets the hatred and envy of the Pharisees hurt Him; he lets the selfishness and ingratitude of the people hurt him. Thus he suffers all His life for our sins, until the violent death of Good Friday. In doing this, Jesus faced the real world as we know it. We all experience suffering from the sins of others, as well as from our own. Our anger, dishonesty, stubbornness, fickleness—all our sins hurt others, as we each are hurt by others' failings.

From every eye some tears must fall: we cannot escape suffering. Life is like the keyboard of a piano: first a white key, then a black one: a white note of joy, then a black note of sorrow, yet somehow they blend into the perfect song. The very fact that we have teeth—which is good, especially when you have nice straight ones—also means that some day you may have a toothache, which can be pretty bad!

God never told us that this life on earth would be only a mountain peak of joy. Rather, it is the *road to* that mountain peak! And there are plenty of bumps on this road. How much these bumps hurt you depends on how strong your moral and spiritual springs are. Do we say, "God should not dare to plant any rosebushes in *my* garden, because roses have thorns and thorns hurt." If so, are we not saying, "God should not treat me the way He treated Christ, His only beloved Son!"

Wisdom that flouts the wise, folly's own redeeming prize,
Foolish the world's wisdom has become!
Baffling to human pride, we preach the Crucified:
Eternal Love has overcome!

WHERE DO YOU LIVE?

January 4   **John 1:35-42**

It's interesting to see how the apostles first got to know God, through Jesus. In Bethany John the Baptist pointed out Jesus as He walked by, "There is the Lamb of God." James and John followed Jesus. Jesus turned around and said, "What are you looking for?"

That's the question He asks each of us. "What are you looking for? What kind of God are you searching for?" When we go to meet someone we never saw before, we have some kind of picture of him in our mind. And so we each have certain views about what God is like—till we find out we've been wrong. Just like Minnesota's "sky-blue waters." You dip your glass into the water, and find out it isn't blue.

Some say, "You'll find God through religion: get some religion in you." Well, what *IS* religion? A set of rules to follow, to reach heaven? Does it mean, don't be an enemy of God? Stay out of trouble, stay out of other people's hair, don't go off the deep end, don't do this, don't do that? All this is negative. So it's surely not God!

How would you draw a picture of God? An old man with a long beard—with a frown and a big stick—a strict disciplinarian—so that if you giggle in his presence you get hit?

Each of us has his own view of God, based on our own personal experiences, through our parents and teachers and events in our life. Many of us never get beyond the stage of that "first impression" of God, just as we don't get beyond it with people we don't get to know very well. And we're as wrong about God as about people we don't really know.

The answer of James and John is beautiful. When Jesus asks, "What are you looking for?" they answer, "Where do you live?" In other words, "We want to get to know you so well that we're your personal friends."

Then Jesus invited them, as He always invites us. "Come and see." Then John says, "And they stayed all day." Did you and I ever do that? Stay all day with the Lord? In fact, they stayed all their life, they found Him so lovable. They never left Jesus after meeting Him. To overcome our wrong notions of God, let's read John's Gospel. Jesus said that *through Him* we would get to know God, our loving Father!

IT'S YOUR ATTITUDE

January 5   **John 1:43-51**

The Gospel tells us about the calling of Nathanael, who is Bartholomew the apostle. Whatever pessimism or suspicion it was in this young man that made him ask, "Can anything good come from Nazareth?" Jesus saw sterling qualities in the man. He called Bartholomew "a real Israelite," and praised him for his honesty. Perhaps with a twinkle of humor, Jesus wished to shake the cautious young man still further by assuring him, "You will see the sky opened and the angels of God ascending and descending on the Son of Man."

Fortunately for Bartholomew, he did not walk away from this glorious and optimistic promise. Others could not take it: the rich young man, the many followers who walked away sadly, who left

Christ's company forever saying, "His are hard sayings! Who can bear them?"

Faith in the resurrection and glory of Jesus is a deeply personal thing and changes your whole life. It changes the meaning of everything around you, it gives you a tremendous new perspective on living, it broadens and deepens your horizons.

It isn't really joy or pain, winning or losing, sickness or health, good luck or bad that makes a person happy or miserable. It's your attitude toward these things, your understanding of their meaning that counts. Your viewpoint makes or breaks you.

Happy people have troubles, too. A man may try to avert bad luck by buying three pair of trousers with his new suit, then the first week he'll burn a hole in the coat! In what frame of mind will he accept this? That he must find within himself.

To his apostles Jesus predicted persecution and suffering, not to make them pessimists, but to prepare them for finding behind it and within it a meaning and a glory and a promise: "I am with you, and your joy no one can take from you. You are assured victory. They can kill the body but not the spirit. And which one really counts?"

Lord if we are happy that You gave us life, that You gave us the chance to bring joy to others, happy to be close to you by faith and love—no one can dampen our spirit.

THE LAST WORD

The Epiphany of Our Lord　　　　　　　　　**Matthew 2:1-12**

"Rise up, Jerusalem, your light has come,
　the glory of the Lord shines upon you."
He comes, He has come, He is always coming,
　the Lord our God.
Had we but eyes to see Him, ears to hear Him!
"Behold the Lord the ruler has come;
　and the kingdom is in His hand" (Ml 3:1).

He speaks with power,
  because He speaks through all living things.
He is the God of might,
  because He lives and acts forever.
He does not sleep, He does not fail,
  He never stops short to say, "I have done enough."
"We have observed His star at its rising,
  and have come to pay Him homage" (Mt 2:2).
The Lord has appeared:
  come, let us find Him and adore Him.
He lives in all life, He acts in all events,
  He loves in all generous hearts.

He lives amid the stars and galaxies,
He breathes the chaste and gentle summer breeze.
He rides upon the thunders loud and wild,
And weeps beside the cold and hungry child.
He lives beyond the glow of northern lights,
And plays between the moons and satellites.
He speaks through prophets and through radar towers,
And through the children's eyes
  and fragile morning flowers.
He visits man through pain and sickness
  as through glowing health,
Through labor, tears, and poverty,
  and wrapped in nature's wealth.
Everywhere He lives and whispers,
  darkly clothed in mystery,
Hiding in the surge of life,
  beneath the force of history,
Hiding lest by finding Him we would search no more;
From afar we see His star, hasten to explore:
Seek Him while He may be found, call when He is near!
"Speak today and always, Lord, tune our ears to hear,
Light our minds and wake us, Lord! Shall we not perceive?
Thaw our hearts and open us, that we may receive:
Yours is the true message, Lord, the last word;
Ours is the lost word, the wrong and rash and fast word.
Now may we fall silent . . . and listen. . . ."

PRETENDERS

January 6　　　　　　　　　　　　　　　John 1:29-34

John the Baptist sees Jesus coming and he says, "Here is the Lamb of God who takes away the sins of the world." John has seen the Spirit descend on Jesus at His baptism, and he declares Jesus to be the Son of God. The honesty and integrity of John is obvious. He does not seek his own popularity or security; he is only in search of the truth.

The truth of John's testimony concerning Jesus is obvious, too. Who else would have done what Jesus did in coming to John and asking baptism as a sinner? Jesus is not a pretender. We are, however. We all sit in judgment on our neighbors, finding fault with everyone and pretending we are better than others.

Christ did the very opposite. He came to John and to baptism as one who repents of sin and does penance—and He had no sins! How many of us would do that? Do penance for sins we never committed? Suffer for someone else's sins, take the burdens of others on ourselves, take the blame when we're not guilty?

If Christ could make this His life's work, the least *we* can do is not pretend that we're perfect, that when anything goes wrong the fault is always someone else's. But that's human nature: we're all phony balonies! We pretend we're smarter and richer than we are. We pretend we're boss in our family and everyone bows to us. We pretend we have nothing to be sorry for, because we never made a mistake. We pretend we never really get what we deserve, because nobody understands how good we really are.

A good look at Jesus would show us how false we are, how untrue and unreal our ways of acting tends to be. Christ is real, honest, genuine. He came not to pretend or to push ahead at the expense of others. Innocent as He was, He chose to carry on His own shoulders the burdens of other people's failures and crimes, as if they were His own. Could we not be a little more Christ-like, a bit more Christian by being willing to help, by "bearing one another's burdens," by trying to build and to save?

Lord, teach us to laugh at our pretenses, that we may learn honesty from You.

SIGNS

January 7 **John 2:1-12**

"What Jesus did at Cana in Galilee marked the beginning of His signs: thus He revealed His glory, and His disciples believed in Him." St. John is saying, "Actions speak louder than words." Jesus, who was always completely honest and genuine, spoke through His actions as clearly as His words. His deeds were signs of the reality, the mystery inside. And He left signs, visible things, actions that continued His presence.

His human body and all its movements were signs of the divine nature within: His miracles were signs of His power and His plan: what He wanted that power to do for us.

So He comes to a wedding, a happy occasion, a family festival. He turns the water into wine: a sign of His creative power, a sign of His approval of the festive spirit of the occasion, a sign of His generosity, and a sign that with the touch of His divine power He wished to sanctify marriage, to bless this young married couple in a striking and visible way. These meanings were obvious in His action: no words were necessary.

So the Bread of the Eucharist is the sign of Christ's abiding presence with us and within us. When we come to the Eucharist to worship, we come not only to hear words alone. We want not only to hear Him, we want to see Him, to touch Him, to answer Him, to know He is really present.

The reality is here, too. Here is the bread and wine on the altar. Jesus is truly here: He is the living Bread, the living Bread is He. "As often as you shall do this, you shall do it as a memorial to Me." What does this sign, ever present before us, do? St. John sums it up when he writes, in today's Gospel, "Thus He revealed His glory, and His disciples believed in Him." The divine, glorious, risen Jesus is revealed in the living Bread, and our faith in Him is strengthened; His disciples, those who listen to Him, learn to believe in Him.

We come to You with longing, O Bread by Heaven sent;
We would embrace Your goodness, our soul's true nourishment!
It was Your invitation that won our meek consent
To come within Your presence, contrite and confident.

GETTING INVOLVED

January 8   **Mark 6:34-44**

Jesus very clearly tells us in the Gospel to have concern for our fellow men. He gives us an example. He sees a vast crowd and He pities them, "for they were like sheep without a shepherd." He taught them at great length, so long that the Apostles got worried that they might have to feed them. They came to Jesus and suggested He stop preaching so that the people could either get home or into some village to get something to eat.

Jesus simply said, "You feed them." He is saying to them that they should not shy away from responsibility to the poor, the needy. The disciples evidently didn't want to get involved. They were afraid what it might cost them.

Are we afraid to get involved? Do we shy away from responsibility to our brothers and sisters in need? We live in a society that is very independent; every one for himself. Don't get involved. It might get you into trouble. It might cost you some money, and you need all you have to keep up your affluent living.

Jesus says if we want to be His disciples, His followers, we've got to get involved, we've got to be willing to sacrifice for our brothers and sisters, to deny self so as to be able to help them. He makes it quite clear that it is the best way to live, the happiest way. Why? Just look at the reward! What a joy it must have been to be a part of that exciting incident, feeding the five thousand with just five loaves of bread and two fish. And to end up with more than at the start.

Getting involved will make our Christian lives a joy. We will be a part of God's exciting work in the world. And without a doubt we will end with more than we began with, more joy, more meaning, more of God's blessings both spiritual and temporal.

> **Such as My love has been for you,**
> **so must your love be for each other** (Jn 13:34).

THIS WAY OUT

January 9, or Wednesday after Epiphany   Mark 6:45-52

It seems that man as an inventor of excuses is no new institution. It seems that year after year, century after century, God's own people found excuses for ignoring Him.

Some years ago an unknown humorist posted this sign near several exits in the Boston Symphony Hall: "This way out, in case of Brahms."

We can reasonably doubt whether certain music lovers are as afraid of Brahms as certain Christians are of real prayer. And these are "good Christians," those with some sense of justice and duty. Yet there is an effective sign posted on every exit of their interior soul: "This way out, in case of meditation." The very word frightens them. They rather expect to find prayer or meditation as difficult as the cuneiforms of ancient Sumeria.

"Jesus went off to the mountain to pray." Are we afraid to try prayer for fear that our conscience will bother us forever after that? Are we afraid we may discover in ourselves something that must be driven out before God can enter?

To avoid prayer, to postpone those hours with God, is like taking a trip without a single map and without so much as a glance at the highway signs. How can one live, you may wonder, without ever asking, "Why am I here? How did I get here? Where am I going? Where should I be going? How can I find my way? If God created me, what is He like? What does He expect of me? What do I owe to others? Does my happiness depend on them? Does theirs depend on me? How can I avoid failure of my purpose on this earth?"

Suppose I come out of prayer with a desire to find answers to these questions? Suppose prayer has given me a deeper and fuller appreciation of Who God is, the beauty of His creation and its meaning, the marvels of my own immortal spirit, the thrilling promises God has made to me—is this dull, is this punishment or imprisonment? Suppose I come out of prayer and meditation prepared to live truly happy, full of a new freedom, truer to myself, a greater blessing to those around me—is this something to find "a way out" of? Tomorrow a new sign will hang over the entrances of my soul: "This way in, for real prayer."

Lord, teach us to pray. By Your example we see the power in prayer.

THE SPIRIT WORKS

January 10, or Thursday after Epiphany   **Luke 4:14-22**

Have you ever noticed how much Jesus is involved with the Holy Spirit during His life? Not only does Jesus talk about sending the Holy Spirit to us, "to teach us all truth," to "help us recall everything He taught us," and to "be with us always." It is the Holy Spirit that gives power to Jesus in His own ministry.

We recall that at the baptism of Jesus, "the Holy Spirit came down upon Him in bodily form, like a dove" (Lk 3:22). Luke adds, "Jesus returned from the Jordan *full of the Holy Spirit*, and was led by the Spirit into the desert, where He was tempted by the devil" (4:1-2). After Jesus fasted and overcame the temptations, Luke says, He "returned to Galilee, and the power of the Holy Spirit was with Him" (4:14). Then when Jesus went to Nazareth and got up to read in the synagogue, He chose this prophecy from Isaiah: "The Spirit of the Lord is upon me. He has anointed me to preach the good news to the poor."

We notice when there's growth in the life of Jesus, it is by the action of the Holy Spirit. Luke in the Acts of the Apostles shows us that whenever there is a leap forward in the early Christian community, it is also by the action of the Holy Spirit. He is the life and vitality of the Church. It was at His coming on Pentecost that the disciples of Jesus came out in power.

The same Holy Spirit who worked in the life of Jesus and gave such joy and power to His early followers, can work powerfully in our lives, too, if we are open to Him.

> **Come, of all consolers best!**
> **Come, our souls' most welcome guest,**
> **Strength and peace to souls distressed.**
> **In our labors, bring us rest;**

Cool us, when by heat oppressed;
Stay our grief, Consoler Blest!
Blessed ecstasy of light,
Charged with wisdom's radiant might,
Pierce our hearts with inner sight!

CHRIST THE HEALER

January 11, or Friday after Epiphany　　　　　　　**Luke 5:12-16**

We all like seeing things get back to normal. When you're sick with a fever, you look for the day when your temperature will be normal again. When you feel overworked, you say, "It's been so hectic, I'll praise the Lord when things get back to normal around here." If you remember when you were young and away to school, and you came home for the holidays, you were quite the guy for a while: everyone welcomed you home, and you had lots to tell. Then in a day or so, when Mother said, "Come on, get to work, you're part of this family, you know," you felt relieved: things were back to *normal* again!

The leper in the Gospel appealed to Jesus, because he wanted to get back to normal again. He was leading a terrible existence. He had a disease that made everyone avoid him; he could not be with his family or friends, because leprosy was contagious, and it scared people almost to death.

Did you ever stop to think of what a tremendous thing Jesus did for this man? Curing him, getting him back to normal—a thing the leper thought would never happen again!

Did you ever stop to think that this is what Jesus does so often for each of us? He cures us, gets us back to normal again, gives us a freshly cleaned slate and a new start! The leper, of course, would always be remembered as someone who had had leprosy, but—what a joy and favor—he was completely cured!

So with each of us: we have had our bad days, we have made our stupid mistakes, but if we have real faith, the Lord has cured us, and we are free once again.

We need that kind of help, each of us, and we need to help others. Jesus helps us in that way; He keeps His promise to forgive and to heal us and to get us back to normal. But He does demand that we follow His example in dealing with others.

The Lord has so prized us, His death has baptized us:
Christ Jesus, our Savior, has conquered all sin!
Though Satan despised us, and evil chastised us,
Christ gave us hope and strength and power to win!

HE MUST INCREASE

January 12, or Saturday after Epiphany   **John 3:20-30**

The gospels tell us a good deal about John the Baptist. In today's passage from John's gospel we witness a controversy arising between John's disciples and a certain Jew. John's disciples are getting jealous that Jesus, whom John baptized is drawing large crowds. They are afraid their Master's reputation will suffer.

To John the whole affair is completely irrelevant. He answers, "No one can lay hold of anything unless it is given him from above." He indicates clearly that his own mission is meaningless unless it has a divine purpose. He simply says he is not the one, not the expected Messiah, he is only his forerunner. John has it straight. He knows his true relationship with Jesus. And he likes it, accepts it joyfully. He humbly says, "I'm just a best man, at the service of the groom, and I'm happy to have that privilege. Jesus is the one who is to come. It is my joy to announce Him."

John tells us it is Jesus who must become known more and more. He says he's done his duty in announcing Him and now he must recede into the background. "He must increase, while I must decrease."

Excellent advice! We've got to get to know Jesus. He is the one, He is Lord. To know Him is life, Spiritual Life. Not to know Jesus is death. He must increase. Jesus must become more and more important in our lives. He must be Lord of our lives. We must decrease. We must give Jesus all the glory. Like John we must know our place in relationship to the Lord. We can witness with power, like John did, but it's the Lord to whom we draw attention, not ourselves.

O Lord, I want to know You more and more. I want to commit my entire self to Your Lordship.

DON'T YOU LAUGH!

Ash Wednesday   **Matthew 6:1-6, 16-18**

In the Gospel Jesus says, "When you're fasting, don't look glum like the Pharisees, pretending that it's such a great burden to do penance."

Somehow we Christians have gotten the wrong idea about penance, and with it, the wrong idea about heaven itself, and God Himself. We somehow see God as a stern or sour old man, who sits up there waiting to clobber us for doing wrong.

Jesus says here, "That's all wrong; that's false and fake." It's sad to think of how wrong we can be about God and about Christian life.

I can remember a "game" we learned as children. Apparently it was supposed to teach us something about heaven. It surely taught the wrong things. You'd line up a bunch of kids, face to the wall, and then as you poked each one in the ribs, you said, (we were German, and it sounds so nice in German!) "Engel, Bengel, Zucker-stengel, dreh dich um und lach nicht!" Which means, "Angel, devil, sugar-staff, turn around and don't you laugh!" If you laughed, you were going to hell; if you only smiled, you went to purgatory; if you kept a straight sour-pussed face, you were going to heaven!

I guess they wanted to say that will power got you to heaven. It was only a game, but it gave us the wrong picture. Jesus says, "That attitude makes hypocrites, or sour pickles, or else people who aren't interested in heaven at all!"

You can take life seriously without being sour or miserable! People who connect penance with a glum face have a false notion of the life God wants us to live. Jesus says, "I came that you may have life, and have it in all its fullness." Jesus never says, "I came to make you miserable, because my commandments will spoil all your fun." Rather, the Way of Life Jesus teaches brings the only real happiness.

The Lord has said, "Return to me, do not oppress the weak; Assist the poor in charity, no malice shall you speak. Then from the gloom your light shall dawn, and night shall be as day: New life from fountains shall be drawn, new strength will guide your way" (Is 58:9-11).

THE CROSS

Thursday after Ash Wednesday   **Luke 9:22-25**

Jesus and the apostles have much to say on the mystery of the Cross. The daily cross of which Jesus speaks is not only the final road from Pilate's hall to Calvary; it is the whole life of Jesus, and the whole life of every faithful Christian, the task which God has given us to do. St. Paul assures us that the Cross is our joy and our glory; though it is folly to pagans, it is the greatest wisdom to Christians.

The Cross is the way of perfect love and total dedication. All four gospels make this clear: the Cross is the very life of Jesus, and will become the very life of His apostles and of Christians. Jesus never thought of Himself in a selfish manner; His concern was always the work His Father had given Him to do: saving God's people.

Suffering and sacrifice belong to the glory of Christian life, making us sharers in the redeeming work of Christ. We do not help our suffering brothers and sisters in order to take them away from the Cross, but to make ourselves and them more like Christ, perfect in love and saved from evil. We love our share in the Cross, because we love the work of Christ on earth: to restore His people to God and to bring all creation back to its original beauty.

> Faithful Cross, O tree of power,
> Mighty branch that bore the King,
> Lo, your sinews o'er us tower,
> Strength to weakened sinners bring.
> We have strayed, but you have made us
> Rescued children of the Lord.
>
> What crude gibbet He has chosen
> For His awesome sacrifice;
> To support this treasure never
> Fairest altar could suffice!
> Gracious wood and nails of patience,
> Mercy's bountiful award!

A STYLE OF LOVE

Friday after Ash Wednesday   **Matthew 9:14-15**

Jesus says, "After my ascension, my disciples will fast." We must fast? God forbid!

Some people think that Lent is out-dated and out of the question, because for real Penance you have to suffer agony—starvation by fasting, sleepless nights from scourging yourself, the seven-year shakes from an itchy hair-shirt. That false notion of Penance reveals a false god. Penance then is taken as a big *show*, where everybody has to *see* the poor martyr, so they'll praise him for it and call him Saint Miserable.

Some worship that false god of Pride. Others, the false god of Good Health. "I can't do anything for Lent because my health will suffer."

"Well!" answered St. Teresa of Avila, "Who ever ruined his health by keeping his mouth shut at the right time?" And who ever ruined his health by praising someone *else* twice, instead of *himself* twenty times? And who ever ruined his health by being less fussy at the table? By eating healthful food instead of what his little sweet tooth desired? And who ever ruined his health by letting someone *else* go out the door ahead of himself? Have good manners ever ruined anyone's health?

There's so much we can do in Lent without harming our health! In fact, it will *improve* our health, bodily and spiritually. Laziness does *not* contribute to good health. What is better medicine than good hard work, especially the kind that includes regular physical exercise? What is better *mental health* than charity to our neighbor, giving of our love to those in need?

Lent is the time to *improve* our *style* of *love*, and beautify ourselves by doing it. A beautiful soul shines through outward actions.

Lord Jesus, teach us the true spirit of Lent. The spirit of fasting, which is the spirit of giving up whatever is not of You. And the spirit of celebration, which is the ability to rejoice heartily in Your presence among us.

FORMULA FOR HEALING

Saturday after Ash Wednesday   **Luke 5:27-32**

Levi, or Matthew, was once a greedy man, an I.R.S. official, a hated tax-collector. At the time of Christ, these men could get away with pocketing any amount of money from the taxes they collected. No one checked on them. They ran their own extortion game, and it was really crooked.

We remember how Jesus came to Levi's tax office one day. Jesus knew there was only one thing He could do with a corrupt tax man: get him out of that line of work! So Jesus said to Levi, "I have a new job for you. It's a lot less money, but the retirement benefits are heavenly."

We know that Jesus worked a great spiritual healing in the life of Levi, who became Matthew, apostle and evangelist. And Matthew was one of the men who in writing down the Good News gave us the secrets of Jesus in the field of healing. Jesus told us how we can be healed, spiritually, mentally, emotionally, and even physically. Why do I lump these all together? Because we are, each of us, one human nature. If some say that sixty per cent of our pains are mental and emotional stress, this should not surprise us. You can't separate body and soul in this life!

The secret formula for healing may come as a surprise. Jesus said, "Love your enemies and pray for those who persecute you, so that you may become sons and daughters of your Father in heaven, for He makes His sun shine on bad and good people alike" (Mt 5:43). Are you there? Do you hear what Jesus is saying? The all-powerful perfect Father offers His healing power to all of us alike: good and bad.

Now put this together with Matthew 6:9-14. Here Jesus says, "This is how you should pray: Our Father who art in heaven . . ." After teaching us this prayer for forgiveness, He adds, "If you forgive others the wrongs they have done to you, your Father in heaven will also forgive you. But if you do not forgive others . . . ," He warns, then neither can you experience the healing effects of forgiveness in your own life.

Lord Jesus, don't we know well enough that hatred and resentment are destructive, while love and forgiveness

are the world's greatest healing formula? You showed
us this in your own life, and we will experience it in
ours, once we really put it to work.

REAL LOVE

First Week of Lent, Monday   **Matthew 25:31-46**

We talk a lot about love in Christianity, and rightly. It is
undoubtedly essential. Old and New Testaments, Saints' Writings,
theology ancient and modern, Christians and pagans alike—all agree
on the primacy of love. But we talk so glibly of love, as if it were very
simple, as if it made no demands other than the overthrow of
everything else, as if it were an immediate cure-all. It *is* a cure-all, in
fact, when it is *really love*. That is the thorny problem: we cannot rid
ourselves of the childish notion that love is simply a gushy emotion.
The notion is fortified by slick magazine stories, movies, novels, the
whole complex of our pleasure-mad culture.

Well—isn't virtue supposed to be pleasant? Yes and no. Given the
tendencies of all human flesh, true love is as painful as pleasant. It is
frightfully demanding: total giving of yourself calls for the utmost in
patience, humiliation, in difficult decisions, and often in acting
contrary to your own selfish desires. Hasn't every married couple
noticed that within a week after the honeymoon? If there's real love
and deep happiness, someone's always giving in. Self-giving becomes
the joy of love, certainly, but who denies that it's painful? The very
attention and interest in another demanded by love causes an anxious
kind of concern. It's the very opposite of jealousy or self-pity, but it is
a real form of suffering. Real love suffers what the other suffers.

**Lord Jesus, when we truly respond to Your love by
loving one another, then already now, in this world, we
receive Your blessing in the Gospel: "Come. You have
my Father's blessing! Inherit the kingdom prepared for
you from the creation of the world."**

THE FORGIVENESS MARATHON

First Week of Lent, Tuesday　　　　　　　　**Matthew 6:7-15**

The great prayer Jesus taught us, the Our Father, ends with a petition for forgiveness, and a promise to forgive. This is followed by the Lord's warning that we cannot be forgiven by God unless we forgive others. In another place Jesus insists that this must be forgiveness "from the heart" and forgiveness of everyone. If Jesus makes it so important in our lives, then we need a regular spiritual exercise in "reality forgiving," a deep and personal act of forgiveness that is real.

Let's call this exercise "The Forgiveness Marathon." Many good spiritual directors and psychiatrists recommend and prescribe this therapy of the heart:

Be seated in a chair, and place an empty chair right next to you. Now in your mind clearly see a person seated on that chair, a person who has hurt you and whom you have not really forgiven. Maybe it is your Mother or Dad or wife or husband or brother or sister. Someone you are still inwardly angry at. See that person very clearly, right now.

Now talk to that person. Say, as you name that person with love, "I forgive you completely for whatever you did, for being unfair to me, for rejecting me, for belittling me, for neglecting me." Be sure to bring out all the hurts, all the sore spots. Often this causes tears, healthy tears! Some people have to put so many persons on that chair that it takes a whole box of kleenex till everyone is forgiven. But there is no greater healing therapy. Those are tears of great relief and healing. You may also be healing your headaches or ulcers or depression, just by really forgiving.

Do this often. Nothing can bring you closer to the love of Jesus. Nothing can bring you greater personal peace and happiness. Just imagine that person seated next to you, that person against whom you harbor resentment. Now forgive and love that person. And complete the session by thanking Jesus for giving you the greatest power of love: the power of forgiving

Jesus, if I am ever going to be like You, I'll have to do a lot of forgiving. For that is what you came to this world to do for us: to forgive and heal each of us!

FORTY DAYS

First Week of Lent, Wednesday   **Luke 11:29-32**

The story of Jonah reminds us of the Scriptural origin of Lent, the forty days of Penance. The forty days is a time of purification, a time when our closer association with God makes us more worthy of Him and brings us spiritual growth.

Jonah preached repentance with a message from God. "Forty days more and Nineveh shall be destroyed." In the Gospel Jesus praises the citizens of Nineveh for listening to the prophet Jonah. They made use of the forty days which God gave them, forty days in which to repent and save their sinful city. Jesus deplores the lack of faith in his own people, who refuse to follow the example of the Ninevites.

Forty days is a sacred tradition in Holy Scripture. The Lord asked Moses to come up to Him on the mountain. Moses was to prepare himself for receiving the ten commandments for the instruction of his people. Moses stayed on the mountain, in the company of the Lord, for forty days.

Elijah fled for his life from the jealous queen, Jezabel, who had promised to send her soldiers to kill him. Elijah came exhausted to the desert, begging God to let him die. But the Lord sent food and water to Elijah, and in the strength of God's food, Elijah survived forty days and reached the mountain of God.

After his baptism, Jesus was led by the Holy Spirit to the wilderness, where He fasted and prayed for forty days.

The forty days that God has given us for prayer and repentance are sacred and precious and full of meaning. Like the Ninevites, we should thank God for giving us the forty days for our conversion. Forty days of Lent: a chance to repent and come personally close to God, as Moses and Elijah did.

Lord Jesus, as You stood transfigured, changed, glorified before Your disciples, Moses and Elijah conversed with You as personal friends. May we be transfigured, changed, renewed this season of Lent, so that we, too, may converse with You always as personal friends.

ASK AND RECEIVE

First Week of Lent, Thursday   **Matthew 7:7-12**

The Bible's praise of God's mercy to all who call on Him has been echoed through the centuries by millions of saints. They recall the Lord's promise that anything asked in His Name would be given: "Ask and you shall receive."

But there is another echo, another sound heard through the centuries: the cry of suffering, injustice, and despair. Cries of prayers apparently unanswered. The Church herself has prayed for unity, for peace and justice, for freedom that men might serve God according to their consciences. What then has happened to the kindness and mercy of the Lord, His goodness to those who call upon Him?

The answer must remain a mystery to us in this life. The psalmist, in reply to his own question, observed that God's wisdom is too sublime for us. We Christians, with the full benefit of Christ's revelations concerning life and eternity, with the full benefit of Christ's example and the mystery of the Cross, can accept the mystery more readily. We feel, at least, that at times people think their prayers are unanswered because they have asked for the wrong things, have made the wrong things important, have perhaps prayed for their own destruction; they are, like the disciples, a "scandal" to Jesus because they "mind not the things of heaven, but of earth."

But that is not the whole story: the mystery remains. Many really good things that really good people have prayed for, hoped for, worked for, and believed in have come to nothing, and the forces of evil remain a mystery to the wisest of us.

We can but look again at the paradox of the crucifix: how the pain of defeat led to the risen glory of victory.

> Many reject the Cross,
> Stumbling block and earthly loss;
> Folly of God is the wisdom true!
> God's weakness is true might,
> His Cross our guiding light.
> O foolish love, our hearts renew!

COMMUNITY SPIRIT

First Week of Lent, Friday **Matthew 5:20-26**

What Jesus says in this passage is, "Your worship must speak clearly to your life. You don't just bring your gift to the altar and think your duty is done for the week."

"No," says Jesus. "If there's something wrong in your family so that your brother—meaning *anyone* in your household—has something against you, then you must make *that* the priority in your life! Get that relationship straightened out according to God's first law of love." That means, we put our own household in order first. If your Sunday worship does not speak powerfully to your life, you are Christian only in name, not in reality.

Christian community has to begin in your family—that's the basic unit. It doesn't stop there, but if it doesn't have its foundation in the family, it will be a building without a foundation, and how long can such a building stand?

The meaning of the Gospel is, you build the Christian community not by your donation, but by your life. If your life is in order, you are making the greatest contribution to the Body of Christ, and your gift will have meaning. But your offering has no real Christian meaning if your life is not Christian.

A parish is a large-scale Christian community, as St. Paul describes in Romans 12, 1 Corinthians 11 and 12, and Ephesians 4. But the parish community can never be in good order if the families are not in good order. If there is not a right relationship between husband and wife, between parents and children, and children and parents, if there is not a deep bond of Christian love within the families, the parish can never be in right order, either.

In the family we can never just take one another for granted, without the deep signs and actions of love. Otherwise the family falls apart, and we do not have a Christian home. Without real Christian homes no parish can be healthy.

Jesus, we understand that when you said, "Go and be reconciled with your brother first, and then come offer your gift," you insist that we keep our family relationships in order. In the family we must begin the right order we need in the larger community.

FEEL LIKE LOVE?

First Week of Lent, Saturday　　　　　　　**Matthew 5:43-48**

"If you would be perfect," said Jesus, "keep the commandments." Asked by a lawyer which was the first and greatest commandment, He said, "Love God above all things, with your whole heart and soul, your whole mind and strength."

"How can I know I love God?" a boy asked us one day. "I don't feel it at all." He was a lad of good mind, his explanation was sensible enough: "I love my parents, my brothers and sisters, and my friends. I can feel that. I feel *at home* with them."

Where do I begin to answer? Shall I remind him that we are orphans, that we are not truly home on earth, that we have gone astray from God and grope about without feeling His love? Or shall I say that we cannot feel love before we *have* it? We must first love, that is, do the works of love and suffer its pains, and then only shall we feel the depth of real love. Or shall I remind him how modern advertising, modern luxury and comfort have warped our feeling of love, have cheapened it, left it weak and sluggish? Much to reflect on, these sincere words of a thinking boy. We have brought him up, we have "educated" him. Have we failed him in so important a matter?

It is a warped mind, isn't it, that takes such meticulous care of a child's body, that fears the slightest infection, and smothers him with comforts—too much rich food, too much fine clothing, too many material gifts. Smothers him—rather, smothers his spirit with neglect, crushes his true feelings of love, shuts him out from God's love.

"I don't feel I love God." Forgive us, Lord; we have been asleep. We have slept through our prayers, we have slept through the reading of Holy Scripture, we have slept through the example of the saints, we have slept through the demands of godly love. The emptiness of our lives has not awakened us, the boredom and frustration have not stirred us, the daily stroke of death around us has not sobered us, the terrors of materialism and bodily enslavements have not aroused us.

Forgive us, Lord! We and our children have been asleep!
"What? Could you not awake and watch one hour with Me?"

TO SAVE OR DESTROY?

Second Week of Lent, Monday   **Luke 6:36-38**

In the New Testament the importance of forgiveness is repeated over and over. St. Paul never lets us forget it: "Owe no debt to anyone except the debt that binds us to love one another . . . Never repay injury with injury. Do not avenge yourselves . . . Forgive as the Lord has forgiven you . . . Love never does any wrong to one's neighbor . . ."

How many Christians would dream of such fanatic love? What do we habitually do? For the least injury we fume, we rave, and we say, "Wait till I get my hands on that guy! Will I get even!" Not only do we repay injury with injury. That's too little. We make sure the payment is worse than the injury. Not tooth for tooth, like in the ancient court of the Hebrews, but three teeth for one! and front teeth for molars!

Tragically, our usual Christian love is thus: "He insulted me! How did he dare? Therefore I won't leave a shred hanging on him!" One injury, one inch of hurt pride, and we riddle our neighbor like a tea-strainer. We look upon one another—family, friends, husband and wife, neighbors, fellow-workers—as someone to fight with and come out the winner.

How quickly our children learn the sad lesson! A little girl looked upon her younger brother as someone to fight with and beat up. She was older, had longer finger nails, and what have you. Her mother said, "Hildegarde, don't beat up on Elmer! Don't you know, God sent him to us from heaven?"

Hildegarde answered, "Aw, he wasn't sent. He got *pushed* out!"

And this remains our lifelong attitude. Rather than respect one another, we are often busy trying to push each other out of any chance for heaven!

> **Jesus, Your example is quite different. You keep insisting that You did not come to destroy, but to save. To love the unlovable, to restore the ruins, to rescue the sinners. We've got too many destroyers on the waters of life already. What we need are more life-boats, more people who are out to *save* people!**

YOUR TEACHER

Second Week of Lent, Tuesday   **Matthew 23:1-12**

In the Gospel Jesus says that He knows we need a teacher, but He doesn't want us to pick the wrong one. Those who teach or preach and do not practice what they preach, as Jesus says of the Pharisees, have actually chosen the wrong teacher themselves.

We surely need good teachers. With our world's problems as bad as they are, we need excellent teachers, who can show us the way to go in solving the problems. We have all kinds of teachers and experts who claim to have the solution to the world's problems. But how successful are they? They all talk about peace and love and harmony and justice—but where are they?

Instead of stability and order, we have broken homes, divorce, crime, broken lives, emotional illness, many problems that breed an atmosphere of confusion, sin, and violence. If anything, the news media make us hardened to these evils, so that we begin to accept them as unavoidable. We breathe the foul air almost unknowingly. But the evil is there, and great loneliness and fear result. A teenager said recently, "I don't have one real friend." Many people feel this way.

Drugs and alcohol are attempts to escape the problem. But they only deepen it. The result is insecurity, fear of the future, lack of direction. People don't know where to go or what to do.

We have the Lord's own words in the Gospel: "Only one is your teacher: the Messiah. Only one is your father: God, your Father in heaven." Only there will you find your solutions. It is the Lord, and only He, who can solve our problems. So Isaiah writes, "I, the Lord, teach you what is good. If you listen to me, your prosperity will flow like a river." Forceful image! The power to cure our ills is given us, but we must accept Jesus totally to experience His power!

This is our real problem: we put all kinds of obstacles in the Lord's way. We try to find easy substitutes for Christ, but they don't work.

**Lord Jesus, You are the answer—if we would only give
You a chance to show us!**

SERVE THE REST

Second Week of Lent, Wednesday   **Matthew 20:17-28**

In the Gospel a concerned mother is looking out for her children's future. Jesus dares to answer the mother's request by suggesting that her darling sons would be better off taking back seats rather than front seats in His kingdom. When the other ten apostles grumbled against the two brothers for that bold request, Jesus gave them the same answer. "Learn of me," Jesus had said, "for I am meek and humble."

Humility is one of the bad words in modern vocabularies. A desire for it, or even a study of it is one of the great taboos of our smart society. For who is "crazy enough to take the abuse" attached to humility? Let's be fair: a large part of the touch-me-not attitude toward humility is simply a radical misunderstanding of what it is.

We throw so much dust and smoke in our urge to express ourselves, that we becloud the very best in human self-expression! The fact is, real humility is attractive and always will be, and it always saves its owner from innumerable and tragic pitfalls. For it rests on the solid pillar of deep, genuine honesty. Like it or not, the ever-modern generation must return to this priceless virtue as the only authentic expression of the best in human personality.

Free discussion is important. We are fortunate that Zebedee's wife asked this favor for her sons. It gave Jesus the opportunity to teach a most important lesson. It is valuable to hear one another, to disagree with one another, to feel the need to convince one another. But—to paraphrase the Lord's teaching—it can only succeed when it is done with the deepest charity and mutual respect. Notice the deep kindness and the practical realism of Jesus' answer. It is the answer of a deeply humble man, who respects the hopes and aspirations of his fellow men.

All successful interchange requires the open-minded attitude of humble men. Real humility is not a veneer; it is nothing artificial or false.

"Anyone among you who aspires to greatness must serve the rest, and whoever wants to rank first among you must serve the needs of all." Thank you, Jesus, for

advice that will solve countless problems in human relations!

RICH MAN, POOR MAN

Second Week of Lent, Thursday   **Luke 16:19-31**

Jesus in the Gospel today hits upon the tension that exists between the rich and the poor in the world. He is quite obviously siding with the poor. We can be sure Jesus would still speak in the same way today. Maybe a different story, but the same message. There is too large a gap between rich and poor. We are all God's children, we are brothers and sisters of each other in his family. We just cannot tolerate the present injustices where brother exploits brother and leaves him destitute.

Jesus is challenging us to gospel living. Are we witnesses, true witnesses to his teachings or not?

Remember, the poor are always with us. Every time that we see or hear of someone poorer than ourselves whom we could help and don't, Christ is present; He is in our midst. If we don't reach out our hand of love, He goes on his way hungry and thirsty and naked. We probably won't be hearing trumpets blasting or a lot of angels flying around, but the judgment has taken place just the same. We've failed the test.

So where is Jesus really present among us? In the Eucharist, surely; in his Word, just as truly. But what about the no less real presence of Christ Jesus in all those Lazaruses we meet up with? In the Eucharist Christ is present in the Bread. In the poor he is present just as much in the absence of bread.

> **Had the rich man been the poor man's friend,**
> **He would have come to a happier end.**
> **O Jesus, help us to catch on**
> **To Matthew, Mark, Luke and John.**

NO IMAGINATION

Second Week of Lent, Friday   **Matthew 21:33-46**

Jesus said to the Pharisees, "The Kingdom of God will be taken away from you and given to people who will produce the right fruit."

We may well wonder how the world has survived the infections with which man has polluted it, the depravities, the lies, the betrayals, the injustices. "Behold how the innocent are murdered, and no man stops to consider," said the ancient prophet. How many times had God to repeat that cry through the centuries, in every nation, on every continent! The prophets themselves, the chosen people, men, women, children of greatest holiness and charity, the most beautiful of God's creatures were most often victims marked for slaughter, victims to teach and prepare fallen man for his crime of crimes—the rejection of Innocence itself, the execution of the Son of Man. And He, the head of humanity, the "first-born of every creature," said, "Whatever you do to the least of my brethren, you do to me."

Mankind's record of crimes is a horror to make the very stars scream, to turn back the sun, to darken the earth, a record shocking enough to stop crime forever—we might hope. But "still too dull to learn, too slow to grasp the lesson, the sinner goes on in his busy wickedness" (Ps 92). An even-greater army of bloodied martyrs marches behind the Son of Man, its ranks swollen year by year, its number legion in our own century.

"Must then a Christ perish in torment in every age to save those that have no imagination?" asks the spirit of Cauchon in Shaw's *Joan of Arc.*

Thousands of Christs have perished in every age, and millions in our own age, and still "senseless man does not understand this. Though the wicked flourish like grass and all evildoers thrive, they are all destined for eternal destruction, while You, O Lord, are the Most High forever" (Ps 92).

Lord Jesus, give us Your light, that we may not blindly reject You, the cornerstone of our whole structure.

PRODIGAL SON

Second Week of Lent, Saturday   **Luke 15:11-32**

The parable of the prodigal son is really the story of the forgiving father. Jesus told the incident to show us how God feels about those of us who know we are sinners, but want to return to God. He loves us and wants to celebrate that happy return with us.

It is very revealing to note what happened just before Jesus told this story. Luke tells us, "the sinners were all gathering around Jesus to hear Him." Why? What had Jesus done to attract these sinners, these people whom the Pharisees called the good-for-nothings of society?

Jesus had just held out an invitation and a challenge. He had told the parable of the great supper, in which God invites many, but they all find excuses and fail to come. So then the king sends out his servants to invite others, because the first invited guests are busy making excuses. After this parable, Jesus challenges His audience to dare to be His disciples, because they are going to have to carry the cross with Him. And this attracts the sinners to Jesus! He is at the same time inviting them and challenging them to a new life, a greater life than they have ever known.

Just in case any of His listeners wonder, "Does he mean *me*?" Jesus tells the parable of the wayward son and the forgiving father. The parable says, "No matter how you think you have failed, your heavenly Father will receive you back with love, and He invites you to that new life in Him."

That is the invitation and the challenge which Jesus is holding out to each one of us. God's unfailing and unquestionable love for each of us comes through in the parable. We should note the role of the son in Christ's story. The father could not have forgiven the son, if the son had not returned to his father to receive it. The son was open and ready for forgiveness, because he was honest enough to see himself as he really was. He saw that his life was empty, that he had thrown away his real blessings for false ones, and that he would be infinitely better off returning to his father.

> He saw, as we must each see, Lord, that we really do need our heavenly Father.

THE OLD HOME TOWN

Third Week of Lent, Monday   **Luke 4:24-30**

Remember the old song, "Those good and gentle people in my old home town?"

What happens to the greatest of all men, Jesus Himself, when He comes to those good and gentle people in *His* old home town? They treat him terribly. They refuse to listen, they're not at all open-minded, they show hatred and envy, and they even plot murder against Him. "They expelled him from the town, intending to hurl him over the edge of the hill." Small minds and closed hearts, the same sad rebellion experienced by the prophets of the Old Testament.

Don't you think you and I would do much better than that if Jesus came here to preach, even if this *weren't* His home town?

Well—we *do* have many a chance to accept the Son of God—or to reject Him. How well do we come out? How *could* Nazareth reject Jesus, the all-holy and loving one, their very Creator and Lord? Well—there was a certain spirit in that town, a narrow, prejudiced spirit which was responsible for their awful mistake. It was a spirit of criticism and envy.

They said, "Where did He get all this wisdom? His parents are only Mary and Joseph: they're nothing—just a carpenter and wife." These people refused to see any special good in others. Jesus later called them "blind leaders of the blind."

Here was the spirit of small-minded gossip. St. John later says, "They plotted how they might destroy Him." Eventually their pride and envy did make them murderers, killers of the innocent.

This has a lot to teach us. St. Paul says, "Brothers, be careful how you treat your neighbor, for as you accept one another, so you accept Christ." If we're out to hurt our neighbor, we are really hurting ourselves.

> **Unworthy guests are we, Lord, though we desire to be**
> **Your servants by Your grace, Lord; we rose from poverty.**
> **But You have dared to take us into Your family;**
> **Your own you chose to make us: supreme Your charity!**

PSYCHOLOGY OF FORGIVING

Third Week of Lent, Tuesday   **Matthew 18:21-35**

Jesus says, "Forgive seventy times seven times." Then He tells a parable which indicates "torture" if we do not forgive. What excellent psychology! Most people who are tortured mentally have been hurt and have refused to forgive.

Any psychologist or psychiatrist can tell you of persons—and sometimes their whole families with them—who suffered mental torture and even mental and emotional illness by refusing to forgive. Jesus knew very well that a deep and realistic spirit of forgiveness is essential, not only to our spiritual health, but our mental and emotional health as well.

That is why Jesus instructs us to love others, even if they have hurt us. Forgiveness is the love of those who have hurt you. If you don't do this, it is not God who punishes you; you punish yourself; you torture yourself by nursing the resentment. You suffer so much so needlessly.

You hear people say, "You know, God used to answer my prayers so wonderfully, until the time I became bitter about a person who hurt me and my family. I refused to forgive, and after that, my prayers just seemed useless." How many blessings we miss, if we refuse to forgive. How much peace and joy we miss.

Jesus showed us how to forgive. As He was nailed to the cross, He said, "Father, forgive them." Nothing but love in His heart, even at the very worst hurt He could ever suffer—complete rejection and murder. When you forgive, you have a very personal part in the healing ministry of Jesus. Jesus made forgiveness so much a part of His teaching, because His was a ministry of healing and saving.

Now if you say, "I cannot forgive," you may be right. Of your own power, maybe not. But you can ask Jesus to come into your life and forgive *for* you. The spirit of Jesus is the spirit of forgiveness. So then we know where the spirit of not forgiving comes from! Satan! Jesus has won the victory over Satan, and if you find it too hard to forgive, remember, Jesus has won that victory for you. Ask Jesus to put His spirit into your heart. If you really want it, He will answer that request.

JESUS SPEAKS

Third Week of Lent, Wednesday   **Matthew 5:17-19**

The Gospel passage today is a small piece from Christ's beautiful and powerful sermon on the mount. They are words used by Jesus as He instructed His disciples and the people on the mountain side.

Today, as we read these words, He still gives us the same instruction. It is good for us to remind ourselves that the Gospels are not just a recalling of past events in Jesus' life, not only a recalling of words spoken by Him.

Jesus is still present in the Gospels, in His Word, in a very unique way. And as we read a gospel passage we become aware of the special way in which He comes to us today. Sometimes He comes as Healer, sometimes as Friend or Comforter, sometimes He comes as Teacher

Jesus today comes to us to spend a little time with us as Teacher. He brings us one of the lessons He gave in that sermon on the mount. And He teaches us with the same authority and divine presence as He did on the mount.

"You are the light of the world," He says to us. We do have the light of faith. We have the light that can dispel darkness, the darkness in which one can see no further in life than the immediate pleasures and comforts of the day. We have the light that can dispel the darkness of gloom and despair which stem from not being able to see God's Hand, God's Will, in sickness, in the death of a dear one. We have the light which can dispel the darkness of bitterness, of resentment, of unforgiveness. The light of faith can enlighten our minds with meaning, with joy in the midst of sorrows, with forgiveness in spite of hurts.

But that light must be more than the light of knowledge through faith. It must be a burning light in our way of living, it must shine forth in our love, in our good works, in our apostolic zeal, in the way our actions by example draw other people closer to God.

Thank You, Jesus, for speaking to us today, and for promising us Your Kingdom if we listen to Your message.

HE WAITS TOO LONG?

Third Week of Lent, Thursday   **Luke 11:14-23**

"Though Jesus had worked many signs in their presence, they did not believe in Him."

"He loves too much and waits too long," says the impatient Christian. "He lost His chance," says the professional organizer. "He could have organized a rebel group, enforced radical reforms, incited zealots to stage a massive coup."

With the right diplomacy, with motivated miracles, He could have set the world aflame—a desire He Himself expressed.

"He waits too long—I told you so! Too patient! Bad thing!"

The promotion man agrees: "His enemies had nothing on their side. He had the color, the mind and might, the idealism and the magnetism." What a stirring and shaking liberation He could have sparked. "I told you so—He forgives too much and waits too long."

See Christ among His people: a picture of God in His dealing with the world throughout history. He loves us, He gives His life for us—but He does demand a return. He is incorruptible: He demands that we face the truth.

Loves too much and waits too long? Watch Him in action: He is always in command. He accepts insults, but there is judgment in the very acceptance. He accepts rejection because He loves. He receives insults and humiliation because He loves. He suffers and dies because He loves. And what in the end does He demand?

He demands love. "You are to love as I have loved." He holds the key to the mystery—the mystery of divine patience, the mystery of divine wisdom, divine forgiveness.

And those who have not loved too much and waited too long have learned too late.

Patient Jesus, teach us to wait—and to listen.

QUESTIONNAIRE

Third Week of Lent, Friday **Mark 12:28-34**

"Love one another as I have loved you." The New Testament is full of advice on how we should love as God loves, and imitate the patience of Christ. It's healthy to make ourselves a questionnaire at times, to find out how we're doing on the law of love. In your Christian love today, you might forgive me for choosing a light vein.

First case: you're in a hurry to get moving on an important trip, and the gas station attendant can't get your hood opened, then he smears your windshield more than he cleans it. Do you grumble, "If he doesn't hide, I'll run him over?" Or do you say, "Oh well, I can't please everyone, and everyone can't please me. Hooray for my patience?"

Second case: you're in the supermarket, and you're racing two women with loaded carts to the checkout counter, and you lose the race. Under your breath, do you swear and grunt? Or do you say your morning prayers? The Lord has given you time for it—how do you use it?

Third case: It's breakfast with your family, you feel worse than your usual pleasant self, and one of the kids spills his milk on your plate, while another steals your toast. Do you leave the table in a huff, determined to eat in a restaurant by yourself? Or do you announce, "How wonderful that we all think of others, even in the morning?"

Fourth case: You wake up with a sore throat and a headache and an upset stomach. Do you have the whole house on the run, anxious and fearful? Or do you say, cheerfully of course, "This must be God's way of slowing me down, and brother, is it effective!"

Fifth case: All in one week, the TV set, the sink, two doors, and the car break down. Do you break down, too? Do you in a wild tantrum go out to buy everything new? Or do you say, "Thank God, we still have each other, and we're still alive!"

Even the apostles had their problems with love, and we have ours. If anyone was challenged by the law of love, it was Jesus Himself, by the poor response he got. But He stayed with it faithfully, and eventually His apostles caught the Spirit. "I have given you an example," said Jesus, and after years of failure, they understood. Looking at our failures, may we, too, stay with it faithfully till we begin to experience Christian love and patience.

WHO NEEDS WHOM?

Third Week of Lent, Saturday   **Luke 18:9-14**

Jesus meant this parable, says Luke, for those "who trusted in themselves," those who thought they were "just, and despised others." And how many of us can say "He didn't mean me?"

The Pharisee goes to the temple at the hour of prayer. Perhaps he even went twice a day to pray. 9 a.m. and 3 p.m. were the traditional hours of prayer. He was not an outright liar: he did give ten per cent of his income to the temple, he did fast twice a week, and it was a very strict fast on Mondays and Thursdays, no food and even no water.

With all his fasting and prayer, why doesn't the Pharisee deserve the Lord's praise? Because he despises his neighbor. He is so important in his own eyes that he rejects the thought that anyone not of his clique might also be pleasing to God. In the parable's "prayer" of the Pharisee, Jesus has captured the man's spirit: "God needs me because of my excellent observance of the law, but who needs these sinners, these thieves, cheaters, adulterers, this scum of society?" He has broken the greatest law of all. He has entirely misread his Bible, ignoring God's real message of love.

Far back, behind the proud Pharisee, stands a sinner, an outcast, a "lawbreaker." But this man knows who needs whom. He is not proud of his accomplishments. His head is bowed in shame. But he knows where to turn for justice and mercy and forgiveness. "God, be merciful to me, a sinner."

This man is acceptable to God, says Jesus, because he knows the truth about himself and he faces it with a sincere heart. He also knows God well—the God of love and mercy who forgives honest sinners, sinners who know themselves. He knows, "I need God, I need him totally to cleanse my life, and I trust in Him."

Lord Jesus Christ, Son of the living and loving God, be merciful to me, a sinner.

OPEN OUR EYES

Fourth Week of Lent, Monday   John 4:43-54

"Unless you people see signs and wonders, you do not believe." Galilee wanted signs and wonders, but not repentance. It wanted a color spectacular, rather than a change of heart. People came to Jesus too often because they were desperate or because they wanted to see a miracle. Here is an example of the age-old temptation of preferring fun and thrills to anything solid or lasting: razzle-dazzle rather than substance.

Blindness of heart is so utterly stupid; yet we are all guilty of it again and again. We are fond of rejecting reality for what is pleasant and easy. A young man had a bad cough, and finally went to the doctor. The doctor X-rayed the patient's lungs and came face-to-face with the grim reality. "You have a bad lung condition: you'll need surgery. It may be painful and costly."

The man said, "I'm scared of that, and anyway, I can't afford it. Isn't there an easier way?"

"Sure," said the doctor. "I could simply touch up the X-ray pictures and say, now everything's fine."

Many a time the only easy way out of a problem is that superficial: we touch up the picture and forget the reality beneath it. We get occasional glimpses of what's wrong with us, but we don't face the facts. We simply close our eyes and forget it.

Open eyes at the end of the rope are really too late. A pilot radioed the control tower from his airplane: "I'm out of gas at sea, four hundred miles from shore. What should I do? Urgent!" This is what you call the end of the rope.

The answer he got from the control tower: "Here are your instructions . . . Repeat after me, 'O my God, I am heartily sorry for all my sins . . .' "

Is it really necessary for us to wait that long before doing something about our shortages? Just what are we doing with the opportunities God is giving us?

Open our eyes, Lord, that we may live. Open our ears, that we may learn. Open our hearts, that we may listen.

I HAVE NOBODY

Fourth Week of Lent, Tuesday　　　　　　　　**John 5:1-16**

We have here that beautiful incident of Jesus curing the sick man at the pool of Bethesda. It was another one of His Sabbath day cures which seemed to upset the Pharisees so much.

This pool had the reputation for cures. It seemed to have had springs in it which bubbled up occasionally and people attributed healing power to these springs. Popularly it was said that an angel of God came to disturb the waters. The first sick person in the pool after such a bubbling was said to be cured of any ailment he had.

Now one man there had waited thirty-eight years to be cured. Jesus saw him lying there on his mat and knew his condition. He said to the man, "Do you want to be healed?" The sick man said to Him, "Sir, I have no one to put me in the water after it has been disturbed. By the time I get there, some one else has gone in ahead of me." Jesus simply said, "Get up, pick up your mat and walk," and he did. He was cured. What Jesus was telling the man who said, "I have no one," was, "you don't need anybody; you've got ME. That's all you need."

Isn't that often our problem? We feel we have nobody, nobody loves us, nobody cares for us, when all the while we can have the Lord Jesus touch us just by being open to Him and to His love.

When problems overwhelm us, when we are down and out, when everybody else seems to get ahead of us and nobody cares, there is just one answer. Turn to Jesus. Let Him be Lord in our lives and soon we will find a new peace, even in the midst of our troubles.

To You I lift up my soul, O Lord, my God.
In You I trust; let me not be put to shame (Ps 25:1, 2).

MY FATHER'S BUSINESS

Fourth Week of Lent, Wednesday   **John 5:17-30**

Jesus had cured on the Sabbath several times. The Jews cannot accept this and start to persecute Him. First Jesus answers by asking why He, the Son, cannot work on the Sabbath, since His Father certainly does. His creative act goes on everyday. This upsets them even more because Jesus is now speaking of God as His Father, making Himself God's equal.

Jesus answers by speaking of the relationship of the Son to the Father. As the Father does, so does the Son. The Father loves the Son. He will show Him even greater works, greater even than curing the sick. He will raise the dead to life, a work that the Father has been doing in every act of human creation.

All through this passage Jesus indicates the love relationship between the Father and the Son. He says He doesn't act on His own, but does what He sees the Father doing. He acts only according to the Father's will. He is in complete harmony with the Father.

As a twelve year old boy Jesus had already said to Mary and Joseph, "Did you not know that I must be about my Father's business?" Now He shows that regardless of the persecution and opposition He encounters, He will keep on doing the work of His Father, the works His Father gave Him to do. "I am not seeking My own will, but the will of Him who sent Me."

We too have a work to do. We all have a mission to fulfill. We must not seek our own wills, but seek to do the Lord's will. As He was faithful in doing His work in spite of opposition, we too must be faithful in doing ours, regardless of difficulties, opposition or human respect. On this will depend our personal love relationship with the Lord.

Lord, help us to hear Your word and to have faith in Him who sent You, so that we might possess eternal life.

FIVE WITNESSES

Fourth Week of Lent, Thursday   **John 5:31-47**

Jesus in this Gospel passage names five witnesses to His divine mission, five witnesses that proclaim Him the Messiah, five witnesses that testify to the truth of His words.

The first witness is God the Father, who sent Jesus (v. 31, 32, and 37). Those who have God's word abiding in their hearts will recognize the Father's witness. This is a convincing testimony to those who are sincerely open to God.

The second witness is John the Baptist, a human witness in which His listeners had rejoiced (v. 33-35). He had pointed out Jesus as "the One who is to come, the Lamb of God who takes away the world's sins."

The third witness was the wonderful works of Jesus: His healings, His miracles, His very goodness (v. 36). This testimony, Jesus says, is even greater than John's. His works speak for themselves. "By their fruits you shall know them."

The fourth witness is Holy Scripture: the psalms, the wisdom books, the writings of the prophets. Jesus tells his listeners to "search the scriptures" because they also testify to Jesus. He is fulfilling all that they say about Him.

The fifth witness Jesus cites is the great prophet, Moses, their lawgiver. Moses wrote about Jesus, and "if you believed Moses, you would then believe Me."

This was the Lord's well-ordered answer to the Pharisees, who were forever objecting to His works of healing on the Sabbath day. They should have known well enough that God's providence, His loving care of His children, does not come to a sudden halt on the Sabbath day. Jesus says so: "My Father is at work until this very day, and I am at work as well as He." They understood His meaning, for John tells us they hated him the more, no longer for just breaking their Sabbath tradition, but for "speaking of God as His own Father, thereby making Himself God's equal."

Turn back Your anger from us, Lord, blot out our failures from Your sight!
Your holy city lies in shame, great Zion fallen from its height;

**A desert land the holy place, where once we praised Your
glorious might!**

(Is 59).

HIS ORIGIN

Fourth Week of Lent, Friday John 7:25-30

Jesus said to His people, "So you know me, and you know my
origins? I was sent by One who has the right to send, and him you do
not know."

Whence came this notion of the people that "when the Messiah
comes, no one is supposed to know his origins?" Should not the
chosen people have known that when the promised Messiah came, he
would come from the God they claimed to know and worship? Yet
Jesus says of the Father who sent Him, the God of His people, that
they did not know Him.

This was surely not the fault of their prophets and saints, who
always insisted that they trust in the Lord, not in man. Why did God's
people not know Him, and therefore not recognize the one He sent,
the promised Messiah?

The Old Testament contains many a boast that they, of all
nations, knew the true God, and knew Him very well. And if the
sacred writers seem at times to look at God from afar, to set Him at
too great a distance from His people, they can shock us a moment
later by making Him almost too human, by thinking of Him in terms
surprisingly earthly. And even though they were not prepared to
understand the mystery of the Messiah as God-made-man, they were
prepared to expect a Messiah who was man.

Why, then, would they not accept this man, whom the Father had
sent?

Was it not because He was too much like the God they claimed to
know, and too little like the worldly standards they had set for Him?
Was it not the case of a people saying—and maybe even thinking—
they knew and worshipped the true God, but actually worshipping
their own graven image of Him?

They could not accept the "scandal" of Jesus, the "scandal" of their God, who had stripped Himself of His divine riches to become one with the poor; their God, who chose to be born of the poor and take on incredible poverty and insignificance; their God, who in His divine love could not take anything for Himself, but live a life of complete self-giving.

Lord Jesus, do we really know you better? Do we really accept you as our Messiah?

HUMBLE ARE THE MIGHTY

Fourth Week of Lent, Saturday   **John 7:40-53**

"Surely the Messiah is not to come from Galilee."
"Do not tell us you have been taken in."
You can always identify truly great persons by their humility. Those who have true inner worth need not fear stooping to the most lowly. It is the small, petty, puny person that fears humiliation, that disdains the smell of poverty, that shows annoyance when not given sufficient attention and honor.

The secret of greatness is the secret of genuine humility. It means forgetting my own importance and going out of myself in order to remember the importance of others.

How easy this should be when we see Christ's utter debasement, His free choice to live in the greatest poverty, ignored by His neighbors and later rejected by His townsmen. They could not bear to see "the carpenter's son" coming by all this wisdom and power to heal. "Why begin now?" they meant to say. "For thirty years He was nothing. He was but a sweating, poorly-clothed village lad. If He is someone great, He would never have been born and raised here in Nazareth, of all places!"

They missed the very point of Your choice, Lord. You were so great that You could well afford to empty Yourself. Even in Your public life, Jesus, when after thirty hidden years the time came for You to tell the world who You were, You accepted no rewards, took no offers of glory, made no display of earthly power. Like a homeless refugee, You could truly say You had no place to lay Your head. Your home was indeed the universe. You had no need and no desire to accumulate anything less.

Such was Your humility, Jesus, because of Your infinite superiority. The quality of humility is like the quality of mercy observed by Shakespeare: "it is mightiest in the mightiest."

Silent, poor, He worked among us, till His words with deeds fulfilled,
Christ surrendered to His people, met a fate His love had willed:
Gibbet crude became an altar, where the Lamb of God was killed.

(from the *Crux Fidelis*).

THE AMERICAN KILLER

Fifth Week of Lent, Monday   **John 8:1-11**

I wonder how many of you have ever heard of a fierce little creature, called "The American Killer." It is found in the southern states of our country, from Texas to Florida. This tiny American Killer attacks human beings: another name for it is the hookworm. You know what this killer does? It crawls to a high elevation on the ground, waiting for human flesh to come along. When a barefoot person steps on it, it pierces his foot and soon enters his bloodstream. It even attaches itself to the ankles or legs of persons lying on the ground. The worst part is, the person himself usually doesn't notice it at all. Through the bloodstream this tiny worm enters the intestines and even into the lungs. It is said to have teeth as sharp as a tiger's. Each worm consumes one-half cubic centimeter of human blood in an hour. These worms breed and multiply; the victim slowly bleeds to death internally.

What the hookworm does to man physically, certain sins do to man spiritually. The life-blood of spiritual strength in us is our reverence for God and our fellow man. The sins that drain away this essential of love and respect are the most deadly. And what fills the bill better than the rotten old sin we call gossip? Nice names for it are criticism, passing judgment. It eats the heart right out of the good that's in you and in your neighbor.

Notice the Pharisees in the Gospel (or in the story of Daniel). They claim to have caught a woman in sin. What is their reaction? To forgive? To help? To sympathize? All they want is to condemn. "Moses said such a person should be stoned to death." There was an ancient law of this kind, but it presumed a fair trial before official judges. In the Book of Daniel, Susannah was falsely accused, and the accusers were themselves found guilty. Jesus, who knew what was inside each person, saw a similarity here. The very accusers of this woman were in fact greater sinners themselves. Thus He said, "Whoever is without sin among you can throw the first stone."

None of them dared to throw a stone. Would any of us dare?

Lord, let my words about others be words of love and forgiveness.

AM I IN THE WAY?

Fifth Week of Lent, Tuesday   **John 8:21-30**

Jesus said, "He who sent me is with me; He has not left me alone, because I always do what pleases Him."

The only real source of unhappiness is our constant foolishness in placing obstacles between ourselves and God. As soon as we desire to possess things for ourselves, instead of desiring to give ourselves to God, anxiety is born and the assurance of happiness flees.

The famous conductor, Arturo Toscanini, had a phenomenal knowledge of the music performed by his orchestra, down to the finest details. One day at a rehearsal, as the orchestra reached the climax of an overture, Toscanini suddenly shouted, "Stop!" And when they stopped, he asked, "What was that noise?"

There was a puzzled silence, until the first violinist solved the riddle. "Sorry, Maestro," he said, "That noise was yourself, humming."

"Oh, yes," answered Toscanini, enlightened. "So it was, so it was."

He had gotten between himself and his orchestra, and the strange sound disturbed him. Strange sounds disturb us, too, when we get between ourselves and God.

Then if, like Toscanini, we stop to ask, "What was that noise? What's wrong here?" will the Lord not answer, "Sorry, my dear, that noise was yourself, getting in the way and spoiling a beautiful harmony. Your pride has caused this confusion. You are making your own unhappiness. Why not try loving others genuinely, without intruding yourself so much? Why not try appreciating the mystery of the divine plan, without spoiling everything by trying to improve upon it?"

> **Lord, Your kindness spans the heavens,**
> **Great Your love beyond the sky,**
> **Firm your justice as the mountains,**
> **Wisdom reaching low and high.**
> **Your true children know Your greatness,**
> **Strength and peace in You they find;**
> **Confident, they sing Your goodness,**
> **Lord and Father of mankind!** (Ps 36).

A TYRANT

Fifth Week of Lent, Wednesday   **John 8:31-42**

Jesus says, "If you live according to my teaching . . . you will know the truth, and the truth will set you free."

Man is born a tyrant. He is a slave to greed and vain-glory all his life, unless by a miracle of grace he allows Christ to set him free.

This doesn't mean he has no desire to *appear* virtuous—unselfish, generous, kind, humble, and set free. But cross his path at the wrong place, and you shall feel the violence of man's slavery to self.

We have experienced this often enough, living among humans. We have noticed it most often, perhaps, in ourselves. Know yourself—as Socrates advised—and you know that man is a born tyrant, wrathfully jealous of all that he thinks is his own.

There is only one kind of person who cannot be thus invaded and stirred to tyranny: he is that rare creature who has become in the fullest sense "a child of God," as St. John writes. He has been filled— and consequently emptied—by God's love. There is no more greed, no arrogance or vanity, no false desires, no wall around self. He may be attacked, but not disturbed; invaded, but not angered; persecuted, but not conquered. Such persons we call saints when their struggle to become thus emptied of self begins to produce true effects.

All of us are either saints or slaves. Slaves indeed, though we act like tyrants. Who is free, but he whom Christ has emptied? Such a person's path cannot be crossed, for the path is not straight, rigid, or unbending. It is forever elusive, forever winding this way and that, as the breath of the Spirit prompts it. It follows a mysterious route: the Will of God. When you try to cut off this path, when you attack or restrict it, it bends for you; it makes room, it strikes out in a new direction, and every new detour hastens it more surely to its goal. It is colloquially stated thus: when life hands the saint a lemon, he makes lemonade.

Jesus, let us experience Your living truth: that truth will set us free.

LOYALTY

Fifth Week of Lent, Thursday **John 8:51-59**

One of the most touching stories of loyalty I've heard is that of a writer who was the father of a family, and through no fault of his own lost two jobs in one year. The second time this happened, his wife comforted him as best she could, and his three little boys stared quietly.

Late the next morning he went into his study, and in the waste basket he noticed the broken remains of three piggy-banks. On his desk was a pile of quarters, dimes, and nickels, with a note in a little boy's handwriting. "We believe in you, Dad."

This is loyalty: a trust in the face of the greatest odds.

Such should be our loyalty to Christ; because such is His loyalty to us. And what an example He gave us of loyalty to His Father! How truly He lives up to His name, the Son of God. What a Son He was! "I do only what the Father has taught me . . . I always do what pleases Him. . . Were God your father, you would love me . . . It was He who sent me . . . If I glorify myself, that glory is nothing. He who gives me glory is the Father . . . I honor my Father and keep His word. . . ."

He never got too smart for His Father, though indeed He was equal to the Father.

Did you ever notice how *personal* Jesus was in all that He did? He seldom spoke of obeying a regulation or rule, or ethical standards, good politics, or the proper thing to do. He often spoke, however, of pleasing His Father, obeying His Father, keeping His Father's commands. All that He did was done out of a deep personal loyalty to His Father.

And that's our job. A Christian doesn't obey an abstract law, a line of print in a book, an ethical standard or a political expedient. Jesus in fact condemned playing politics, playing the hypocrite, acting only to be seen by others. He knew how people were squealing on Him to the Pharisees, how they put all His actions into a bad light, how they were misusing His honesty and loyalty. Yet He will not be corrupted by mob pressure. He is a man of power, but He cannot be talked into abusing it. He obeyed His Father in every detail, and is not afraid to say so.

THE WORD

Fifth Week of Lent, Friday John 10:31-42

Through the history of salvation we come to see the power of God's word. His word creates all things; His word to Abraham creates a new people, the favored of God; later His word rescues these people from slavery through Moses; when they fall back into sin, His word continues to save them; His word brings the good news of a coming Savior. When the Redeemer appears, His word effects endless works of power: He heals the sick with a word, He drives out devils, He multiplies bread and changes water to wine, He calls back the very dead. His mighty word promises His own resurrection and ours, and His word, resting on bread and wine, extends His presence among us for ages to come. His word establishes a new people of God, and forms them to the perfect image of man. What power there is in the word of God!

The sacredness of the word is too easily lost on us. Too many meaningless and hypocritical words have deadened us. We need real effort—study and meditative prayer—to purify and ennoble our use of words, our very choice of words, and our appreciation of their power. We hear so many worthless, deceptive, vile and evil words, that we are always in danger of underestimating the value of the word.

The word is mightier than armies; the idea outlives all physical force, and well may we rejoice in that, or else how few people in history ever knew freedom and love! In the days of most abject slavery and oppression under the worst tyrants, there always appeared gloriously free and heroic spirits.

About that powerful word Jesus said to the Pharisees, "You do not have the Father's word abiding in your hearts, because you do not believe the one he has sent."

> **Word of the Cross of Christ,**
> **Who for all was sacrificed,**
> **Weakness of God and true strength of man,**
> **Wisdom we cannot know,**
> **Folly to man below,**
> **Embrace us in your mighty span!**

VICTORY ROAD

Fifth Week of Lent, Saturday   **John 11:45-57**

"From that day on there was a plan afoot to kill Him." The Pharisees, as the prophets said, had "cut Him off from every way of escape" (Ps 118), and in doing so, they had forced Jesus onto the road of His supreme victory—so it seemed. But He had chosen this road from the beginning.

Thus the Christian's victory song: "Jesus is risen; all things are set right." The world has no such glory to offer. What the world offers is very brief, very passing, very uncertain. What the Church offers remains forever, cannot be lost by treachery, deception, ill-fortune or accident. It depends entirely on the will of man as conformed to the Will of God, on man's well-grounded hope in Christ. Whoever hopes in Jesus and desires to share the victory of Jesus, is assured of it in advance.

If there is suffering and sorrow, there is the example of Christ's Passion. If there is apparent defeat or failure, there is the Lord's assurance that when we live united to Him there is no such thing as defeat or failure. Not only the Resurrection, but the Cross itself is victory. The Cross is self-giving united to victory as the Resurrection is the fulfillment of victory.

In the face of evil the Christian remembers there is no victory without struggle. He hopes to come before his Lord like a warrior who has endured much, who has overcome such great difficulties that his love and his loyalty cannot be doubted. "I would do it for you again, any time," said a dying soldier to his captain on the battlefield. He had risked his life; he had lost it—but he had already given his life willingly. The risk itself was proof of his loyalty. The true Christian will do as much for Christ. The tasks undertaken are proof of his loyalty, and whatever happens, victory is his.

> **Christ Jesus brought us life,**
> **Cross of shame has won the strife,**
> **He chose the weak to confound the strong!**
> **No human tongue can boast,**
> **Praise God, creation's host,**
> **To whom all life and strength belong!**

DO WE BELIEVE?

Holy Week, Monday   **John 12:1-11**

The crowd came "not only because of Jesus, but also to see Lazarus, whom he had raised from the dead." As He sat at table with His friends, Martha, Mary, Lazarus and His disciples, there must have been deep joy in the heart of Jesus. That joy came from Christ's faithful love for His heavenly Father and the Spirit, and for all the people present at the banquet.

In some cases it was a forgiving love, a love Jesus had already taught us, for we become aware of the human frustrations at this friendly banquet! Mary, the contemplative who has sat at the feet of Jesus listening to His teaching, now anoints the feet of her Lord. And Judas, the unbelieving and traitorous apostle, voices loud objections. The Pharisaic hypocrisy which Jesus often denounced has invaded His own band of apostles. "Why was this perfume not sold in favor of the poor?" Jesus is well aware of the deception and the thievery behind this pious front.

And while there is the consolation of increased faith in the people because of the resurrection of Lazarus, Jesus is also aware of what this great sign has done to the Pharisees. They have frequently demanded "signs" from Jesus, proofs of His divine mission, credentials for His teaching. Now that Jesus has given them the most convincing of signs, how do they respond? John tells us "they planned to kill Lazarus, too," for people were believing in Jesus since He had brought Lazarus back from the dead.

Remember the parable Jesus had told of the rich man and Lazarus? Was the choice of name not a prophecy? In the story, when at last the greedy man saw the result of his worldly life, from hell he begged Abraham to send the poor man, Lazarus, back to earth to warn his brothers. "No," said Abraham, "If they will not believe Moses and the prophets, they will not believe even if someone should return from the dead" (Lk 16:31).

And how is our faith, Lord Jesus? What sign do we demand before we truly believe and live by that belief? After we have listened to the power of Your teaching, what further sign do we need?

PILGRIMS

Holy Week, Tuesday **John 13:21-33, 36-38**

Jesus says, "I am going where you cannot follow me now; later on you shall come after me." He refers to His departure from this world—and theirs. And yet, His work in this world is far from finished. But He has taught us, as His saints have, that those who accomplish real good in the eternal records of God are seldom those who see the results of their work in this life.

Yet love makes them go on in spite of apparent failure and bitter opponents. That does not say the temptation to discouragement is ever so far away. How many great mystics, experiencing within themselves the passion of Jesus, exclaimed, "Ah, much good it does to bleed so copiously, to receive so many blows, so much rejection and spittle, so many lashes, to suffer such intense pain!" As St. Augustine writes of Jesus, "Daily he stretched out His hands to an unbelieving and ungrateful people."

"Yes, Lord," we answer. "If we wish to be like Jesus, we need to remember, we are pilgrims and strangers on this earth. We should not expect to see the results of the good we do. How many great men ever did? We dare not on that account give up. Too many have shrugged their shoulders, have lost their zeal and fallen into spiritual decay, because they found no visible effects of their efforts."

Jesus Himself warned us that because the world is heaped with scandals, "the charity of many shall grow cold." He Himself did not stay in this world to witness the fruits of His work. It was enough that He had done His Father's Will. He taught us that it is not our earthly success but our trusting perseverance that counts. The life of Jesus and the lives of the saints teach us this: Love to the end, and remember, results will come in God's good time, not in ours.

> **For in His Will is our true peace,**
> **His truth our life and way;**
> **Will pain and sin and darkness cease?**
> **In heaven's endless day!**

AN EMPTY LIFE

Holy Week, Wednesday   **Matthew 26:14-25**

This Gospel passage begins and ends with Judas, the betrayer. When we think of Judas, we think of the tragedy of despair and a lost life, an empty life, a loss too large for most of us to understand.

Ordinarily we manage to survive with small, selfish aims, with enough success and satisfaction to compensate for our failures. Many people even survive on the pleasure they derive from complaining, scolding, and criticizing.

If we must find meaning in the very goal of life itself, as when a very great sacrifice is suddenly thrust upon us—are we prepared for it? How often we hear of those who are not. We read, for example, of a high school student who in despair committed suicide. His popularity rating was excellent: president of his class, winner of honors and awards, captain of the football team, idol of the girls—what more could a high school boy want?

What more could he want. God forgive our blindness. In desperation he took his life. It was not the aftermath of a quarrel, not a painful humiliation, setback or defeat, no death in the family or among friends that might have accounted for depression. At first there was no explanation at all. Of course, no one was able to report on the state of his soul. No one, that is, but himself. He left a brief note: "I no longer have anything to live for. I cannot rise out of my despair."

Not all the health, the talents, the popularity, the money, the friends—not all of it was worth living for. The young man was right, but he ended his search too soon.

"I cannot rise." Even this, his last desperate cry, was true and genuine. I myself cannot rise—but God can raise me up, as surely as He has raised up all His saints who gave up this world by rising above it. I cannot heal myself—but Jesus heals!

> **Oppressed by sin and wicked ways,**
> **We floundered, sinking to the grave;**
> **Yet begging God through nights and days,**
> **We learned the Lord is strong to save:**
> **His healing word we thank and praise** (Ps 107).

THE LAST SUPPER

Holy Thursday   **Luke 22:15-19; John 13:1-15**

As He sat down to the "last supper" table, Jesus said to His friends, "I have greatly desired to eat this passover with you." What was that great desire of Jesus? What desires of Jesus did the institution of the Holy Eucharist fulfill?

St. Thomas Aquinas says, if we examine the words of Jesus in the Gospels, at least five purposes or desires of Jesus appear:

1) So that we would not forget Him. "Do this in memory of me" (Lk 22:19). Jesus says by this, "Keep me ever in your mind and in your heart."

2) So that He could be our food, our spiritual strength and healing. "I am the Bread of Life; whoever comes to me shall not hunger, and he who believes in me shall never thirst" (Jn 6:35). "This bread is my flesh, given for the life of the world" (6:51).

3) So that by the Eucharist He could be our sacrifice, and win forgiveness of sins for us. He would be our peace offering, our gift to the Father. "This is my Body, which will be given up for you" (Lk 22:19). "This is my Blood of the new covenant, which is being shed for man, for the forgiveness of sins" (Mt 26:27-28).

4) So that we could personally experience His deep love for us and His presence with us.
Jesus had indicated that He wanted a personal friendship with each believer, each person who accepted His love. "Whoever eats my Flesh and drinks my Blood abides in me and I in him" (Jn 6:56). "As the living Father sent me, and as I live because of Him, so whoever eats me will live because of me" (6:57).

5) So that we may share in His Resurrection. "If anyone eats of this Bread he will live forever" (Jn 6:51). "Whoever eats my Flesh and drinks my Blood has eternal life, and I will raise him up on the last day" (6:54). Holy Communion is our personal share in the power and glory of the Risen Jesus.

So the Eucharist, the Bread of Life, is the Church's way of continuing what Jesus began at the last supper.

Jesus, thank You for this wondrous mystery, the Bread of Life, by which we can be so near to You and experience Your strength, Your forgiveness, and Your healing power. Thank You for the share in Your risen glory which You give us in this Sacrament.

LIBERATION

Good Friday   **The Passion from John's Gospel**

The theme of Good Friday's liturgy is liberation. We are free because of Christ's love for us. If we do not deeply understand that His sacrifice brings us the great gift of freedom, we miss the greatest joys of Christian life, and we cannot possibly appreciate our own worth.

We are free now to make our lives worthwhile, eternally glorious because of Christ's surrender to the cross. We are free now because our love and our good works have a lifelong meaning and an eternal day of fulfillment. We are no longer slaves to human limitations and to death as the gloomy end of all. We are eternally free, and that eternal goal has deeply affected time itself; it has changed our whole life and its every detail. Eternal meaning has reached into the smallest moments of time.

Every word and gesture of the Good Friday liturgy celebrates mankind's liberation. The atmosphere of sorrow is grief over our failure to yield ourselves to this new freedom; we continue to block the way to our new freedom by sin. Jesus has won the prize, but we make it ineffective in ourselves by closing the door to Him.

Nevertheless, He has freed us. From the prophet Hosea we hear the jubilant song of liberation, "He will heal us . . . He will bind our wounds . . . On the third day He will raise us up, to live in His presence" (6:1-2).

Let us follow Him to Calvary, then, where we will learn to know God, who is Love. In Gethsemane Jesus says to the police, "If I am the one you want, let these men go." This was to fulfill what He had said, "I have not lost one of those you gave me." To the high priest Jesus says, "I have spoken publicly to any who would listen . . . There was nothing secret about anything I said." To the Roman governor Jesus says, "The reason why I came into the world, is to testify to the truth. Anyone committed to the truth hears my voice." On the cross, at the end of the three hours' agony, Jesus says, "Now it is finished." Then He bows His head and surrenders His spirit, as He has already surrendered His whole life for our liberation.

> **"The fruit of the tree betrayed us, but the Son of God has set us free."**

REBIRTH

Holy Saturday

"This is the night in which Christ burst the bonds of death and came forth as Conqueror from the grave." This is the great Passover of the Lord, His passing through death to eternal life.
"God said, 'Let there be light,' and there was light."
This is the festival of rebirth, the joy of new awakening.
All nature stirs anew, with new life the very earth is quaking,
The spring is illumined with the risen Christ, a new dawn is breaking!
"Why do you seek for the living among dead?"
He is risen and He is here—
In the fresh, youthful bubbling of the coffee pot,
In the warm spring breeze before the sun gets hot,
In the child-like joy of the bird's morning song,
In the cool river gurgling as it happily flows along,
In the clean rain falling, washing green the young sod,
In all new discoveries, which are new discoveries of God.
In the risen birds of spring and Early Bird riding under heaven,
In the honest sinner's struggle to purge out the old leaven,
In the new hope risen from the old sin and shame shriven,
In the new peace risen from the old hate and grudge forgiven,
In men of good will, who encouraged by His death and resurrection,

Will work anew and again for justice, order and peace under His direction.
"The Master of Life, First-born from the dead; come, let us adore Him!"

VICTORY

Easter Sunday

"Victory" was the message of the risen Jesus to His disciples on Easter Sunday. On the road to Emmaus He asked them, was not the divine plan of victory—suffering, agony, death and resurrection most fitting? Jesus said, "How slow you are to believe all that the prophets have announced! Did not the Messiah have to undergo all this so as to enter into His glory?" Then, going back to Moses and all the prophets, He interpreted for them every passage of Scripture which referred to Him (Lk 24:25-27).

Lord Jesus, what a day of glory was the day of Your resurrection! For this day You came into the world: for Your resurrection, and for that of all Your saints. This day is the beginning and the proof of our resurrection; the glorification of those who become other Christs. For this we were born; for this You created sun, moon, and stars; for this You gave us a mind and a will: to hope for and to love and to anticipate that day. Our life would have no meaning, but in the fulfillment of the resurrection.

Truly, if we knew the glory, the splendor, the beauty of our resurrection, no one would ever be satisfied with another day on earth.

Risen Jesus, glorious and resplendent, You are with us in the Holy Eucharist, our hidden God, high above the heavens. And is it not true, You come to us in the Eucharist in order to prepare us for the resurrection? Is it not Your desire to come to us frequently, as the pledge of our future glory? For You said, "Whoever eats my flesh shall have life everlasting in himself, and I will raise him up on the last day."

Tell us, Mary, what you saw this morning!
"Tomb of Christ the Risen One I see,
Angels, and the empty shroud between them:
He is risen, gone to Galilee!"

THE WOMEN'S MESSAGE

Octave of Easter, Monday   Matthew 28:8-15

"The women hurried away from the tomb half-overjoyed, half-fearful, and ran to carry the good news to his disciples. Suddenly without warning, Jesus stood before them and said, "Peace!" Then Jesus told them, "Go and carry the news to my brothers."

The women have been most faithful to Jesus, even during His bitterest time of suffering and His painful death. They remain at the foot of the cross, suffering with Him. Now the reward of their loyalty: they are the first to bring the Good News. They are the first to report what the disciples still cannot comprehend. They bring the Easter news that Peter will finally announce in his Pentecost sermon under the power of the Holy Spirit: "God freed Jesus from death's bitter pangs, and raised Him up again, for it was impossible that death should keep its hold on Him."

This great morning the women are privileged to bring the world the best news it has ever heard. "Have you searched for hope and strength against the fear of evil and the fear of death? You shall not be disappointed! Today we announce an event that answers all your pain, your questions, your despair! Today is the central point of all history: it is the climax, it is the mountain peak of the faithful: Christ Jesus has risen from the dead!"

What surprise, what joy, what confidence rings through the world from this Easter morning! All the persecuted, all the despondent, all the crippled, the blind, the sick, the dying, the imprisoned, the tortured, the abandoned—all suffering people can rejoice today! They shall laugh one day at all they have ever suffered. For Jesus has confirmed His promise: "Whoever believes in me shall live forever." Jesus has conquered death, and so shall His believers. They shall rise perfected, joyous, beautiful, strong, healthy, free for all eternity. What else matters now, after this Good News?

All tragedy has been swallowed up. Only one sadness remains: willfully failing to join Jesus, so as not to rise with Him.

> **Death and life were drawn in awesome battle;**
> **Christ, the Victor in that fearful strife,**
> **Passed through death to rise again immortal,**
> **Conqueror forever, Lord of life!**

SEE JESUS

Octave of Easter, Tuesday   **Acts 2:36-41; John 20:11-18**

In today's Gospel the Lord appears to a woman, Mary Magdalene. It is Easter morning. When Mary recognizes Jesus, whom she first thought was the gardener, Jesus says, "Do not cling to me so. Do not act as if I shall never return; do not think I will no longer be present." Jesus has entered a new mode of existence. We must see something now beyond His physical presence: we must be attached to Him by faith. It is by the sacred signs, the sacraments, that we touch Him and are touched by Him.

We also meet Him in our fellow men and in the world. If we are people of faith, we have eyes which really see, ears which really hear, hands which really touch.

The reading from the Acts of the Apostles speaks of Baptism. We have been baptized and have this faith which brings light, joy, wisdom and understanding.

But do we live with this light, joy and wisdom? Do we live as resurrected persons, saved and still being saved? Or do we act as if we were still unredeemed, confused, indifferent and without joy?

In faith like Mary we have seen the Lord. We see Him here, in the word proclaimed and in the bread offered and received. We see Him in each other and in the world. As Christians we should be fully resurrected, people who live life to the full.

As the deer longs for the living waters,
So my soul longs for the Lord's embrace.
Soul athirst for God, the living Presence,
When at last shall I behold His face?
Deep the waters roar and rush upon me,
Through the waves I pray and onward plod;
Breakers, billows pass me, and they lead me
Safely to the Presence of my God (Ps 41).

SURPRISE

Octave of Easter, Wednesday   **Luke 24:13-35**

Life is full of surprises. Today's Gospel recalls how two disciples came back to Jerusalem to tell of their big surprise. The disciples had been sad and disappointed. These men thought all their hopes were gone. Jesus was supposed to save their nation from the Roman empire, but then He had let Judas and the police capture Him without a fight, and He was murdered.

On Sunday two men are taking a seven-mile hike to Emmaus. They are sad and confused over the loss of Jesus. A stranger comes up to meet them, saying he doesn't know why they are sad: then the first surprise: the stranger explains why Christ had to suffer and die *before* he could win his victory.

When at the journey's end he consents to have supper with them, this surprising stranger takes bread and says, "This is my Body, given for you."

The second surprise: He had been with them all the way, and they did not recognize Him. Isn't this our life, too? We fail to recognize how close the Lord is to us all the time. Maybe we don't even recognize Him in the breaking of the Bread, the Eucharist. We also fail to recognize how God is there always, helping us through others.

One of the sad and happy surprises each of us will have some day, is finding out how much other people did for us—and we did not appreciate or recognize it. How many people prayed for us, how many good examples were given us that we ignored, how many little favors were done for us day after day by our own family and by others, and we took it all for granted, never appreciated it, never returned the favors.

We are all one in the Body of Christ. We either help each other on the way, or our actions help to keep others away from God.

See how much Jesus had done for His followers. Yet they failed to recognize it. That's why they were sad: they failed to understand.

We can learn from them, Lord! We can learn how suffering and sadness lead to joy, because in You they find true meaning. We can look forward to that Resurrection and reunion with You. There we'll see that You have been with us all along the way!

SNEAK A LOOK

Octave of Easter, Thursday   **Luke 24:35-48**

Today's Gospel is the special message of Jesus to discouraged Christians. Are you fearful, doubtful, depressed? Do you wonder what your daily devotion and faithfulness is worth? Do you keep asking yourself why the *good guys* finish last? Then what you should do today and many days is, sneak a look at the back of the book.

What Jesus means is, He took on all your problems and more: the problems of the rest of His people, too. He took on all the burdens of our sins, brought them up to the cross with Him, shed all His blood and died to free us of these burdens.

Here Jesus stands, gloriously risen, shocking even His closest friends and disciples, so that they think He must be a ghost. But Jesus dispels that timid notion. "Why do such ideas cross your mind?" He asks. "Touch me, and see that a ghost does not have flesh and bones as I do." Then He let them feel the glorified wounds in His hands and his feet. When they still seemed unable to believe this great news, He sat down and ate lunch with them.

Why does this sad story of rejection and murder end so well? Well, you see, Jesus was in a perfect love relationship with the Father. He trusted the Father completely. He said, "I always do what pleases the Father." Jesus knew something we don't know, and He tells us, "If you knew what I know, you would always put God first."

What did he know? "God is all Love, and only the best ending is in store for you when you are tuned in to perfect Love." John came to understand that. He wrote, "Perfect love casts out all fear."

In His very death, Jesus had conquered. He defeated sin, self, and Satan, and so He rose victorious. Now He says to you and me, "All right, I have conquered the world. Now it's your turn!"

Now hear the message of the Lord, your ransomer, the Holy One:
"I am your teacher, I, your God: I send the Word, my only Son.
If you will listen to my voice, a stream of life shall be your peace,
In waters cool you shall rejoice, my tender mercies will increase."

DIVINE GENEROSITY

Octave of Easter, Friday   **John 21:1-14**

If I have any doubts regarding the power of Jesus to help me in my needs, or His generosity in doing so, I can recall any of many simple scenes in His life.

After the Lord's Resurrection, when He no longer lived in the same way with His disciples, the funds had run low. So low, in fact, that Peter felt he had to go back to the fishing trade. Other apostles went along. All night they caught nothing. At dawn Jesus stood on the shore waiting for them, although they did not at once recognize Him. To tease them, He called out, "Young men, have you caught anything good to eat?"

I can imagine with what dejection Peter answered, "No!"

Then Jesus put his trust to the test. "Cast your net on the other side," He ordered. Can't you imagine most fishermen answering, "Who says so!"

But expert fisherman Peter obeys the Lord's suggestion. When a man at last learns to lose that "self-confidence" so respected by the world, he is ready to find true confidence. His reward? St. John tells us that the net nearly broke from the weight of the catch, and when the disciples came to shore, they counted 153 fish. What a powerful symbol of the Lord's generosity!

It calls to mind the same Jesus, seeing the plight of the young couple at the wedding of Cana. The Lord's Mother made the request for them: "They have no wine." We can see in the large size of the six stone water jars, how generous the response of Jesus was!

When the same Jesus fed five thousand people on the seashore, after all had been satisfied, twelve baskets of leftovers were gathered.

Shall you be less generous to me, Jesus, when Your Mother asks for my needs? Let others talk of their earthly goods; my security is in the generosity of my God.

NEW LIFE

Octave of Easter, Saturday   **Mark 16:9-15**

As God created the world to bring forth life, so Christ in redeeming the world restored it. His Resurrection is the celebration of life itself. It is life's answer to the mystery of death. "Unless the grain of wheat fall into the ground and die, it remains alone," said Jesus. "But if it dies, it brings forth much fruit. Whoever loves his life, loses it. And whoever hates his life in this world keeps it into life everlasting" (John 12:24-26).

We ask ourselves, "Why must we have sickness, disappointments, loneliness, failure and frustration?" Christ came to be a part of the mystery by His own life.

We have heard people of faith and good life express their bewilderment at the great sufferings of innocent peoples and nations. Our century is surely the century of martyrs; we have had millions of them. But worse, perhaps, is the living martyrdom of more millions of enslaved people—a life of endless fear, weariness, boredom, poverty and pain.

"It would seem that God abandoned these unhappy people," said a religious lady.

"Yes," answered a young man, "if you forget what happened to His Son on Calvary."

Christ had decided to become one of us; thus He, too, subjected Himself to the law of human achievement—the things of greatest value demand the greatest sacrifice; they have a high price and often a heroic price.

Sorrow today is for joy tomorrow. Death today is resurrection tomorrow, if we have found the key. "Blessed be the Lord now and forever, the God who bears our burdens and wins us the victory" (Ps 68). He has paid the price, but we must share the price with Him if we are to share the victory.

> **Christian people, lift your grateful voices:**
> **Christ the Paschal Lamb with joy we praise!**
> **Victim who returns us to the Father,**
> **He, the Innocent, our ransom pays.**

RESCUED PEOPLE

Second Week of Easter, Monday   John 3:1-8

"No one can enter into God's kingdom without being begotten of water and Spirit." Baptism is our entry into unending life, by joining ourselves to Christ's work of redemption. Born into the race of mankind, we inherit mankind's blessings and curses, the good and the evil. We inherit our race's sinfulness, its fallen state. But we also inherit its glorious opportunity to find rescue from these ills.

It was Christ who conquered Satan's hold on our race. In Christ's saving Cross, sin died and the new life of grace was born. Christ built the new bridge to eternal life. To share His victory, we join Him in a similar passage through death to life in the sacrament of Baptism.

Jesus took our weaknesses and burned them away in His

consuming love. By his absolute dedication to the Father's will, the breach is healed. He rises, the new creation, the head of all renewed and redeemed mankind.

Baptism begins our active share in the redeeming work of Jesus Himself. We must continue this great experience of passing through death to life, in our own lives, day by day. We must keep putting to death the old corruption in us, and be forever putting on the new man, risen and beatified by the work of Christ in us.

To this new glory God has called us in Christ Jesus. Are we responding? Do we live like people rescued from sin's darkness and basking in the new life of God? If we do, the difference will soon be noticed.

> With Christ we descended, our sinfulness ended,
> And buried with Christ, now with Him we arise;
> With death He contended, and victor ascended:
> We join ourselves to Him, our hope and our prize.

LIFTED UP

Second Week of Easter, Tuesday   **John 12:31-36**

Jesus said, "When I am lifted up from the earth, I shall draw all men to myself." St. John, who writes these words of Jesus in his Gospel, sees this as a prophecy of great importance. He pauses to say, "This statement of Jesus indicated what sort of death He was going to suffer."

John doesn't mean only that Jesus will be crucified, that He will be lifted up on a cross for all to see. But when he quotes Jesus as saying, "When I am lifted up I will draw all men to myself," he sees the power in that death of Jesus; he sees the great drawing power of the crucifix. That great love of Jesus for us on the cross will attract millions of people to Jesus through all the ages that the world will go on.

That death of Jesus is so special because He raises Himself from the dead! There He is lifted up as the one who freely dies, who wants to suffer and die for us, and who lifts Himself high again in that glorious resurrection.

St. John sees the power of that cross, which wipes away our sins, but which also is the cause of the glorious resurrection of Jesus. The Body of Jesus is glorified on the Cross today. It is now His glorious and risen body. As St. Augustine writes, "That Cross which was the derision of His enemies is now displayed on the foreheads of kings. The effect has proved His power; He conquered the world, not by the sword, but by the wood." And St. Paul writes, "Jesus humbled Himself, obediently accepting even death, death on a cross. Because of this, God highly exalted Him, and gave Him the name above every other name."

Sing, my soul, the Savior's battle, praise the Lamb now glorified!
On the Cross a noble triumph: praise the Master crucified!
Tell the world how our Redeemer by His love was slain and died.
Glorious tree, though once ignoble, You alone He chose to own
As His sign of love and conquest; honored now in every zone,
Sign of mercy and self-giving, you are love's victorious throne.

THE LOVE OF GOD

Second Week of Easter, Wednesday   **John 3:16-21**

"God so loved the world that He gave His only Son."
"I have loved you with an everlasting love, and now in mercy I have drawn you to myself" (Jr 31:3); "Torrents of water cannot quench love, floods cannot drown it" (Sg 8:7). There is no sound in the world, there is no word in the universe closer to God than Love. It is a word terrible and strong, a word more dazzling than lightning, a word with more meaning than all the books ever written, a word forever falling from the lips of God.

We hear how fearfully Jesus speaks of the "cooling of love" in the days when people will forget for what He stands (Mt 24:2). We read that tremendous chapter of St. Paul, in which love is pictured as a person unable to die, suffering everything, believing everything. We are warned that without love all is vain; that it would mean nothing to be a martyr, to burn at the stake without love; that love is patient and kind, in no way envious or malicious, having no vanity, no ambition, not even seeking what belongs to her, a stranger equally to anger and pride, an enemy of every evil thought—in a word, that love is God Himself (1 Cor 13).

"God is love, and he who abides in love abides in God, and God lives in him" (1 Jn 4:16); "The whole earth overflows with the Lord's goodness" (Ps 33).

> **Lord God, is there any room in Your heaven for me? Heaven is God, and God is love. Can I, then, enter your heaven and be at peace before I have become perfected in love?**

> **We pray You, Jesus, risen King,**
> **While saints and angels praises sing,**
> **Raise up Your sign of victory,**
> **Your Cross, for high and low to see:**
> **The Lord, whom envy crucified,**
> **Has risen and is glorified!**

TREASURE

Second Week of Easter, Thursday   **John 3:31-36**

Jesus says, "The one who comes from above is above all; the one who is of the earth is earthly . . . The one who comes from heaven testifies to what he has seen and heard."

Jesus often spoke of heaven as of a treasure, but a special kind of treasure. Heaven cannot be hoarded by misers; heaven cannot be wrested away from us by robbery, or betrayal, or shady dealing, or trickery of any kind. We cannot lose it by some outrageous accident.

The earthly man thinks happiness consists of having what others cannot have. But truth and time have proven him wrong.

Do we understand how fortunate we are to know that the true

treasure of life is that "which comes from above," that heaven is the only complete and satisfying treasure? In heaven we will find everything that is good; all that we know to be beautiful, delightful, pleasing and worth loving. No matter what our tastes happen to be, no matter how much our idea of heaven differs from that of our neighbors, God indeed has the power to fill every desire.

Heaven is far from the proverbial golden city with a silver fence around it. Heaven is God. Heaven is all of God's perfection and joy. The Lord says in the Book of Revelations, "Behold, I make all things new . . . and there shall be a new heaven and a new earth" (Rv 21:1). God will have all things fit to welcome the risen and glorified saints. Yet they would never be satisfied if they could not have God Himself. They will never see enough of God, nor even of each other, in the glory God sheds over heaven.

Dear Lord, could this splendor ever wear out? Impossible, for Your beauty is infinite and eternal. A modern songster knew enough to sing that "love is a many-splendored thing," but Your love is unlimited splendor. No one shall ever see all Your beauties; no one shall ever tire of them.

OUR LOAVES AND FISH

Second Week of Easter, Friday   **John 6:1-15**

The miracle of Jesus, multiplying the loaves and fish, is surely an impressive incident. Great is the promise of Jesus which it introduced. But let's dwell today on another element of the event. Have you ever thought about that little boy involved? Take a look at him. He has brought his little sack-lunch along. He has been carting this bag around all day. The bread is probably half crumbled, and the fish is getting smelly. His lunch is kind of a mess by now.

But Jesus accepts it, He takes it, He thanks the little boy, and look what He does with it. This is you and me, too. We've been carting around our own little mess—our bit of faith and hope, our few efforts, not really impressive. They're getting smelly and crumbly, too. But Jesus accepts us, anyway; if we offer what we have to Him, see what He can do with us.

Notice that Jesus takes the little boy's bread, He gives thanks, and He breaks it—and then everyone has enough, and there's still so much left over. Think of the happiness Jesus brought that little boy: to take that mess of his, and give him so much in return. Of course, the boy had to trust Jesus. He had to believe in the goodness and the power of Jesus. His faith was needed.

The same Jesus is able and wants to use what each of us has to offer Him. Sometimes He has to break us, too. He has to shake us up, to make decent Christians of us. But if we let Jesus do that to us, if trust Him to take us and what we have, there will always be plenty left over: twelve baskets from a crumbly handful.

None of us has really much to give God. We're not that great. Often we have little more to offer than our foolish pride, our stupid mistakes, our fears and our problems, but Jesus is willing to take even that. If He took our sins upon Himself, than surely He will take whatever we trust to put into His Hands.

Naturally we should offer Him more than only the bad things we have. How about the good things? Our talents, our joys, our loved ones, our work, our time. This Gospel incident will tell us what to expect: more than we ever dreamed of.

Jesus, You are never cheap with us! You pay back a hundredfold the little we offer!

DON'T BE AFRAID

Second Week of Easter, Saturday   John 6:16-21

As He comes walking on the water, Jesus says, "It is I. Do not be afraid." How often the Lord tells His people, "Do not be afraid! I am always with you!" Over three hundred times in the Bible we hear that message from God: "Fear not! For I am with you; I, the Lord, will rescue you! Don't be afraid: it is the Lord."

In the Life of Jesus, the Lord can be recognized by these words. Gabriel said to Mary, "Fear not, Mary. You have found favor with God." The angel says to Joseph, "Joseph, don't be afraid to take Mary as your wife." You can trust my word that Mary has conceived by the Holy Spirit. When the shepherds come to adore the newborn Son of God, they probably tell Mary and Joseph what the angel said to them. When they quote those familiar words of the angel: "Do not be afraid," Mary and Joseph nod knowingly. Yes, that was the Lord speaking! He always begins that way!

At the very end of Christ's life on earth, on the glorious day of His resurrection, He walks up to the holy women with the same message, "Don't be afraid! You have been chosen to carry the good news of my resurrection to my disciples!"

How often the Lord needs to remind us, "Don't be afraid. Trust me. Does anyone on the whole earth love you more than the Lord does?" Isaiah writes (49:14-16): "The people of Jerusalem said, 'The Lord has forgotten us.' The Lord answers, 'Can a woman forget her own baby, and not love the child she bore? Even if a mother would forget her child, I will never forget you. I have written your names in the palms of my hands.' " What a tender picture of God's unfailing love.

How little we trust in Him! Matthew and Mark, speaking of this same nighttime scene on the water, tell us how impressed Peter was at seeing Jesus walk over the water in this storm. So Peter calls to Jesus: "Me, too, Lord!" Jesus agrees: "Yes, you, too, Peter!" But seeing the waves and feeling the wind, Peter is seized with fear! "Lord, save me!" And Jesus said to Peter what He says to us: "What? Still so little faith? Why do you doubt me?"

HEALTH AND HUNGER

Third Week of Easter, Monday   John 6:22-29

People generally consider your appetite some measure of your state of health. If you won't eat, something isn't working right. As our appetite for food fails us, so our strength fails. On the other hand, mothers know that if their youngsters clean up all the food on the table, they're probably very healthy, for the moment.

So in John's Gospel we see that the crowd of five thousand whom Jesus fed was rather healthy physically. Even after they had been filled with the wonderful bread Jesus had multiplied for them, they still were not satisfied. They wanted more. Jesus had to slip away, but they followed Him across the lake to the town of Capernaum.

There Jesus laid the truth on them. He said in effect, "You're hungry physically, but you're not really hungry where it counts. It's spiritual hunger that makes the whole difference in your life! You should not be working for perishable food, but for food that remains into life eternal." What a powerful statement Jesus makes. If you're going to be more than flesh, if you are to count as a real person, then you have to hunger for the true food, the living power-house that God has to offer.

Ever since Jesus made these powerful statements in the Gospel, you and I know how to measure our condition, our progress, our degree of health as a human being. We are measured by the hunger we have for God's most personal gift to us: our hunger for His Son Jesus. In the divine circle, the divine family, the more we truly hunger to be personally united to Jesus, the more fulfilling is the Eucharistic Bread. The deeper our experiences of the Lord in Holy Communion, the stronger our faith becomes, and the more frequently we seek Jesus in the Bread of Life.

> **"As Moses fed God's people in the desert,**
> **The Bread of God comes down to man at last.**
> **Who comes to Me shall never thirst or hunger:**
> **Herein are hopes, desires and dreams surpassed."**

A FRIENDSHIP MEAL

Third Week of Easter, Tuesday   **John 6:30-35**

"It is my Father who gives you the real heavenly bread," says Jesus.

"I am the bread of life."

When God calls us together around Christ, it is not only to speak to us, but to have a banquet with us. The shape of the Eucharistic Liturgy is fundamentally that of a meal, an extension of the Paschal Supper and of the friendship meal of the Hebrews on the Sabbath Day. This does not eliminate the sacrifice element of the Mass. The sign into which Jesus chose to put His work of salvation is that of a sacred banquet.

The meal was an essential part of the temple liturgy and religious gatherings of the Old Testament. It was a religious action. The things sacrificed were eaten in the House of God as a symbol of the Messianic promise. "You and your families shall eat and make merry because the Lord has blessed you" (Dt 12:4-7); "The lowly shall eat their fill," says Psalm 22. "Lord, You have spread a table before me," we find in Psalm 23. God invited His people to a friendship meal.

Christ used these same symbols to anticipate the coming kingdom of His followers on earth and in heaven. He said, "I give you a kingdom, that you may eat and drink at My table" (Lk 22:29). Again He said, "If anyone opens the door to me, I will come in and have supper with him" (Rv 3:30).

The Eucharistic banquet is a continuation of the Old Testament message. Isaiah said, "Come to eat and drink and be filled." Holy Mass is the banquet that indicates the Savior's arrival and the coming of His kingdom. The apostles gave proof of their mission by saying, "We ate and drank with the risen Lord" (Ac 10:41).

> **While mingling water with the wine,**
> **We ask to share Your life divine;**
> **You shared with us—this cup the sign,**
> **We are the branches, You the Vine.**

HEALING POWER

Third Week of Easter, Wednesday   **John 6:35-40**

When we call Jesus our Lord, our God, our King, we refer to

many things about Him, but especially to His divine power. Jesus revealed His power as Lord in His public life especially by healing all who touched Him. There were thousands of physical healings—the sick, the crippled, the blind—but many more mental and spiritual healings: people in the grip of evil, serving the devil, were healed. Sinners were freed and became the most loyal followers of Jesus.

Do we really take note of this power of Jesus the Lord in our own life? We find this same Jesus in all His power and love in the Holy Eucharist, still with us, still our loving Lord and Master.

Now more than ever, people want and need to experience the saving power of Jesus in the Holy Eucharist. We know from the Gospels that Jesus meant this Sacrament to be our healing, our freedom to live as sons and daughters of God. In the Eucharist, Jesus has given us Himself in a form that we can touch and experience, just as He was touched and experienced in His public life. Because we are human, we need to touch and be touched. So often it is a healing touch. Jesus, in His beautiful human wisdom, left us His Body and Blood so that we could touch him and be healed! "I myself am the Bread of Life; no one who comes to me shall ever be hungry."

Jesus remembered those words at the Last Supper, and so He said, "This is My Body, which is given for you. This is My Blood, to be poured out in behalf of many for the forgiveness of sins."

Do we believe this, so that we expect our sins to be forgiven? Do we thank Jesus for His forgiveness, because we trust He has kept His promise? Obviously the Church wants us to approach Jesus with a deep faith that really expects healing from Him. That is the weight of the Church's words, "Lord, I am not worthy to receive You, but only say the word and I shall be healed."

> **Though parents might forget a wayward child,**
> **The Lord will not forget His children's needs;**
> **He sees His loved one fall, by foes reviled,**
> **And hears him, when for help and strength he pleads (Ps 27).**

PERSONAL EXPERIENCE

Third Week of Easter, Thursday   **John 6:44-51**

Why did Jesus say, "The bread I will give is my flesh, for the life of the world," and "if anyone eats this bread he shall live forever?" Because we need that exact experience of God and of Jesus. Experience is essential in human life. We learn most by experience.

Mark Twain said, "If your little boy wants to carry home a cat by the tail, I say, let him! That experience will teach him more than a thousand words of warning." It's said, often enough, that we need to learn the hard way by hard experience. It's often a tragedy we cannot repair. People who have to learn the evils of drugs or of alcohol by unhappy experiences are paying too high a price. How often it results in ruined lives that never are repaired.

Good experience is also the deepest and most effective way to learn. What would the word "rain" mean to you if you never walked in the rain or got caught in it? Or "snow" or "storm" or "fire," if you were never warmed by fire, or chilled by snow, or buffeted by the force of a storm? What would "love" mean to you, if you never experienced it? If no one had ever loved you, or you had never loved anyone?

Jesus knew we needed to experience Him personally and deeply. It would not be enough only to hear about Him or read His words. We had to experience His life and His love moving in us. This is what builds our faith: the personal experience of it. The personal touch of the One who is most faithful.

> Your presence, Lord, my soul will ever seek,
> My Savior, do not hide Your face from me;
> Of God, who rescues me, my heart will speak,
> Do not forsake me in adversity!
> With sacrifice of praise I will rejoice!
> In You my bulwark holds on every side:
> The Lord has heard the pleading of my voice!
> Within Your presence, Lord, I will abide (Ps 27).

LIGHT AND STRENGTH

Third Week of Easter, Friday   **John 6:52-59**

St. Thomas More was one of the most gifted men in history. He was a brilliant philosopher, author, and statesman. The King promoted Thomas More to the high position of Lord Chancellor, a kind of chief justice of the nation. It goes without saying that Thomas was a very busy man.

Yet he never missed daily Mass and Communion. He was asked more than once how he could take off the time from his heavy schedule. He always answered, "Exactly because I have so many responsibilities. These can be most distracting, and so I need Holy Mass and Communion to pull myself together. There are many temptations in my kind of work, but Communion sees me through them. I have difficult affairs to manage, but in Communion I find the light and strength to do it well."

This is one of thousands of answers, from many of the greatest men and women in history. They all admitted readily, "We could never have managed alone. In Christ we found the strength to do the things you call great accomplishments." Jesus left us Himself in the living Bread to be our spiritual food, our pillar of strength, our daily healing and consolation. He wished to share His presence with us, in a way we could find simple and accessible. What great man in history became so approachable as the Lord Himself, when He chose to dwell in the living Bread? In a half million churches around the world today, He is present, He has offered Himself for us, He has joined in friendship with His faithful ones.

His listeners found that first promise of the Eucharist "a hard saying," because they never suspected the deep, personal quality of His love, they never guessed at the universal extent of His openness to all, they hadn't suspected His power, or the glory of His coming resurrection.

> **And what do we allow You to do for us, Jesus? Does our faith grow? Does our love deepen? Does the joy of the risen Lord stay alive in us? Is it making a difference, as we find more and more opportunities to share with You?**

MORE FAITH

Third Week of Easter, Saturday   John 6:60-69

Jesus knows that the Eucharist demands faith—more and more faith. So He says, "It is the spirit that gives life; the flesh is useless. The words I spoke to you are spirit and life. Yet among you there are some who do not believe."

The saints with their healthy hunger for Christ are much more satisfied and nourished with the Eucharistic Lord than we are. Some of us may even be near the zero point, as Jesus suggests. We really need more faith and are starving for it.

Lost hunters or campers start out by looking for directions or shouting for their friends. But the longer they're lost and the worse things get, the more they simply hunger for food. So with us: as things get spiritually worse, we're no longer helped by friends or position or possessions. We're simply starving for something lasting, a food that's permanent, the Bread of Life.

We have to allow our faith-hunger to grow. If we have no spiritual appetite, then like a sick person we won't find Christ very appealing. How can we develop a healthy spiritual appetite? St. Paul answers, "Lay aside your old way of life and the rotting self which deteriorates through illusion and desire, and put on a fresh, spiritual way of thinking. Put on the new man." In other words, get your priorities straight: put the important things first. Or as Jesus says it, "Have faith in the One God sent you."

We know that trust in a friend grows by experiences shared together. We begin to lean on that friend for support and advice and a sharing of problems as well as joys. In time faith and trust are there! That is how our spiritual appetite becomes healthy: by frequent contact with Jesus. The more we share with Him, the stronger the friendship becomes. The more we eat the Bread of Life, the greater the fulfillment of His presence. More friendship and fulfillment bring stronger faith and growing spiritual health.

> **"Do you want to leave me, too?**
> **"Lord, to whom shall we go? You have the words of eternal life."**

SHEPHERDS

Fourth Week of Easter, Monday   **John 10:1-10**

Jesus said, "I am the good shepherd."

Not many of us are shepherds nowadays, but we all have responsibilities, as shepherds did. All the prophets, as well as Jesus, used the shepherd theme as an image of responsible leadership, of devotion to duty, of people caring for their neighbor. Bad shepherds were those who used or exploited their neighbor for their own selfish ends or ran away from their problems.

All the prophets spoke of the Lord God as the true shepherd who really cares for His people. Never will He misuse, exploit or abandon them. The branch of David, which the prophets said would bring forth the true shepherd, is the family of David, from which Jesus came. He, the true shepherd, gave His life for His sheep because He really cares.

So the true Christian is a shepherd, or merely a sheep. He is one who cares for the good of others as Christ did. We see in the Gospels that although Jesus and His apostles needed rest, they continued to care for the people.

We tend to grow tired and complain about having to do more than our share for the good of others. Always a smaller percentage of the people have to shoulder the extra work that the larger percentage neglect to do. If you feel over-burdened, you are in good company. Jesus was heavily burdened, too. If the leaders of His time had done their job well, Jesus would have had a much lighter load, too. He would not have had to deal with rejection by religious leaders in addition to the many needs of the people. But Jesus cared, when others did not, and He paid the price. He died for us all. "The good shepherd lays down His life for His sheep."

If He carried so much more than His share, why can't we? Can we not at least do some of our share of the Lord's saving work?

> **In your joy and pain I still live on,**
> **And wherever you go, I am there!**
> **To my loved ones I am ever drawn,**
> **Seeing, knowing, with a Brother's care!**

CHRIST AMONG US

Fourth Week of Easter, Tuesday   **John 10:22-30**

"The works I do in my Father's name give witness in my favor." Jesus reveals Himself in terms of action. His self-giving poverty is action—a living, moving, performing generous love. And so Jesus becomes known to us throughout history, as acting—alive in His living Church, in His Sacraments, in His acting members.

Jesus does not accept any external trappings of kingship: no crown, robes, throne, retinue or palace. These are static things, showpieces of one who desires to *be* a king rather than to *act* like a king. Jesus acts: He is voluntarily poor because that is the effect of love in action; it is the result of what He *does*.

He acts in us, too! He wills that we Christians be the extension of His action through time. We are now the eyes and lips and hands and feet of Christ in the world. Such is His generous love that He wants and plans for us to be Christ Jesus in this world this very day. Many will never see Christ unless they see Him acting in us.

Jesus manifests Himself in actions; we must manifest Him in actions, too. The real Christian is Christ endlessly searching for people in need of help. Not a mere kindness done here or there to the needy upon whom we happen to stumble, but the urgent, unflagging search of love.

None of us are rich—not really. We are poor, all of us. You and I are poor, helpless little ones—and we are so little! But Christ accepted us. He asked us to continue His work through our time in our life. Because He so honored us, we accept and honor one another.

Are we aware of our fellow men in a Christian way? Do we as a group—a family, a neighborhood, a clique—really accept others in Christ, with Christian openness and generosity?

> We're only pilgrims on the way, Lord, on the way.
> We've come to You to rest today, to rest today.
> We must go on, we've hills to climb and miles to go,
> But we are slow, Lord Jesus, oh, how well You know!

WHO IS THIS?

Fourth Week of Easter, Wednesday   **John 12:44-50**

There is a knock on the door; I open it. Two well-dressed men are waiting for me, and tell me I am to come with them immediately. They take me to a limousine manned by two men in uniform. They drive me to the city hall, where a large crowd of people has gathered — for what reason? I have no idea. The police hustle me to the balcony of the city hall, and stand me before a well-dressed, dignified person. I have never seen him before; I am unable to say who he is or where he comes from; but he is clearly someone very important. Now they tell me, "You have been chosen to deliver greetings and a message to his highness on this great occasion."

Of one thing I am sure: there will be very little said, if anything, and my "message" in any case will make no sense, until I find out who this person is, and what my position toward him happens to be. I cannot "carry on" with him in such ignorance.

In the Gospel Jesus tells us that He has come to reveal God the Father to us, so that we can speak to Him and speak of Him as one whom we know. "Whoever looks on me is seeing him who sent me. I have come to the world as its light, to keep anyone who believes in me from remaining in the dark."

God the Father has sent His Son Jesus to us for this very purpose. So Jesus says, "I have not spoken on my own; no the Father who sent me has commanded me what to say and how to speak."

If I am to speak to God my Father and my Creator in prayer, I must know Him, and know my relationship to Him. Jesus came to reveal this to me. How often have I thanked Him for this wonderful revelation?

Lord, teach me to pray. Help me to understand clearly who I am, and help me to understand, as far as humans can, who You are.

WHO IS MASTER?

Fourth Week of Easter, Thursday   **John 13:16-20**

"No servant is greater than his master," says Jesus. "Once you know this, blessed are you if you put it into practice." In other words, "Man is not greater than his Creator. What a happy world we'd live in, if people understood this in their hearts."

Unfortunately, the "slave" has set himself up as master—and then everything begins to go wrong. The unhappy people crushed under the atheistic heel know by painful experience how wrong life can be. Atheistic "law" has become a cloak for the outrageous betrayal of human dignity and freedom. Tyranny is the result of slaves pretending to be masters. Slaves who forgot that "no messenger outranks the one who sent him."

In the free nations, just laws have been abused so much by unjust citizens that true law is left in confusion, and most of us must agree with Goldsmith that "Laws grind the poor, and rich men rule the law." The slaves pretend to be masters, looking upon the true law as a disagreeable enemy of their false freedom, ignoring and ridiculing the true justice of God in favor of their money-greed and pleasure-hunger.

But the divine order cannot be ignored without inevitable ruin. When the law of God is no longer deeply engraved in their hearts, peoples and nations experience the gradual loss of good order, justice, peace, and freedom.

There is no hope for the servant but in the law of the Master. Man cannot become God. The fearsome spectacle of murdered millions, of enslaved people, of the appalling sufferings of the poor and the dashing of their just hopes—all this should have awakened us to an unprecedented reverence for the law of God. But has it?

All human life is permeated with a crying need for divine law. Nations have brought catastrophes on themselves by ignoring God's word, and rare is the individual who has not experienced the price of godlessness.

Lord, as we review every cause of our unhappiness and unrest, every failure that we want to forget and not repeat, is it not true that faithfulness to Your law would have saved us? From

every defeat we've suffered, Your commandments would have
rescued us!

WAY, TRUTH, LIFE

Fourth Week of Easter, Friday   **John 14:1-6**

In this remarkable Gospel passage, St. John wanted us often to
return to that upper room, where Jesus sat at table with His first
followers the night before His death. These young men had just
shared in the first Eucharist, the Bread of Life, in which Jesus had
already surrendered His life for us, in a giving of His Body, a symbolic
death that would be real death for Him the next day.

Jesus then prayed to His Father, "Father, I want those whom You
have given me, to be where I am. I want them to see the glory which
You have given me." Jesus was saying in effect, "Tomorrow I will
pass through death and I will stand in eternity. I want my friends to be
with me. Just as I ask my Father not to leave me alone in death, so I
ask Him not to leave my friends alone in death." And so Jesus
promises to prepare a place for us, so that where He is we also may be.

Let us notice how Jesus goes. We need to, because He says, "I am
the Way, and the Truth, and the Life." He shows us the Way to this
eternal joy; He tells us the Truth about it; He gives us this Life, for
only He has the power.

What *is* the Way? It is the Way of the Cross. There must be some
sorrow and suffering, some carrying of burdens, some sacrifice and
grief. This was The Way Jesus went, the day after He spoke of it and
made the great promise. But that was not the end of the way: far from
it! Three days later it was the Way of a Glorious Victory, an amazing
resurrection, a life of joy, power, peace, and love.

He is The Truth: He is the answer to all the puzzles and trials of
life. He *is* the Life for which we are created. He is the all-powerful
Creator, and He is the meaning and the purpose of life. He, in His
boundless love, promises that we are to share in that powerful,
unending, glorious life. The only requirement: that we follow Him,
full of faith: "Whoever believes in me will have life everlasting."

"I shall prepare a place for you in glory,
That where I am my friends may also be.
Be not afraid, let not your heart be troubled,
As you believe in God, believe in me."

WITH FAITH

Fourth Week of Easter, Saturday   John 14:7-14

Philip had a very practical mind. When on the shores of Galilee Jesus asked him where bread might be bought to feed the audience, Philip answered that there wasn't enough money in the company to feed this big a crowd. No doubt he was amazed at how Jesus solved the problem. He was probably no less amazed when at the Last Supper he asked another practical question, "Lord, show us the Father and we'll be satisfied," and Jesus answered with a rather firm reprimand. It was a demand for faith in his Apostles, and we know that with the overwhelming help of the Holy Spirit, Philip lived by that faith. He gave his life for it, too, being crucified in Asia Minor.

How is our faith, yours and mine? Thomas learned eventually. How about us? Doctor Victor Frankl, a psychiatrist, writes, "To live is to suffer, to survive is to find meaning in the suffering. If there is a purpose in life at all, there must be a purpose in suffering and dying." And this is something we are all certain to experience.

If we don't see the connection between suffering, death, and resurrection, then life means nothing. "O foolish and weak of faith," said Jesus at Emmaus. "Was it not necessary for Christ to suffer and so enter His glory?" Is there another way?

We see people suffering everywhere—poverty, war, earthquakes, floods, fires, and the whole range of what we all suffer from other people—unkindness, hatred, false accusations, injustice on matters of income and family needs, lack of gratitude or appreciation. Yet all these trials unite us and our fellow men to Christ's victory, if we see it with faith. Faith gives us courage and a sense of values, and puts a divine meaning into everything.

Let all who trust in God rejoice,
His kindness praise with glad acclaim,
His mercy sing with cheerful voice:
He blesses all who love His name.

PROOF OF LOVE

Fifth Week of Easter, Monday   **John 14:21-26**

We continue reading and reflecting over Jesus' farewell address at the Last Supper. As we read we sense a very tender spirit prevail. Jesus tells His apostles how they can share life with Him even though he departs from this world. He also promises them the Holy Spirit who will abide with them to console them and instruct them in everything He told them.

Jesus here makes it very clear what the conditions are for sharing life with Him, with the Father. Only if we obey the commandments He has given us do we love Him. But once we have proven our love by this obedience we will be loved by the Father. Jesus will love us to the extent of revealing Himself to us.

Obedience is the proof of love. If we love someone, we desire to do his will, to conform ourselves to his plans and wishes as much as possible. So it is in our relationship with the Lord. We must be loyal disciples. "Anyone who loves Me will be true to My word" (v. 23), Jesus says, and goes on to say that both the Father and He will make their abode in such a one.

Do we perhaps have difficulty in prayer? Does the Lord seem far away or entirely absent? Are we doubtful whether He really dwells in us? There are times when He does keep away from us the sense of His presence to build up our faith and trust. But another reason we don't find the Lord in prayer may be that we are not true to His word, not doing His will in our lives. Maybe we are not living the law of love as He gave it to us. If so, we know what we must do to have the Lord reestablish His dwelling place in us and once again reveal Himself to us.

Happy the man who delights in the law of the Lord, and meditates on it day and night (Ps 1:2).

MY PEACE

Fifth Week of Easter, Tuesday   **John 14:27-31**

"My peace is my gift to you. I do not give it to you as the world gives peace."

What peace was yours, Jesus? You found no peace as the world gives even in the seclusion of your small home town. Those who should have known you and loved You most personally turned against You; the mob tried to lynch You—to stone You and throw You headlong from a cliff near your own home. You, the Prince of Peace, never experienced worldly peace.

How dare we ask You for this blessing? Only because You insisted that we share Your peace. What was your peace—when You asked the Pharisees, "Why do you seek to kill me?" What peace did you enjoy—as they picked up rocks to throw at You and You hid Yourself and left the temple? What peace did You feel—as You informed Your twelve closest friends that one of them was on the verge of betraying You? By what pact of peace had Your own chosen people rejected You? What peace comforted You—as You prophesied Your cruel sufferings and violent death?

The one peace which Your every word and action bespoke was the perfect peace of being one in purpose with Your heavenly Father. This was Your peace—not as the world gives it—the peace of a right conscience, the peace of unity with God's Will, the peace of an unsoiled love. We understand to some extent what You mean by Your peace, Jesus, when we speak of "making our peace with God." By that we mean freeing ourselves from all selfish rebellion and restoring our errant wills to union with our Father's will.

Yours is the only true peace, Lord, understood clearly by Dante when in his *Paradiso* he exclaimed, "In His Will is our peace."

Go forth today with shouts of joy,
God's love like rain on dying ground
Will bring us peace, by God's good will:
We long to hear the happy sound!

VINE AND BRANCHES

Fifth Week of Easter, Wednesday   **John 15:1-8**

"I am the vine, you are the branches. Without me you can do nothing." Jesus tells us, "God is your total source of life. You are in absolute need of Him for true human life and growth." St. Paul understands this very well. He says, "God, with all His abundant wealth in Christ Jesus, will supply all your needs" (Ph 4:19).

God is interested in my whole person, in my every need, no matter what. Matthew and Mark in their Gospels tells us, "In the evening, they brought Jesus all the sick, and those with every kind of affliction, and He healed them *all*" (Mt 8:16).

By the comparison of the vine, Jesus tells us that it is God's purpose for us to live abundantly, to have a full life: "I have come that you may have life, and life in all its fullness" (Jn 10:10).

God, who is in me, is greater and more powerful than the devil, who is in the world. John writes, "You belong to God . . . for the Spirit who is in you is more powerful than the spirit in those who belong to the world" (1 Jn 4:4).

God wants you and me to be winners. He wants us to have the power to overcome every evil in our life, every attack of Satan to destroy our relationship with God, and to destroy our spiritual growth and vitality with it. So Jesus holds out the victory. He says, "Remain in union with me, and I will remain in union with you. Unless you remain in me, you cannot bear fruit. Whoever remains in me, and I in him, will bear much fruit."

Jesus promises that we will receive great power through this relationship of love with Him. He says, "If you remain in me and my words remain in you, then you will ask for anything you wish, and you shall have it." But note the condition: we must really and truly be one with Him—one in mind and heart with the Lord. Then His power will flow into us, and the promise will come true.

> **The Lord has come to be our life's companion,**
> **A banquet for His friends He shall provide.**
> **Unless you eat the food of life eternal,**
> **With Christ the Lord you cannot long abide.**

WHO EVER LOVED?

Fifth Week of Easter, Thursday   **John 15:9-11**

We only doubt God's love if we ourselves have never really loved. If we don't really know what love is, we think of it as a hot, fleeting passion which song, movie and novel flaunt before us. We think, to speak plainly, that selfish passion is love.

In the minds of the truly great, love is far from a passing infatuation. It is a firm direction of will. Love as Shakespeare saw it was that overwhelming power in man which made him faithful to death amid the greatest struggle and sacrifice. Love was a force of spirit that surpassed all flesh:

> Let me not to the marriage of true minds
> Admit impediments. Love is not love
> Which alters when its alteration finds,
> Or bends with the remover to remove:
> O, no! it is an ever-fixed mark
> That looks on tempest and is never shaken;
> It is the star to every wandering bark,
> Whose worth's unknown, although his height be taken.
> Love's not Time's fool, though rosy lips and cheeks
> Within his bending sickle's compass come;
> Love alters not with his brief hours and weeks,
> But bears it out even to the edge of doom.
>   If this be error and upon me proved,
>   I never writ, nor no man ever loved.   (Sonnet CXVI)

If man can be so sure of the unshaken, eternal strength of love, what must be God's love for us! A love which can die or weaken with any change is no love, says Shakespeare. It is the star which guides us back to truth when we wander. Such love does not pass with time's "brief hours and weeks," but faithful as God from whom it comes, love "bears it out even to the edge of doom." No sacrifice is too great for real love.

Love that is worthy of the name will always have this eternal quality. Eternal Love became flesh, and in Jesus we came to see real Love. The saints understood this love, lived by its faithfulness, and carried its bright flame to the very "edge of doom." If their love is not real, then Skakespeare is right: no man ever loved.

Jesus, You are eternal Love in the flesh. In You we see perfect Love.

HE LOVES YOU

Fifth Week of Easter, Friday   **John 15:12-17**

Throughout His teaching, Jesus assures us of His love. He commands that we love one another, as the Father loves Him, and He loves us. "God loves you and listens to you," He says, "Never forget it." Do we make this a living fact in our daily life? Let's try some examples. . .

When the phone keeps ringing and ringing while you're in the bathtub, remember: God loves you and is calling you to His happiness, and listens for your response.

When you can't find a parking place, and you come across a car stupidly taking up two places, remember: God loves you and listens and looks for a place in your heart.

When you're thumbing through a dictionary, and you forget the word you were looking for, remember: God loves you, and He does remember your name.

When you get your bill from the dentist, remember: God loves you and hears you. When you're on a slow elevator in a thirty-five story building, remember: God loves you and thinks of you all the time.

When the outdoor temperature is 36, and you keep closing the window while someone else keeps opening it, remember: God loves you and He calls the other guy your neighbor.

When you come hot and thirsty to a dairy queen just behind a bus load of kids, remember: God loves you and He loves every one of them.

When you discover, after a long wait, that you forgot to *plug in* the coffeepot, remember, God loves you and listens to you. Plug it in gently, and get your Bible to read about what the Gospels say about love and life and patience.

I hope this has included something for everybody, because the mystery of God's love for us takes so many different forms. Life is so full of wonderful opportunities to learn that God loves you, in spite of all the grim fun you're having!

> **With joy sound the trumpet, shout gladness and sing!**
> **Let hills, seas, and rivers rejoice in our King!**
> **The Lord, our true Shepherd, abandons His throne**
> **To save us with mercy, to make us His own!**

STRONG FOR BATTLE

Fifth Week of Easter, Saturday   **John 15:18-21**

"If you find that the world hates you, know that it has hated me before you." Jesus spoke a deeper truth here than we realize. Not only worldly persons, but the world's "things" hate us, too. The soothing "creature comforts" of the world hate us. They refuse to bring us happiness or peace. We like the easy life: eating, sleeping, entertainment, pleasure. We know well enough that the easy life has never produced a saint. But what hurts is that the easy life has never even brought happiness!

So we have the choice of being either saturated with unhappiness and unrest, or becoming "strong for battle," as the psalmist says, prepared for spiritual warfare. Sooner or later, and more than once, God will test us to see what we are worth.

Are we actually victims of the ancient pagan error that earthly goods in abundance are the sure sign of God's blessing on a nation and its people? Has our understanding advanced so little in three thousand years?

Or isn't it true that the saints have always been and always will be the people most blessed by God? Now, have any saints been raised up by the Church for veneration because they boasted of the greatest material comforts?

"No rest on earth! There's peace enough in heaven!" has been the battle cry of the saints. They have made Jesus the pattern of their life: "If you find that the world hates you, know that it has hated me before you. No slave is greater than his master."

What is the pattern of Jesus? "Our God has reigned from the Cross," the Church tells us in her liturgy. But nowhere are we told that this glorious throne of Jesus was the latest in design for comfort and convenience.

> Yes, God chose us fools, confusing the wise,
> ⸗The strong ones of earth are weak in His eyes,
> That flesh may not glory before Him!
> The lowly He lifts, whom great ones despised,
> And those who are small the Lord has so prized
> That pride will be keen to adore Him! (1 Cor 1:27-29).

APPRECIATION WEEK

Sixth Week of Easter, Monday   **John 15:26-16:4**

Jesus promised his apostles that He would send them the Holy Spirit, who would teach them all truth and help them recall what He had said. This seemed to imply that they had not grasped the full meaning of His coming, that they had not been able to appreciate what He had done for them and for all of us, that they really did not yet understand. The apostles would have been the first to admit this!

Only after the Holy Spirit came did they begin to understand their part in the redeeming work of Christ. The Spirit of truth showed them what Christ's supreme love had done for them, and what their love for fellow men could do, to take part in Christ's work of saving the world. The Holy Spirit taught the apostles their own value, their own potential, and the scope of their great challenge.

That is what the Holy Spirit wants to do for us, too. He wants us to share in the tremendous love of the Trinity by seeing the good in our fellow men. Genuine Christ-like love makes people good. Generous, kind, thoughtful help of others makes you better, and has an effect on everyone around you. Just see what it will do to your family if you make this week "Appreciation Week" at your home.

We are much too critical of one another in a useless way, that is we don't help matters by it. If we tear down without building up, do we really want anything to improve? The apostles were weak and ignorant and selfish, but Jesus built them up by what He did. His example and His criticism was constructive; He helped them grow.

So we can be Christ-like by loving others. (Not just liking them emotionally.) We love by seeing the good in each other and building it up. Love must give rather than take away. When we appreciate others with kindly respect, we make them better, as Christ did. By generosity we make both ourselves and others better. It may take years, but eventually it works. Real Christ-like concern for others is bound to produce much good. See what it did eventually for His apostles.

Jesus, bless our "appreciation week," an effort to know You and know each other better.

PROVING THE WORLD WRONG

Sixth Week of Easter, Tuesday   **John 16:5-11**

As Jesus keeps talking to His apostles about leaving this world He notices that they are overcome by grief. They just don't seem to understand why He must go. He tells them the sober truth. If He doesn't go, the Paraclete, the Holy Spirit, will not come to them. He will go and send the Spirit to them.

What will the Spirit do when He comes? He will be their counselor, their consoler. He will guide them in their relationship, in their encounter with the world.

The Spirit will prove the world wrong about sin, about justice, about condemnation. He will show by the divine, just and holy life of the Church which He will guide, that Christ was sinless, that He was just, that He did not deserve condemnation. Those who refuse to believe in Him, to obey His commands, are the guilty ones. They are the unjust. They are the ones who stand condemned.

Which side are we on? Are we truly sharers in that divine life by our faith, our obedience, our love? Are we among the just of Christ, the righteous? Do our lives bear witness to the holiness of Christ whose members we are?

We have received the Holy Spirit just as the apostles did. He is our advocate too. He is our guide and our consoler. He gives us instructions, guidance and the strength, the courage it takes to live with Christ, with His Church. We need not suffer condemnation. It is the world that is condemned every time we witness to Christ as Lord in our lives by the power of the Holy Spirit.

Lord, we thank You for sending us Your Spirit. May He help us to live holy and righteous in Your presence.

THE SPIRIT GIVES LIFE

Sixth Week of Easter, Wednesday   **John 16:12-15**

This gospel, as well as every gospel, is God's message directed to every one of us. God inspired the Evangelists in such a way that their words are really His. Are we truly aware of that when we hear the Gospel read to us, or when we read the Bible? That's exactly what the charism of Scriptural inspiration means.

If God is the author, how can He fail to move us directly every time we hear His Word and expose ourselves to His influence? "The

Holy Spirit will guide you to all truth," said Jesus. "He will have received from me what He will announce to you." This promise of Jesus at the Last Supper indicates that the Spirit will continue to impress the words of Jesus upon our hearts, if we are open to Him. The Holy Spirit will continually give the words of Jesus a new impulse and a vital power. For Jesus intended that we live by His words daily.

"The letter kills," Jesus said, "Only the Spirit gives life," because He is most completely alive. When we hear a passage from God's word read to us, or when we ourselves read the Bible, we must see it not as an abstract text to be dissected. We must see that it is God Himself coming into our tent to speak to us face to face, as a friend comes in to converse with us.

If we listen to the Lord in this frame of mind, His word will be living and active in us; it will produce results, it will cure our ills, it will raise us from the dead. If we receive His word by the power of the Spirit, His word will feed us and strengthen us all day long, just as the living Bread feeds us to make us strong.

> **Come Holy Spirit, make us alive with faith and trust,**
> **let us be amazed at the influence You can have on us.**
> **Give us your peace and joy and strength, that we may**
> **truly live and act by the power of Your Word.**

> **O Spirit, come, Creator blest!**
> **Come to our hearts, most welcome guest!**
> **Bring us Your light and gracious aid,**
> **Strengthen our souls, which You have made.**

ASCENSION OF THE LORD

Sixth Week of Easter, Thursday　　　　**Feast of the Ascension**

When you were down and out and everything was going wrong, what brought you out of it? When you found yourself very materialistic, very concerned about money and success in your work, and the bottom fell out of your plans, what saved you?

When you felt the sting of failure and worried about the future, did you have that rare friend to tell you gently, "You'll be all right when you get your sights up?"

This is why Jesus ascended into heaven. While He was on earth, His followers just could not raise their sights. "Lord, will You restore the political power to Israel *now*?" What a question.

So Jesus said, "I must return to my heavenly Father. That's where *your* sights should be. But since they are not, I will send you the Holy Spirit to fill you with spiritual power—to raise your sights."

That is what the event and the feast of the Ascension of Jesus is telling us: "Look up to the real goal of your life; set your sights directly toward that heavenly Father, your Creator. Jesus gives you the perfect example. His whole life is directed toward God the Father. The Ascension is the closing chapter, or rather, the opening chapter of His new and more powerful presence in the Church."

> **Jesus, Redeemer of man,**
> **Son of the Father most high,**
> **Born before ages began,**
> **Born before stars of the sky:**
> **Sharing the Father's pure light,**
> **Hear, as Your children draw nigh,**
> **Groping unsure through the night:**
> **For Your redemption we cry!**
> **Remember, Lord of the earth,**
> **You took the body of man,**
> **Joining our race at Your birth,**
> **Filling the heavenly plan!**
> **Born through the Virgin's consent,**
> **Lifetime among us You spent:**
> **Lord, by Your humble descent,**
> **Raise us to join Your ascent!**

DIVINE HUMOR

Sixth Week of Easter, Friday   **John 16:20-23**

Jesus says, "Your grief will be turned into joy."

How do you explain the joy of the saints in the very face of torturous suffering? How can you explain the feelings of St. Paul when he rejoices at all his troubles? Just where is the joke, in all the pains and trials of the saints? How can we "joyfully offer sacrifice?"

We must investigate this "divine humor" of the saints. What makes something humorous, anyway? Well—why do we laugh when we see a small, scrawny man walking down the street hand in hand with a huge, husky woman as his partner? The humor is in the lack of proportion. They don't appear to belong together. Humor often grows out of some absence of proportion.

That is the divine humor of the saints. That is the paradox Jesus spoke of when He told His disciples, "Your sorrow will be turned into joy." The saints saw this as a divine joke: they knew how little they were paying for the kingdom of heaven. They rejoiced over the amazing bargain they had discovered. There were humiliations, pains, and some drops of good blood—but they were a small price for God's magnificent heaven. "What exchange can a man give for his soul?" asked Jesus. What can we answer Him, but to laugh at the thought of exchanging anything?

Perhaps only saints can truly laugh at their earthly hardships. For only they see how truly small they are, how out of proportion with what they purchase. They see, as St. Paul did, that "the sufferings of this life are not worth comparing with the glory that is to come."

Jesus, you said that our sorrow would be turned to joy. You promised to show us the glory You reserve for those who can laugh at how little they are asked to pay for it.

GROWTH

Sixth Week of Easter, Saturday   **John 16:23-28**

Jesus describes the kingdom of God as a tiny mustard seed that grows into a large shrub. Growth is the great mystery of life. It has its joys and its sorrows. We all looked forward to growing up, and all the privileges that go with it . . . freedom to make our own decisions, and the whole bit. We thought then we'd know everything and could do everything.

But we found out it's very painful to grow up. There were plenty of physical and psychological growing pains. It's not so easy to have to depend on yourself, instead of on others, and many people never do make that adjustment.

A sad and worried college student sent an urgent telegram to his parents: "Am without funds or friends. Please help."

His father immediately wired back, in two words, "Make friends."

A shocker like this is actually a blessing in disguise. It makes a young person grow. To grow we must often be compelled to work out problems for ourselves. Once we have the need and the good will, it's amazing how much we can accomplish that we never dreamed of. This is what Jesus meant by that powerful and symbolic statement, "If you have faith you can move mountains," and again, "Believe and you shall receive whatever you ask." It was an impressive way of saying, "If you have confidence in God's power and in the potential He gave you, you'd be surprised at what you can accomplish."

It may be hard at first, but these are the normal growing pains. What a grand feeling, once you get your second wind!

> His holy Word created me,
> My Master, I adore Him;
> He guides my life through stormy seas,
> With thanks I come before Him.
> On Him I call, my God and All;
> In joy and pain He schools me,
> With love He wisely rules me.

I HAVE OVERCOME

Seventh Week of Easter, Monday   **John 16:29-33**

Has a religion teacher with a little originality asked you, "What was the last thing Jesus said to His disciples at the Last Supper?"

And did you fail to give the answer he wanted? He claims that Jesus said, "If you guys want to get into the picture, you'll have to get on this side of the table."

That's not just a giggler. It bears a symbolism that makes you think! Isn't it true that at the Last Supper the disciples were just not on the Lord's side of the table at all? They were still quarrelling about which of them would be the greatest in His earthly kingdom. They were miles away from Jesus at that supper.

Now Jesus comes with the biggest shocker: "You will suffer in the world. But take courage! I have overcome the world."

You can imagine how that *threw* them. Peter said to John, "Did you hear what He said?" James said to Jesus, "Lord, would you run that past us once more?"

Jesus said, "I don't mind. I said, I have overcome the world!" Do you know what the disciples were thinking? "Well, it doesn't look like it! The crowds don't understand Him, all the big businessmen in Jerusalem are against Him, the politicians have turned Him off completely, a minute ago He revealed that the smartest one of us is going to betray Him, and now He says, I have overcome the world.!"

But you and I can sneak a look at the end of the book, and we see that Jesus was right. This is the only story where you sacrifice all, your true love is rejected, you give up everything and they kill you for it, but you don't lose at all. You are the uncontested champion, the number one winner for all time.

This is why the Gospel is Good News! It tells us that Jesus holds in His powerful hand the victory over sin and death. The Gospel tells us that "Jesus is Lord." He is Lord over life and death: He has it all, He has conquered, He is forever undefeated.

> **Hear the shout of victory,**
> **We have lived to see Him rise,**
> **We will join His company,**
> **See the Lord with our own eyes,**
> **Alleluia, victory!**

HE PRAYS FOR US

Seventh Week of Easter, Tuesday   **John 17:1-11**

The Gospel today is part of Jesus' prayer for His apostles. He prays to the Father and asks Him to protect them—not to take them out of the world, but to guard them from evil. When Jesus says the world hates his followers, by "World" He means the worldly, the godless, the faithless. Since His apostles do not belong to such a world, they are hated. They are, however, to stay in the world among people, the good and the bad, to be a good influence, to be an example and reminder, to bring all men and all things back to God.

Of course, there is a risk involved. Rotten apples in a barrel can spoil the good ones. Bad example can influence good people. So Jesus prays for us to His Father, "Guard them from the evil one . . . Guard them by means of truth." Then He adds, "As you have sent me into the world, so I have sent them into the world."

Today, this very day, in the Liturgy of the Word, in the Eucharist, Jesus is praying for us, just as He did for His first followers. He prays to the Father to protect us, to consecrate us by means of the truth, to keep us from going wrong in spite of the dangers we are sure to face. He reminds us in His prayer that we might be hated at times for taking a Christian stand in our pagan times, for seeing things in the light of Christ's teaching rather than by what the worldly consider convenient. This need not disturb us as long as we work and act with true Christian love.

St. John in his first letter reminds us, as we approach Pentecost, "The way we know that we abide in God and He in us is, that He has given the Holy Spirit to us." The Spirit's gifts to us are peace, joy, strength, courage and understanding. We need not fear anything, if we are open to the Spirit and live in the Spirit.

> **Holy Spirit, Lord of might,**
> **Shed on us Your wondrous light,**
> **Brought to us from heaven's height!**

PRAY ALWAYS

Seventh Week of Easter, Wednesday   John 17:11-19

Of all men that ever lived, there is only one who did not need to pray. There is only one whose perfections were such that He owed no more to God or to Himself. For this man *was* God: He was Christ, God and man.

Yet when you examine the Gospels, you see how often He prayed! St. Mark tells us, on several occasions "Jesus spent the night in the prayer of God." Again, after a long evening spent in healing the sick, Mark says of Jesus, "Rising very early in the morning, He left the city and went to a desert place, and there He prayed."

St. John in his Gospel gives us four detailed chapters of what Jesus said at the Last Supper. Much of it is the long prayer of Jesus to the Father for His followers, all who would come to believe in Him.

St. Luke indicates what a habit of prayer Jesus had. For he says that after the Paschal Supper, Jesus went out "to the garden of Gethsemane to pray *as was His custom*. And there Jesus said to His disciples, "Stay here and pray, so you may not give in to temptation." Then He left them, and going off a distance, He knelt down and prayed. Notice that St. Luke, who was a medical doctor, was the one who inquired and found out that Jesus had sweat blood in His prayer at Gethsemane, so great was His anguish. Luke adds, "And being in agony, He prayed the longer." How hard it is to pray when we are suffering. But Jesus prayed all the longer!

In His parables, Jesus taught us perseverance in prayer. He told us we need prayer as a lifelong habit. And he taught this most clearly by His own example. Lord, teach us that prayer is our natural way of keeping our friendship with You alive and active.

> We come, O Lord, to You, the living fountain!
> We've far to go, up hill and rugged mountain.
> We listen to the waters flow, O Lord, today:
> We drink with You, and feeling strong, go on our way.

THAT ALL MAY BE ONE

Seventh Week of Easter, Thursday   **John 17:20-26**

We come to the closing words of Jesus' prayer to the Father, sometimes called His High-Priestly prayer. His final words are a prayer for all believers in every age. It is a plea that all these believers be one with the oneness of the Father and the Son.

Evidently Jesus with a measure of divine foresight looks into the centuries to come and sees many believing in Him. Through the work and preaching of those apostles sitting there at His side the good news would be spread far and wide. Others would follow them and carry the message to the ends of the earth.

Yet He sees the disagreements, the turmoil, the divisions, sometimes even the hatreds that occur amongs His believers. He is sad about that and prays to the Father for unity among all His followers.

This unity, this oneness and love amongst Christians is to be a sign to the world. It is to prove that Jesus was sent by the Father, who loves us as He loves His Son.

In the early Church we hear that there was such great love, such oneness, that even the Pagans said, "See how these Christians love one another." As if to say that there is something special about them. It is more than a mere human love and friendship. It bears witness to God's work among them. It is a sign of something genuine and true.

We know our divisions today. We know that only through sincere love and by God's power through prayer can we become one. As Jesus prayed that all might be one as He and the Father are one, we, too, should implore the Father for mercy, forgiveness and unity.

> **Father, Jesus, Holy Spirit, as You are one in love,
> make us all one in faith and love.**

DO YOU LOVE ME?

Seventh Week of Easter, Friday   **John 21:15-19**

A third time Jesus asked him, "Simon, son of John, do you love me?" Here we see Jesus again as the great spiritual healer. Peter feels guilt and remorse. He needs a deep inner healing. He is tense and worried about his sin of denying Jesus three times on Holy Thursday night.

But the risen Jesus is also the healing Jesus and the forgiving Jesus. Though Peter may not understand his tensions and guilt feelings, Jesus knows. So He asks Peter three times, "Do you love me? Do you love me more than anyone else?"

Peter answers, "Lord, you know everything; you know well that I love You." And Jesus heals him, then sends him out to heal all of us: "Feed my lambs, feed my sheep." We see Peter passing on the good news of healing to the crippled man at the temple gate (Ac 3:1-10). Peter tells the man, "I have neither silver nor gold, but what I have I give you! In the name of Jesus Christ of Nazareth, rise up and walk." The man was healed and his response was wonderful. St. Luke says, "He went into the temple, walking, jumping about, and giving praise to God."

That is the way our story should read! No matter what sins we're guilty of, no matter how weak we've been, or how foolishly we have denied Jesus in our lives, Peter shows us that there is healing for us by the love and power of Jesus. That's the good news of the Gospel.

Do we believe, really believe, that Jesus can heal us? That He can heal those bad relationships in our families? That He can burn out those selfish, misdirected movements in us that spoil life for us? Aren't we all like the honest woman who said, "Wherever I go, I must take myself with me, and that spoils everything."

But why don't we learn this greater truth from Jesus? "Wherever I go, I can take Jesus with me, and that heals everything." That's really good news. He loves me, and He has the power to save me from my spoiled self. Praise Him!

> **Jesus, You can change us. You have the power, and You have the love for us.**

EACH ONE IS SPECIAL

Seventh Week of Easter, Saturday   **John 21:20-25**

As we come to the close of the Easter season we read the last words of John's gospel. They contain a beautiful lesson for us.

In His final appearance as the Risen Lord, Jesus had just told Peter how he was to suffer persecution and final martyrdom. Since Jesus said nothing about how John was to die Peter became curious and asked, "But Lord, what about him?"

Jesus never did give the satisfaction of direct answers to idle questions of mere curiosity. The gospels agree on this (e.g., Lk 13:23 ff.). So Jesus gives Peter a puzzling answer: "Suppose I want him to stay until I come, how does that concern you? Your business is to follow Me." He does not satisfy Peter's nosiness, his idle curiosity. He tells him just to make sure he follows in His footsteps, finally to crucifixion.

Why are we so curious about the affairs of others? Why do we wonder about God's ways in His love for each of us as individuals. Jesus is saying to Peter: "You are Peter and John is John. I can't treat you both alike. I must respect your individuality, your special gifts."

So often we are a bit jealous and upset because God seems to treat others more lovingly than He treats us. How can this be? God is love. God's love is limitless to every one without exception. We must learn to accept His love for us and the way He loves us, even though sometimes we can't understand it, we feel less loved than others.

God is a jealous lover. He wants each relationship He has with His sons and daughters to be completely personal and unique.

Thank You, Jesus, for loving me in a very personal way. I am happy to be special in Your eyes.

THE HOLY SPIRIT

Feast of Pentecost   **John 20:19-23**

"Receive the Holy Spirit. If you forgive people's sins, they are forgiven." Jesus says that He gives us the Holy Spirit for the forgiveness of sins. This is to be the mission of the Church, which the apostles are to lead. They are to do the very work of Jesus on earth: save His people from their sins. Thus they will continue His redeeming work. To forgive in Jesus' name they must be filled with the Holy Spirit.

John says of Jesus, "He breathed on them." This is a sign, a sacrament, to indicate that Jesus is conferring the Holy Spirit on His disciples. The new Catholic rite of forgiving sins reflects this connection of the Spirit with absolving sins:

"God, the Father of mercies, through the death and resurrection of His Son has reconciled the world to Himself and sent the Holy Spirit among us for the forgiveness of sins."

We can apply the words of Jesus on Easter Sunday to our own daily personal life. He gives the Holy Spirit for the forgiveness of sins. It is a special gift to His Church, but also a special reminder to each member of the Church. If we are to be true Christians, other Christs, our sign of personal friendship with Jesus is our forgiving Spirit. For this difficult task Jesus gives us the power of the Holy Spirit. Conversely, if we have received the Holy Spirit, then His influence in our life will show when we forgive the sins of others against us.

The Spirit is always present with Jesus in His earthly life. After telling us that the very birth of Jesus is brought about by the power of the Holy Spirit, Luke mentions five more times in his Gospel that Jesus is filled with the Holy Spirit and led by that Spirit throughout His public life. If we are to be 'imitators of Christ,' as St. Paul urges us, then we must be filled with the Holy Spirit.

St. John has Jesus telling us four times at the Last Supper that He will send us the Holy Spirit, to guide us, to be our close companion, to lead us to all truth. So Jesus Himself tells us that our Christian life should be spirit-filled, as His life was. "When the Holy Spirit comes upon you, you will be filled with power" (Ac 1:8).

GOD'S FAMILY

Feast of the Holy Trinity

We might have thought that before God created the angels and before He created the people on this planet, He must have been alone out there somewhere. But when God sent His Son to save us, we learned that God was never alone. He was always a family, a sharing community of three. The Father loves the Son, who is the perfect image of the Father's mind, the Word of God. Between them there is perfect harmony, full love. Their infinite love generates a third Person, the Holy Spirit.

The three Persons in God are so united in love and submission to one another that the three act as one, always in perfect harmony. That boundless love of God spills over into all His creation, so that God's love for us, too, is unlimited. God loves each one of us totally. We divide our love and put limits on it, but God loves fully, completely, endlessly.

So the mystery of the Holy Trinity tells us a lot about that tremendous thing we call "love." Real love, true love, lasting love— not any of its cheap substitutes. God created us in the image of His own most excellent Trinity. What does that mean? He created us not to be alone, selfish, lonely individuals, but to be persons in community, just as He is in the family of His Trinity. He made us to give of our best to one another, as He gives.

Just as each person in the Holy Trinity is different yet living in perfect harmony, so are we different from one another, but created to live in loving harmony. Just as there is a fully open communication of thought and love in the Trinity, so should it be with us, who are created in His image.

Pope John XXIII was talking to a large crowd of people in St. Peter's Square one day and said, "When you return home, give each of your children or your parents a great big hug and tell them, this is a little of the love which the Pope sends to you." So let me say, "Whenever you show how much you love someone in your family, those you love most in all the world, remember: this is just a little of the love which the Most Holy Trinity has for you."

NEW PASSOVER

Corpus Christi   **Mark 14:12-16, 22-26**

We never tire of reading and rereading the various Gospel accounts of the last supper. We find here our greatest heritage as Christians—a heritage that is renewed every time we celebrate Eucharist, and more especially celebrated each year on Corpus Christi.

The Gospel very clearly connects Jesus' last supper with the Passover. No doubt in doing this Jesus wants to show that he is about to celebrate his own passover. Henceforth in the new covenant this will be the Memorial Meal, a memorial of our passing over from the slavery of sin to the freedom of the sons of God. This deliverance, this freedom Jesus won for us on the Cross by his death and resurrection. The new passover meal, given to us at the last supper in his own Body and Blood, would not only commemorate the redemption of the Cross but renew it even daily in our very midst where we can take part in it in a very real way.

Jesus gave some very definite instructions to his disciples who were to prepare for the meal. This was to be very special. In Luke's Gospel account Jesus says "I have greatly desired to eat this Passover with you before I suffer."

This is still true today. Jesus greatly desires to celebrate Eucharist with us. He wants to give himself to us. But He wants us to prepare. Eucharist must be special. We must have a great desire to come together for this meal. We must want to do it well, to be open to the Lord's word, to respond to Him with praise, to receive Him, Body and Blood, in deep faith. "Take this, this is my body. This is my blood."

Lord, how can we ever thank you enough for the gift of Eucharist, the gift of your very self in bodily form.

MYSTERY OF LOVE

Feast of the Sacred Heart of Jesus Second Friday after Pentecost

Love, the holiest and highest earthly good,
Love, most desired and most misunderstood,
Love, most spoken of and most abused,
Love, most sought—when found, most often misused,
Love—who ever really loves?

Good parents, who have worked and suffered for their little ones?
Who have given all for these demanding daughters and those thankless sons,
Who have deprived themselves and left themselves for this child from the day of his birth,
Is their love not the most natural and fundamental and strongest on earth?
But even this love most noble is tainted with excess,
And loving concern too easily becomes over-protectiveness.
For when the child grows older and needs much help to mature,
The once true love unexpectedly becomes a caricature,
And what was great generosity, once strong and secure
Becomes in the face of imminent loss, timidly demure.

Then must we learn true love again from Jesus, source of all good will,
From His creative and redeeming love, learn the true Lover's skill:
Love of Christ, open, forgiving, untouched by slightest shadow of selfishness,
Unprejudiced, totally generous, ingenious with a twinkle of elfishness,
Ever hiding and reappearing, ever loyal and trusted while yet shocking and mystifying,
Ever respecting His creature's freedom, Love renewing and purifying!
With what tenderness and strength He firms His gentle word with deed,
With what glory He surrounds us with gifts, provides for every need!

To Ezekiel He says, "I will go on looking for these sheep of mine."

"I will rescue them," He says, "from the snares and ravines into which they have strayed,
From the dark mists that fell on them when my love was betrayed.
I will bind up the broken limb, nourish the wasted frame." (Ezk 34:12-26)
Praise the Lord of infinite mercy! Sing praises to His loving Name!

> **"What mother could forget her son,**
> **Or cease to love her little one?**
> **But if she failed him, even yet**
> **Would I, the Lord your God, forget?**
> **See what is here—and understand—**
> **Your name inscribed upon My hand!"** (Is 49:15).

GOOD NEWS

First Week of the Year, Monday   **Mark 1:13-20**

As we begin the ordinary time of the Church Year we read Mark's Gospel first. It is the shortest and most concise. Our passage opens just as Jesus comes out of the desert and begins His public life. He proclaims that the reign of God is at hand and urges us to repent and believe the good news.

Good news? Where is the good news? All that one seems to see in the news media is bad news: wars, bombings, terrorism, riotings and such like. Is there no good news to be reported?

Jesus came to bring good news. That is what the very word "gospel" means in Old English. When Jesus was born it was announced as "Tidings of great joy." After His resurrection those who wrote about Him, His life, death and resurrection called it gospel, or simply "good news."

What is this good news that Jesus brings? Is it a hope of great wealth and prosperity? What is this reign of God that Jesus says is at hand? It is a promise of love, a promise of forgiveness, of healing, of new life. Jesus came to bring the love of the Father to His children on earth. He showed this love in all His works, in His healings, His forgiveness, His compassion for the crowds.

How ought we to respond to that good news? Jesus tells us. He says in this gospel passage, "Reform your lives and believe in the good news."

Have we been taken up too much with the bad news? Do TV, daily papers, secular magazines and novels take up so much of our time that we have none left for the good news, God's own Word? Jesus says, "Reform your lives." Get your priorities straight. Look around. See the good news. Become aware of God's love, mercy and compassion at work all around. Respond to that love. Share it with others. Be a messenger of the good news. Then you will see that the reign of God is already in our midst.

I will proclaim You, O Lord, among the nations, and I will sing praise to Your name (Ps 18:50).

A NEW TEACHING

First Week of the Year, Tuesday   **Mark 1:21-28**

The Gospel passage for today is the first account of exorcism, of Jesus driving out a devil, in St. Mark's Gospel. There are four such narratives in Mark. It is interesting to note that this narrative is surrounded with statements of the authority with which Jesus taught. "The people were spellbound by His teaching because He taught with authority, and not like the Scribes." This before the narrative.

Then Jesus rebuked the devil sharply saying, "Be quiet! Come out of the man!" And with a loud shriek he came out of the man. The Gospel goes on to say that all were amazed and began to ask one another: "What does this mean? A completely new teaching in a spirit of authority. He gives orders to unclean spirits and they obey." And so Jesus' reputation for teaching with authority spread throughout the countryside, confirmed by His authority over evil spirits.

Too often we consider ourselves Christians when the going is easy, when Christ's teaching agrees with our easy way of life, when it doesn't disturb our complacency. But when His teaching is hard, when it hits us right between the eyes, we tend to overlook it, consider it outmoded. We fail to recognize the supreme divine authority with which Jesus speaks in the Gospels. When He speaks about love, justice, the poor, about giving a coat to our neighbor who has none if we have two, we hold back. We apply different values. We fail to act as Christians. We are unwilling to sacrifice our comfort in order to live by the authority of Christ's Gospel.

We love Your teaching, Lord, because You teach with divine authority.

JESUS HEALS TODAY

First Week of the Year, Wednesday   **Mark 1:29-39**

Mark's Gospel is in a sense the Gospel of the miracles of Christ. In the very first chapter which we have been reading this week we already find mention of them. The first miracle in Mark's Gospel was related in yesterday's Gospel, the first account of exorcism, of driving out devils. In today's Gospel we have a very short account of Jesus healing Peter's mother-in-law. This is followed by such statements as, "they brought Him all who were ill, and those obsessed by demons . . . those whom he cured who were variously afflicted were many, and so were the demons He expelled." Certainly this indicates that the miracles of healing were very many.

As we read a Gospel narrative such as this, do we realize that this Jesus is the same Jesus whom we meet at the Eucharist, whom we receive in Communion? I wonder whether we think of the fact that this Jesus of the Gospel, the God-Man who has risen from the dead, is alive as God and as man among us. If we do, then why are we often lonely, afraid, sad, as if nobody cared about our troubles, about our sickness, about our various concerns? Christ certainly cares as much about us today as He did about the people who lived in Palestine during His sojourn on earth.

It does seem a bit strange that we, who have been given the

precious gift of faith, lack the trust in Christ's goodness and power that our faith warrants. We need not necessarily expect miracles to solve all our problems. But we certainly should have the confidence that with Christ's help our own efforts will either alleviate our troubles, or if it not be God's will, that Christ's grace will bring light to our understanding, help us to see His will in our trials and give us a peace and calm that no earthly crisis can take away. Let us bring our ills to Christ, the healer, as the people of old.

Make us realize, Jesus, that You are as much a healer today as in gospel times.

HE HEALS

First Week of the Year, Thursday   **Mark 1:40-45**

A leper approached Jesus with a request, "If you will to do so, you can heal me."

The Gospels stress the power of Jesus to heal. He touches all the sick and they are healed. There are physical and psychological healings. But always there are demons to drive out, too. The Lord has come especially for spiritual healing.

Only He can heal our spiritual ills. It is He who takes away our weaknesses. We cannot do it by ourselves. God is the one who can free us from the slaveries of sin: He heals us. "Do it yourself" does not apply to our spiritual life. For inner healing the main formula is, "Give God a chance to do it."

The good news Jesus preaches is that He heals our ills. To repent means "to turn to God," not simply to aim at "a better self," which may merely mean selfishness with a nicer name. It is not I who make myself better: only God does that.

Repenting—turning to God—leads us to a healing outside ourselves, Jesus doing the healing. This saying is true: "When God works, we can rest; when we work—alone—God rests."

God works for us, for instance in the Sacraments, not only forgiving our sins, but also healing us of our spiritual weaknesses. In reality we are working, too, when God works in us. We rest in one sense, but in another, we are opening ourselves fully to Him. The more open we are, the more we "get off our chest," the more things surface, like the plates in a cafeteria coming up automatically. We do plant the seed of healing by open honesty with God. Repentance is a full turn toward God with complete attention to His work in us.

> **The Lord has said, "If you repent,**
> **Your wounds will soon be healed,**
> **For then shall light and grace be sent,**
> **My love shall be revealed."**
> **Our God will answer when we call,**
> **The Lord shall bring us aid:**
> **Our God was ever kind to all**
> **Who heard Him and obeyed"** (Ps 58:8-9).

NO SIN IS PRIVATE

First Week of the Year, Friday   **Mark 2:1-12**

Most of us are too accustomed to thinking of penance as a very private, individual matter. Sin, forgiveness and reparation are, indeed, personal affairs, but they are just as much community affairs.

Today's Gospel story from St. Mark tells us about the paralyzed man whom Jesus cured and whose sins he forgave telling him to sin no more. This man had been a burden to his neighbors. Look at all the trouble they went through to lower him through the roof to get him in front of Jesus for a cure. His sickness was very clearly a community concern. Jesus cured him and sent a sound and able man back into the community.

This occasions a public debate. Can man forgive sins in God's name? Jesus says "Yes," and He uses this very public miracle to illustrate His point.

We can apply this event to ourselves in the sense that by sin, by being in a sinful state, we are unable to help ourselves like the paralytic. The community, the Church which is the spiritual community, should be concerned about our need. And the Church in Christ's name is concerned about healing our spiritual illness.

All of us are a part of the community of God, we all are involved in forgiveness of sin. When a man, even if not conscious of deliberate sin, goes to confession, he is giving witness that he is a member of the penitential Church. He is giving witness that he is making reparation, doing penance, by confessing not only for himself, but for all those who have failed to respond to God's invitation.

Every sin of ours is an offense against all the other members of the Church. By sin we are failing to exercise our ability to make others better, to give grace from our actions to the whole Church. Hence we hurt everyone. And so the need of penance in the Christian community, as a way of changing our attitude. Penance needs follow through, kindness to those we have hurt, correcting unfair criticism, extra work to repair wasted time and all kinds of reparation. Sin has all kinds of community repercussions. So our penance must be community orientated.

Thank you, Lord, for making us aware of the communal dimension of penance and forgiveness.

LEVI'S FREEDOM PARTY

First Week of the Year, Saturday   Mark 2:13-17

Levi is another person who proves what can happen to us—if we are willing to pay the great price.

Jesus saw Levi at his tax office. "Follow me," He said. Levi had a lot in common with the rich young man to whom Jesus made the same offer. But the other man refused because he couldn't leave his treasures behind.

Levi was rich: it went with his lucrative occupation. Tax collectors were hated—partly out of envy. Which of their poor over-taxed victims would not gladly have traded jobs? Levi was rich enough to throw a grand welcome banquet for Jesus and His disciples. He had been a slave to money, and now his new freedom was worth celebrating. It was Levi's farewell to the "good" life, as Americans call it, the "selfish life," really.

But there are always the envious, the self-appointed critics around to spoil a good party. Explain as you like, they cannot or will not understand.

Jesus used the occasion to make clear the reason for His coming, as well as for the party. He came not to condemn, but to forgive. He came to "call not the self-righteous, but sinners."

When we find it hard to see a friend or acquaintance become a success in a good sense, when we feel a twitch of envy at a friend's happiness—especially when we think he hasn't deserved it—it'll be well to remember the Lord's words. He came to bring peace and joy and forgiveness to your neighbor as well as to you.

"Blessed are the merciful, for they shall obtain mercy."
I hear you, Jesus. And I truly hope You can apply that
blessing to me.

CHANGES

Second Week of the Year, Monday   Mark 2:18-22

Jesus compares His presence among men during His public ministry to the presence of a bridegroom during the marriage feast.

This is a time for rejoicing with the bridegroom. There may be times later when in facing the realities of life as a husband and father the bridegroom will need sympathy and compassion. But for the time being all is joy.

So with Christ. While He is with His disciples He doesn't want them to fast. Jesus wants His disciples to be in a state where they can more easily undergo the changes in their person needed for assimilating and understanding the new teachings He is bringing.

Jesus is not condemning fast or other corporal penance. But it must have its right time and circumstances. It must be undertaken prudently. There are times when fasting could be wrong, imprudent, foolish. If fasting keeps a mother from taking care of her children, it is wrong. If it keeps anyone from doing his duty towards neighbor in any way, it is wrong.

There are times when the occasion requires that we have all our strength, both mental and physical, to meet a crisis, a change. Necessary changes are not easily accepted, especially if the groundwork has not been done. In some way we must already have changed ourselves, at least in attitude and openness, before we can accept necessary and good changes.

This seems to be what the Lord means when He says, "No one sews a patch of unshrunken cloth on an old cloak . . . no one pours new wine into old wine skins . . . no, new wine is poured into new skins."

The joy of new life which comes from good life-giving changes has its place in the Christian's life. Its appropriate celebration precludes fasting at such a time. But this joy, this new life, as a rule, only comes after some penance, some denial, a certain dying to self.

We thank you, Lord, for teaching us the truth about fasting and the joy of New Life in You.

LAW ABOVE THE LAW

Second Week of the Year, Tuesday   **Mark 21:23-28**

This story of Jesus and His disciples plucking kernels of grain and eating them on the Sabbath as they walked to the Synagogue appears in all three Synoptic gospels almost word for word. We see the rigorist Pharisees protesting that they were doing a work forbidden on the Sabbath. Preparing food was one of thirty-nine forms of work listed by the Rabbis as against the Sabbath rest. That they should even consider plucking of a few grains of wheat or corn as work shows their rigorist interpretation of the Law.

The rigorist is really out to condemn the innocent to make himself look good. Jesus' answer shows his great concern for human needs, his much more human approach to law.

Jesus asks the Pharisees whether they never read in the Scriptures about how King David because of the human needs of his men, their natural hunger, considered it right to do something otherwise forbidden, to enter God's house and eat the show bread, which only the priests were permitted to eat under normal circumstances. What Jesus is saying is that there is a law way above the written laws, be they of God or man, a law which the Creator placed into the very nature of man: urgent legitimate human needs surpass the law.

As we reread this passage, and reflect upon it, we gradually come to know Jesus better. We see Him more clearly as both God and man. We see how truly and wholesomely human He is, with concern for even the little needs of people. We see how truly divine He is, filled with true wisdom to immediately see through the weakness of the law, filled with divine love, concerned for man to the extent of saying: "Even the day that is to be spent in my honor must not in any way hurt my beloved people, especially the least of them."

O Jesus, Lord of the Sabbath, Your love is beyond all telling. Your law of love is our joy and our salvation.

THE SUPREME LAW

Second Week of the Year, Wednesday   **Mark 3:1-6**

"Is it permitted to do a good deed on the Sabbath—or an evil one?"

Jesus' curing the sick on the Sabbath was a rather frequent occasion of dispute with the Pharisees and seems to have caused considerable tension between Him and the religious authorities. Besides the actual healing act, which was rigidly considered to be against the law of the Sabbath, the healings aroused clamorous crowds and there were processions of other sick persons seeking to be healed, all of which greatly disturbed the so-called Sabbath rest.

But Jesus is teaching a lesson here. Laws are fine—the Sabbath Laws, should not interfere with charity, with doing good to neighbor. And so Jesus at times overrules the Sabbath laws and challenges the

Scribes and Pharisees. They have no choice but to take a stand, either for Him or against Him. Either they are for His law of love or not.

We, too, have to take a stand regarding Christian love. Are we willing to change our established ways, our customary routine to do an act of charity? Will we help out a neighbor, who is in critical need, even though it means not getting to Mass on a week day as may be our custom?

What about our attitude and our actions towards minority groups. Does charity rule regardless of how unpopular it may make us in our accustomed circle of friends? How about the poor, whether financially poor, educationally poor, or poor in personality and looks? What is our attitude? Are we as kind to them as to the rich, the educated, the attractive?

In short, do we have our sense of values straight? Laws are good. They are our guides along the road to life. But the law of Christian love overrides every other road sign, is above every other law, is the ultimate criterion of an authentic Christian life.

Jesus may Your law of love be always the rule in our lives.

MIRACLES AND KINGDOM

Second Week of the Year, Thursday   **Mark 3:7-12**

The Gospel today tells us of the great crowds that followed Christ, people from Galilee, where He had been performing most of His miracles so far, but also, as the Gospel says, multitudes from Judea, Jerusalem, Idumea, Transjordan and from the neighborhood of Tyre and Sidon. All these latter came because of the news of the marvelous things He had done.

Jesus tries to avoid the crowd occasionally. He finds it necessary to retreat once in a while. He spends time in prayer, alone with His disciples. He must refresh Himself spiritually, and so also gives us an example of the need for prayer in our lives.

But mainly Jesus realizes that most of these people that press upon Him are doing so for what they can get out of it, a cure from sickness for self or a dear one, or simply satisfying their curiosity to see wonders worked. Many simply wanted to be able to say they had touched Him.

Jesus has other ideas. His miracles are only to be a means to higher things. A way of giving evidence of God's mercy. Even more so a way of preparing the people to listen to His good news of the kingdom. And so He asks His disciples to have a fishing boat ready by the lake shore so He can avoid the press of the crowd and perhaps speak to them from the boat as a sort of natural stage.

In the same way it is necessary today for the Church to be engaged in social work, to show the mercy of God in action. The Church must have a great love for the poor. As Christians each one of us must be filled with charity for the oppressed, the suffering. But our love must not stop there. We must also bring the message of the Kingdom of God to these poor ones, if not in word, at least by our example. We can all preach with our lives.

Your signs and wonders, Lord, even in our own lives, prepare us to hear the good news.

SUMMONS TO DISCIPLESHIP

Second Week of the Year, Friday   **Mark 3:13-19**

In this gospel passage Mark tells us that Jesus summoned the men He Himself had decided on. This is followed immediately by the phrase saying that these men came and joined Him.

We have here in this one short sentence the call, the summons of Jesus and the response on the part of the Apostles. It is evident that Jesus calls them with authority. He decided whom He Himself wanted. And the Apostles are so strongly affected by His call that they come and join Him. They respond to the call without hesitation, without asking the cost or about what's in it for them.

Jesus then gives them authority to expel demons. They are also to be sent out to preach the good news. But first they need to be His companions, they need to spend some time with Him. Jesus wants to prepare them for their mission. They must first learn what it means to be specially selected disciples of the Lord.

The gospel implies very strongly that it is necessary to be with the Lord, to spend time with Him, before one is ready for action, ready to go out and witness to the good news. Jesus shows this in His own life. Before He began His public life He spent considerable time in the desert in intimate communion with His Father.

As Christians we all have a mission. We are all to be disciples of Christ. Mark's definition of a disciple is clearly one who is a companion of the Lord, who spends time with Him. Here we have a very simple standard by which we can measure our discipleship.

Lord Jesus, how good it is to be in Your presence and to learn from You the joy and the cost of discipleship.

SIGN OF CONTRADICTION

Second Week of the Year, Saturday   **Mark 3:20-21**

Mark in this short passage shows us how upset the relatives of Jesus were with Him and what they considered His insane activity. Evidently they didn't understand what it was all about. They saw the large crowds gathering around Jesus so constantly that it was even impossible for Him and His companions to eat. Perhaps they became a little jealous, perhaps a little shocked.

At any rate they charged Him with being insane and came to take charge. They wanted to put Him away before He embarrassed them any further. But Jesus quickly showed them who was in charge.

Any time the preacher, an evangelist, or even just an ordinary Christian by his way of life contradicts the standards of the world, he is judged. Most people will consider him somewhat off base. Others will have their own consciences pricked because of their own worldly ways, and will quickly turn him off.

Jesus was the first in this line of preachers and witnesses. He contradicted worldly standards. His was a new message. He proclaimed good news, which was attractive to the poor, the crowds, but which went against the grain of the traditionalist Pharisees and embarrassed His relatives.

Yet Jesus persists. He is not afraid to contradict. He came out of love for the people, the crowds, the poor. He does not count the cost of bringing His message, His good news to them.

Are we going to hesitate to witness to Christ because we might be misunderstood? Are we afraid we will be considered abnormal? Jesus is our norm. If He was considered abnormal by the world in His time, it shouldn't worry us to be considered abnormal in our day.

Jesus, You are a sign of contradiction to the world.
May we, too, be signs, witnesses to Your love.

SIGN OF HOPE

Third Week of the Year, Monday   **Mark 3:22-30**

We consider the overwhelming power and beauty of Christ's personality, His great generosity to the poor, the sick, the sinners; we consider the brilliance and power of His teaching, the endless stream of healings, the irreproachable holiness of His life. And we are puzzled.

Jesus asked His enemies one day on the steps of the temple, "Which of you can convict me of sin?" Not the bitterest of His enemies could answer Him. None could accuse Him. Why, then, had Jesus become a "sign of contradiction," why did they consider Him a public enemy? How was it possible for those who professed to be awaiting God's redemption to reject Him when redemption came?

Are we shocked at their blindness, their ignorance, or their apparent bad will? If so, we are simply shocked at our own defects. How often we treat Jesus as a "sign of contradiction." How often we cast aside His teachings. How often we have refused Him and conspired against Him. We always want for ourselves the biggest, the finest, the most. Jesus took the least for Himself.

What His Father required, that He did—at the cost of His

security, His comfort, even of His life. For Himself He took nothing. With a singleness of purpose, with a purity and simplicity that not the greatest of prophets had equalled, Jesus brought a redemption His people were not prepared for! Yet, as we look back and as we look around us, we can truly ask, "What else would have brought true redemption? What other redemption did we need?"

> **You are far too good for us, Son of Man! You did too perfectly what we hope and are never able to accomplish. You will always be the "sign of contradiction." And for that very reason You will always be the sign of hope and redemption.**

FAMILY OF GOD

Third Week of the Year, Tuesday   **Mark 3:31-35**

This Gospel passage of Jesus' mother and his brothers and sisters sometimes causes people difficulty regarding the doctrine of Mary's perpetual virginity. If Jesus had brothers and sisters, must it not be true that Mary had other children besides Jesus? This cannot be concluded from this passage in St. Mark because the Greek words used here for brothers and sisters are used just as well for cousins. So this should cause us no consternation.

We are surprised a bit that when Jesus was told that His mother and relatives were waiting to see Him, He simply said, "Who are my mother and my brothers?" It seems a bit rude, at least somewhat out of place. But He was taking the opportunity to teach a lesson. Gazing around to those seated in a circle He said, "These are my brothers. Whoever does the will of God is brother and sister and mother to Me."

Jesus here does not renounce His natural kinship and the duty of love connected with it, but He radically subordinates it to a higher bond, the bond of brotherhood under God the Father. The Kingdom of God in us makes demands on our commitment which sometimes must go beyond and above all natural bonds of family, nationality or race.

There is no doubt that a natural blood relationship sets up a very close bond. Often it makes one almost willing to transgress God's commandments in order to keep on the good side of a dear one who has gone wrong.

Sometimes families, parents, have such strong ties—even apron strings—on their children that they are unwilling to give them up for the Kingdom of God. They do not realize that there are stronger ties, ties of spiritual bonds, between Christ and their son or daughter or between their son or daughter and others who dedicate their lives to Christ. And these ties according to Christ in today's Gospel must take precedence to the natural family ties. Such is the nature of the family of God.

How happy we are, Jesus, to be Your brothers and sisters.

ON GOOD GROUND

Third Week of the Year, Wednesday   **Mark 4:1-20**

The parable of the Gospel about the seed that fell on various ground is also related in the Gospel of Matthew and Luke. It must have been considered a very important parable, teaching a very important point, in the early apostolic Church. The parable itself, the story of the sower and the seed seemed vague even to the Apostles. Its application was not clear. When the Apostles asked for an explanation Jesus complied because they were all well-disposed to accept the teaching about his kingdom.

Not so with the crowds who were still ill-prepared at this time to abandon their false preconceptions of what they thought the Messiah was to be, an earthly king with an earthly kingdom.

The various ground on which the word of God falls shows us that receiving the kingdom, receiving the word, is not merely something passive. We have to be well-disposed as the Apostles were. We have to be prepared to deny self, to soften our hearts so that the ground on which the Word falls is not rocky, without depth. This means there is a need for openness, a readiness to change if the spirit would move us. It means an awareness of the Word through prayer, reading the Scriptures and attentiveness to the Word as read in the Liturgy.

There is also a need to be free from too much worldly anxiety and concern, desire for wealth, comfort and luxury. Otherwise the message of God will be choked off before it really has a chance to enter the soil of an open heart.

In short, Jesus urges us to accept His teaching despite hardships, despite the need to deny ourselves and turn from earthly desires. He places the message of His kingdom above all the things in human existence which men hold dear.

Soften our hearts, O Lord, that the seed of your word may fall on good ground.

I GET SO BORED

Third Week of the Year, Thursday   Mark 4:21-25

Jesus says, "In the measure you give, you shall receive." A strong hint to those of us who suffer from boredom. What is real boredom? Merely repeating an action regularly? Hardly. We eat and sleep, wash, dress, and primp ourselves, and never seem to tire of these common things. Some have defined boredom as "getting sick of doing nothing." Or better, it is "weariness of doing nothing worthwhile."

I could not sincerely become bored if I knew that my day's work had really given praise to God and brought blessings on my corner of the world. But if I knew I had spent another day trying to inflate my own pride or striving to saturate myself with the world's pleasures, I may well have failed in both and ended sick of myself and of the world.

If I am waiting for others to make my life interesting or exciting, if I am willfully bored, I deserve all the empty feeling that comes with it;

for I am, in fact, empty. If I think of nothing better to do with my leisure than doze or watch television indiscriminately or stand on street corners waiting for excitement, I am empty. If I am incapable of rescuing myself from boredom because I am a flitting butterfly, never content more than five minutes, then I need to listen to the Lord.

He may just say to my problem, "Well, child, if ever you begin to make yourself a blessing to others, you won't be bored anymore. If ever you learn what it means to love God and your neighbor, if ever you begin real prayer, so that you appreciate the very joy of living, life will be anything but boring. Your problem then will be, not having enough hours per day to accomplish the good you desire.

"But if you continue to yawn away your life waiting for pleasures to come, if you keep dragging your feet going nowhere, life will indeed be a bore, and when you die nobody will really be able to say they miss you. The people we miss when they're gone, you see, are those who with their love of God and neighbor, with their persistent generosity, have made life happier for everyone around them."

SMALL BEGINNINGS

Third Week of the Year, Friday   **Mark 4:26-34**

Jesus was a very good teacher. He used examples that could easily be understood by the people to whom He spoke. In today's Gospel He again used the seed as an example.

First He speaks simply how the seed, after being planted by the farmer, sprouts and grows and finally produces the ripe wheat for the harvest. The farmer simply waits not knowing exactly what happens to produce a harvest from little seeds. The reference is to God's kingdom planted in men by Christ. Somehow through grace it has a mysterious growth and is destined to spread throughout the world and yield a harvest of souls.

The second part of the Gospel tells the parable of the mustard seed. It is a very small seed, one of the smallest when planted. Yet it grows up to become a very large plant, a kind of shrub with branches large enough for birds to nest in its shade.

In a similar way the Church, Christ's kingdom on earth, began with a very small beginning. Not many people were truly faithful followers of Christ in His lifetime; only a few Apostles and several women. This was a very shaky beginning—even most of the Apostles were terribly shaken during Christ's passion. Yet from this start, small as the mustard seed, grew up the mighty tree, which is the Church today, a tree under whose protection and shade many have found refuge from sin and worldliness.

God's ways are often a surprise to us. We human beings would have expected that such a kingdom would have to be founded on better ground instead of simple fishermen, intelligent and wise men with ability to organize and administer. But God shows us how vain we are, how much stock we place in human endeavor, human intelligence. What we need is faith, hope and love, trust in God's wisdom and power.

Humanly speaking, the Church is a miracle of God's doing. With mere human effort it would not long have endured. The same applies to us. At times we also need more than human effort. But God has assured us of His help.

Jesus, teach us to trust in You regardless of what the odds are.

PRAYER FOR FAITH

Third Week of the Year, Saturday   **Mark 4:35-41**

Jesus, You teach Your disciples and us to have trust in the power and the love of the Father, as You sleep peacefully during the storm at sea. Your disciples are so afraid of perishing, even though You are right there in the boat with them.

It didn't please You to see their lack of faith as they woke You up. Yet in Your kindness You calmed the storm to put them at ease. "Quiet! Be still!" was all it took from You to stop the wind and calm the waters. How ashamed they must have felt to have doubted You.

Surely it was with great love that You said to them: "Why are you

so terrified? Why are you lacking in faith?" We know, Jesus, You
wanted to teach them to trust in You. You wanted them to know
Your great desire that they accept You wholeheartedly as Lord, as
Master of all.

Lord, there are times when the sea of life becomes rough. There
are storms, there are troubles that surround us and threaten us. You
seem to be asleep at such times, Jesus. You seem to be so far away.

Help us to understand that these are times when You are nearest
to us, when You wait for us to turn to You.

We are sorry, Lord, for the many times we turn to You only after
having tried everything else. Give us the grace, Lord Jesus, to know
and experience that You are the only true answer to all our problems.

Increase our faith and trust in You, O Lord.

GO AND TELL

Fourth Week of the Year, Monday   **Mark 5:1-20**

Today's Gospel story is one of four accounts of exorcism, of
driving out devils, narrated in Mark's Gospel. This incident
happened in Gerasa, across Lake Genesareth, where Jesus had gone
with His disciples overnight. Barely had they landed when a
possessed man came running up to Jesus. The devil recognized Jesus
from a distance, ran up to Him and begged Him not to torment Him,
to let him alone.

We see here that the devil recognized Jesus as the son of God,
admitting that He had the power to drive him out of the man. He
pleaded with Jesus not to drive him away, finally begging to be sent
into the swine. Jesus gave the word and with it the unclean spirits—
they were legion—came out and entered the swine, who rushed over
the cliff and drowned in the sea.

What was the reaction of those who witnessed the incident? The
swineherds ran and brought the news to the townspeople. They came
and saw that the man, whom they knew to have been possessed by
many devils, was now normal in every way. They must have realized
that Jesus had shown divine power to remove unclean spirits.

Yet they didn't want Him around. They asked Him to leave their town. Why? Was it because they lost their swine, their possessions? Or because they were complacent in their ways and didn't want any divine messenger to disturb or confront them?

The cured man reacted normally. He was enthralled with Jesus and wanted to follow Him. A very understandable initial reaction. But Jesus set him straight. He gave him a mission, a new purpose in life. "Go and tell how much the Lord in His mercy has done for you."

Do we dislike spiritual values at the cost of the material things in our lives? Are we like those townspeople? Remember, Jesus cures us many times from unclean spirits, from all kinds of uncleanness. He wants us, too, to go out and tell it to others. We are to be messengers of God's mercy.

> **Your healing power, O Lord, has touched us, too, and we thank You!**

FAITH VS. FEAR

Fourth Week of the Year, Tuesday   **Mark 5:21-43**

In this rather lengthy passage Mark tells a story within a story, something he does on other occasions too (e.g., 3:19-35). The miracle stories about the daughter of Jairus and the woman with the hemorrhage fit together very well. They make a very interesting joint account.

In both cases we have situations that look rather hopeless, yet faith in Jesus is the answer: "Daughter, it is your faith that has cured you"—"What is needed is trust."

We also see in these stories that fear is entirely out of place in the presence of Jesus. When the woman who was cured realized she had been discovered, she was afraid, but Jesus said, "Go in peace and be free of this illness." And when the report of Jairus' daughter's death caused consternation and hopelessness, Jesus said, "Fear is useless."

Jesus shows us His great power to heal. It flows out of Him. There is healing power in His touch. He teaches us something about human touch as well as about His divine touch. He wants us to touch. When we touch we are not afraid to get involved. There is a certain healing in human touch. Until we appreciate that gift of God we won't accept or receive the gift of the divine touch of healing.

The Lord makes it clear that no cases are hopeless in His presence. Do we believe that? When hopeless situations arise in our lives, in our families, do we turn to Him with faith and trust? Or is our first reaction one of fear, despair that nothing can be done? And then we run off to try all the possible merely earthly and human answers.

What does Jesus expect? He wants us to do our best. He wants us to use all the human means at hand, all the normal gifts and remedies He has given us. But this must always be without fear, because He is present; with faith, because He is taking care of us.

O Lord, why are we so weak in faith, so full of fear? Show us that we need not be afraid but simply surrender to your healing touch.

FAITH

Fourth Week of the Year, Wednesday   **Mark 6:1-6**

After having preached and performed many miracles in other parts of Galilee Jesus returned one Sabbath to His native town of Nazareth with his disciples. He taught in the synagogue there, and immediately the crowd of His townspeople were amazed. They knew He was the son of Joseph, the carpenter, and had practiced the trade of carpenter Himself for some years since Joseph's death. Now to hear Him speak so well in the synagogue was a surprise. They also had heard of His miracles performed in other towns.

As the Gospel of Mark here says, "They found Him too much for them." They were skeptical. There was something very strange about all this, they thought. If He is really so extraordinary, how is it that we haven't seen any wonders worked here? Shouldn't we, His relatives and townspeople, have been the first to be favored by such works, if He really has such powers?

Jesus replied to their doubts. "No prophet is without honor except in his native place, among his own kindred, and in his own house."

The reason for this is simple. It takes faith to honor a prophet. It takes faith to be worthy of special favors such as miraculous cures. We see this in practically every Gospel account of a cure, a miraculous healing. "Your faith has made you sound."

Today's Gospel says, "He could work no miracles there . . . so much did their lack of faith distress Him."

The same is true today. Prayers are often not answered by God because there is a lack of faith and trust. If we really pray with faith, trust, confidence in God, our prayers will be answered. It is true, not always in the exact way we expect. But if we are Christians who truly pray with faith we have no trouble seeing how faithfully on His part, God hears us and works wonders in our lives.

Gracious Father, hear us because we trust in You.

OPEN TO HEALING

Fourth Week of the Year, Thursday   **Mark 6:7-13**

When Jesus sent the twelve apostles out to minister in His name, Mark tells us that "they expelled many demons, anointed the sick with oil, and worked many cures." But in this passage Mark also indicates that a response is needed on the part of the person who wants healing. He tells us that Jesus said, "If any place will not receive you or hear you, shake its dust from your feet in testimony against them as you leave." He also says the apostles "went off, preaching the need of repentance."

Jesus knows what we need in order to be healed: a forgiving love. In His lengthy teachings on the need of love in our lives. He tells us in effect, "If you want to be healthy, happy, healed and free, you must love—even your enemies. You will be healed when you forgive everyone from the bottom of your heart."

Our response to the healing power of Jesus requires this:

1. An honest look at ourselves: do I follow Jesus—the way of forgiving love? Or do I follow the world—the way of hatred, resentment, envy, bitterness?
2. Humility: I cannot be healed by my own power. Don't say, "Lord, wait till I get my life straightened out—*then* You can come in." Only Jesus can straighten out my life. Not me! Never!
3. Make a decision: turn around for Jesus—so that He can bring you His wonderful healing.
4. Ask Jesus for forgiveness and healing. Joyfully receive it from Him. Thank Him for it. We need to be better receivers from the Lord; then we'll be better forgivers, too.
5. Expectant faith that the Lord will forgive me and heal me. We can fail, but Jesus cannot. When He said, "I have defeated the world," He meant just that. There is no victory He cannot win. He converted Saul into Paul: a persecutor into a great missionary. He converted tax sharks like Matthew and Zaccheus. In fact, Jesus was accused of enjoying work among sinners. He worked where no self-respecting religious leaders of His time were ever seen.

Jesus, I repent! I trust in You completely, and I open myself to Your healing.

A MARTYR'S COURAGE

Fourth Week of the Year, Friday   **Mark 6:14-29**

The Gospel story today has a very good lesson for us, a lesson of courage.

Herod admired John. He realized he was an upright and holy man. John disturbed him with words, confronted him, yet Herod felt an attraction for John's words.

John the Baptist was, of course, a true prophet. He spoke honestly and courageously regardless of the consequences. John simply told Herod, "It is not right for you to live with your brother's wife." We know what the consequences were. Herod put John in jail. He didn't immediately kill him because he had such a respect for him, he feared him. Yet in his weakness he succumbed to Herodeas' and her daughter's wishes and had John beheaded.

John did not know what would happen to him, but he certainly knew he was running the extreme risk of death when he confronted Herod and his illicit wife. But John was a man of God. John had a true sense of values. John was aware of his calling as a prophet. And nothing would stop him from living up to his commitment.

What a tremendous example for us. How frequently we give way, surrender our principles out of human respect. We know that as Christians we must stand up for Christ and the Gospel message. But we are scared, we are afraid it is going to cost us too much to speak up. We might lose a friend, we might lose some business if we take a firm stand in the community for something that involves Christian and human values.

Let us think of John and other Christian martyrs. Can't we at least suffer a few inconveniences, loss of a few worthless friendships, perhaps a little material loss, in order to stand up for Christ?

O Jesus, the courageous life and death of Your cousin, John, is truly an inspiration to us.

RESTORED YOUTH

Fourth Week of the Year, Saturday   **Mark 6:30-34**

Jesus says, "Come aside and rest a while."

"There is a right time for everything," says Ecclesiastes. "A time to kill, a time to heal, a time to tear down, a time to build. A time to weep and a time to laugh; a time to be silent, and a time to speak" (3:1-7).

"It is related of the Blessed John (Apostle)," writes St. Thomas Aquinas, "that when some people were scandalized on finding him playing together with his disciples, he is said to have told one of them who carried a bow, to shoot an arrow. And when the archer had done this several times, he asked him whether he could do it indefinitely, and the man answered that if he continued doing it, the bow would break. Whence the Blessed John drew the inference that in like manner man's mind would break if its tension were never relaxed."

How many a patient has gone to a specialist to be given sound advice like that. Blessed is the man who is resigned to the seasons of the mind as God created them.

It is not difficult to convince anyone how we must be serious in season. No thinking man or woman is ignorant of the evils that come from not taking our responsibilities seriously.

For many of us it is harder to see the evil of taking everything *too* seriously. We are not so quickly aware that taking ourselves and our importance and our opinions too seriously is evil. It is a very subtle form of pride. We remark at times that someone "worked himself to death" or "worried herself sick," without taking note of the underlying spiritual failure.

> **The human spirit, like the human body, needs relaxation: rest and renewal. The spirit needs joy— cheerful acceptance of Your Will, Lord. A true, confident, loving attachment to You, Lord, is a constant refreshment.**

A PRAYER FOR HEALING LOVE

Fifth Week of the Year, Monday   **Mark 6:53-56**

"They begged Him to let them touch just the tassel of His cloak. All who touched Him got well." The healing love of Jesus went out powerfully to heal all the sick in mind and body. We can touch Jesus this very day, and His healing love will reach us. Let's open ourselves to this power of Jesus by prayer:

Lord Jesus, I invite You into my life today, so that Your healing power may touch me and touch those for whom I pray.

Jesus, You tell me of Your healing love on almost every page of Your Gospel. My heart is moved to respond to You in joyful praise, as I see the overpowering love and tenderness and concern You have for each person who comes to You.

I see in the Gospel that people looked for You eagerly, and when they recognized You, they ran to meet You and to touch You, for they knew what great healing power was in Your arms, Your hands, Your very presence, even the very fringe of Your coat.

If I search for the source of Your power, Jesus, I see You at prayer, and I hear of Your intimate communion with God Your Father. Behind Your healing power is Your healing love, Jesus. Your personal love for the Father is made concrete in Your faithfulness to His commands. You tell me over and over, "I do always what pleases the Father. I have come to do the will of the One who sent Me." It is Your obedience in love to the Father that heals everyone who comes to You. And it is Your forgiving love for sinners that heals their spirits and even their bodies. Whoever comes to You with trust is received with open arms.

Jesus, I ask a share in Your healing love. Weak as I am, I boldly ask You to open my heart completely to You, that I may love Your Will as You loved the Father's. That my spirit of forgiveness may share in the healing power of Your forgiving love. That my response to Your love may be reflected in the healing I experience in my own mind and heart. That my share in the power of Your divine love may pass as through an open door into the lives of others. Amen.

LEGALISM

Fifth Week of the Year, Tuesday   **Mark 7:1-13**

The Pharisees were so afraid and jealous of Jesus' popularity that they were constantly trying to find fault with Jesus and His actions. In today's Gospel it is the matter of ceremonial washings before eating meals. Some of the disciples had omitted this unimportant ceremony, and immediately the Pharisees were aware of it and confronted Jesus with it as if it were a terrible omission.

Jesus criticizes their overconcern for their human traditions to the neglect of the commandments enunciated in the Scriptures. "You have made a fine art of setting aside God's commandments in the interest of keeping your traditions." Quoting Isaiah, the prophet, against them Jesus says, "This people pay Me lip service, but their heart is far from Me. Empty is the reverence they do Me."

Stern words for our Lord. He addresses the Pharisees as fools. And all this because of their hypocrisy and dishonesty. They were keeping their traditions, not out of love of God and neighbor, but to perpetuate their own favored position and to look holy in the eyes of their fellow Jews.

Before we get too indignant at these Pharisees, let us take a look at ourselves. Are we always honest with ourselves, with God and neighbor? When we keep certain commandments or regulations, do we keep them because they are God's will or just to look good to others? Do we simply want ourselves to be considered law abiding Christians because this has its advantages, both in our own self pride as well as socially? Or are we really honestly interested in the law of love of God and neighbor, and keep every other commandment in such a way, and with such an intention, that our acts, our words, our thoughts are all expressions of our Christian love?

All for your honor and glory, O Lord, Our God!

VENOMOUS TONGUES

Fifth Week of the Year, Wednesday   **Mark 7:14-23**

When we stop to reflect upon the offenses committed by our tongues, we are confronted by a long parade of petty vices—pride, envy, revenge, impatience, sloth—every form of selfishness from inflated ambition to thwarted passion. Not only has the tongue gotten out of control, but the virtues of which it should be the instrument of expression have decayed.

"It is what comes out of a person's mouth that defiles him, not what goes in," said Jesus. Think of the evils our tongues can multiply: the lost reputation, the lost right to what all persons hold most dear— some measure of respect and honor, some friends to trust them and to sympathize with them. To be robbed of these goods by venomous tongues is an evil whose extent can literally not be measured. Enough to say that it eventually destroys the victim's hope of reforming himself.

Macbeth, who had long ago silenced his own conscience, who seemed no longer able to shudder at his bloody deeds, was not yet too cold to mourn the tragedy of lost reputation:

> I have lived long enough: my way of life
> Is fall'n into the sear, the yellow leaf;
> And that which should accompany old age,
> As honor, love, obedience, troops of friends,
> I must not look to have; but, in their stead,
> Curses, not loud but deep, mouth-honor, breath,
> Which the poor heart would fain deny, and dare not.
>
> (Macbeth V, 3)

Good men and women instinctively feel the cowardly method employed by the slanderer. His victims are knifed in the back, with no chance to defend themselves. It is in no way a fair fight.

"Man He created to His own image and likeness." Behold, Lord, how we have disfigured the image in one another. Let us remember your words, Jesus, "What emerges from within a man, that and nothing else is what makes him impure. Wicked designs come from the deep recesses of the heart."

WOMAN OF FAITH

Fifth Week of the Year, Thursday   **Mark 7:24-30**

What do you make of the words of Jesus to this Greek woman? Do you think Jesus was in any way rejecting this good person? By no means. He was testing her faith, in order to teach us the power of faith. Jesus asked for faith every time a request for healing was made.

The woman had asked Him for a healing in her daughter. She had not yet expressed her faith. We can only reach God through faith.

Jesus had earlier healed the dying servant of a Roman officer, a pagan. The man had expressed his great faith in those now-famous words, "Lord, I am not worthy that you should come into my house. Only say the word and my boy shall be healed."

Jesus then had said, "I have not found such great faith even in the house of Israel." Now the Lord wanted to show His followers again how great the faith of pagans can be. He tested this woman's faith and perseverance by saying, "I was only sent to the lost sheep of the house of Israel." After all, it was the Israelites whom God had honored with the gift of faith, the gift of His revealed truth in their Holy Scriptures. It was to them that God had promised the Savior.

The Greek woman expressed beautifully that faith and perseverance which Jesus had recommended in several parables on prayer. She said, "Even the dogs can eat scraps that fall from the children's table." Her humility and her trust in the goodness of Jesus are wonderful.

Jesus replies, "Great is your faith. It will be done for you as you desire!" Faith is the power by which we touch Jesus, the power by which we can respond to God's action in us. In His lifetime Jesus came into contact with many men and women of faith by His physical presence: His words, His touch, His powerful acts of healing. And He wishes to continue His presence among us by His words, His touch, His actions. This He does by the Sacraments: there He touches us by word and action, as often as we reach out to Him with faith.

> **Jesus, only by a strong, healthy, living faith can we reach out and touch You. Faith is Your living gift to us; so we must feed it, care for it, give it loving attention. Only then can Your healing power work in us.**

WITH OPEN EARS

Fifth Week of the Year, Friday   **Mark 7:31-37**

"He has done everything well. He makes the deaf hear and the mute speak."

Let us apply these closing words of today's Gospel to ourselves. We would be spiritually deaf and mute except for Christ. Think of what the world would be like today without Christ, without our Christian faith, without Christian influence in the world. Think what it would be like without the sacraments, without Holy Mass, without the graces of Christ.

But thanks be to God, Christ, son of God, has come, has redeemed us, and brought us into a brotherhood under the Father. He has set us on the road of truth under the guidance of the Church. We are no longer deaf and mute. We hear the voice of God in His Holy Word and we can answer. We are given the gift of faith through the sacraments. We listen to God and believe. We open our mouths and use our voices in praise of God, not only in words, but also by living the commandments.

What would we have thought of that deaf-mute in the Gospel, if he had deliberately deprived himself of his hearing and speech after he miraculously received them from Christ? Foolish! Ungrateful! Ridiculous, we would say.

Yet, that is exactly what we do if we shut our ear to the Church's teaching. She is Christ still talking to us on earth today. That is also what we do if we fail to make good use of the sacraments through which Christ is still working among us, speaking to us, strengthening our faith.

We must always be interested in listening when Christ speaks to us through His Church. We should also be willing to speak for Christ when the occasion arises. If God or Christ is attacked, speak out. We have God on our side and have no reason to be afraid to face up to those who oppose us in matters of Christian faith and conduct. We are not deaf or mute.

Grant us courage, Lord, to proclaim your Holy Name!

WHY DOUBT

Fifth Week of the Year, Saturday   **Mark 8:1-10**

Today's Gospel gives us another proof of Christ's loving kindness and His divine interest in our various needs. "My heart is moved with pity for the crowd." He could have sent these people home hungry. But no! Through His divine power He provided a satisfying meal for them.

With such a picture before our eyes, Christ's compassion and His divine power, how can we ever doubt that His loving Divine Providence is watching over us every day of our lives?

But human as we are, we are inclined to doubt, or at least to forget, God's loving Providence. Perhaps some of our neighbors seem to have it so much easier than we. Perhaps we feel like "collapsing on the way" because of overwork and family problems while others seem to have no problems. God seems to be turning a deaf ear to our most earnest prayers.

To remove any such temptations, to murmur, it is well for us to recall to mind the many spiritual and temporal gifts God has already given us. We have the greatest gift we can receive in this life, the gift of faith. We at least know what life is all about through our faith. Many people do not have this blessing. We know why we are here, we know what awaits us after this short spell on earth, we know how we can reach that end for which every heart craves, eternal happiness.

Not only do we have faith, not only do we know our true goal in life, but we also have been given the means to reach this goal. We have the marvelous gifts of the sacraments which help us through the main turns and crises of our lives. Among these is especially the Holy Eucharist, our constant spiritual nourishment, prefigured by the miracle of the multiplication of the loaves.

Truly Christ's heart was moved with pity for us when He instituted the Eucharist. We are constantly invited to come and eat at His table. How have we responded to this most gracious divine invitation?

Your compassion, O Lord Jesus, is beyond measure!

GIFT OF FAITH

Sixth Week of the Year, Monday   **Mark 8:11-13**

It is rather puzzling to read in the Gospel that the Pharisees were looking for some heavenly sign to prove the arrival of God's reign through Christ. We read in the Gospels of the many signs and wonders Jesus worked, which certainly would be sufficient proof that He was from God. But to the Pharisees these signs were unsatisfactory. It seems that there was a current thinking in Judaism that when the Messiah came He would work some sort of unique miracle. Nothing in the Old Testament supports this view, but as with so many other things, the Pharisees had built up a tradition of their own which they considered as important as the Scriptures.

So when they asked for some very special sign, Jesus, quite disappointed in their lack of faith, said, "Why does this age seek a sign? I assure you, no such sign will be given it!" No such sign, that is, no special unique miracle to satisfy their belief that some really extraordinary miracle or wonder would herald the Messiah.

What Jesus in effect is saying is that a request for a sign which has its origin in human distrust simply will not be given.

Faith requires an openness, a willingness to accept ordinary reasons for believing. If curing the sick, driving out devils, multiplying the loaves and other such miracles of divine power are not enough to convince them, then there is a lack of response. Faith must be a free act. Christ will not force it on anyone. Response must come freely, aided by all the signs Jesus already worked.

We ourselves have not seen Jesus work His miracles. We only read about them in the Gospels. But Christ gives us the gift of faith to accept the Gospels as true. That they are quite accurate accounts of Jesus' life and actions has also been historically established. And so we believe. We believe Christ proved His divinity, His Messiahship, by His signs and wonders, especially the culminating wonder of His resurrection.

O Jesus, we are specially blessed because You have said, "Blest are they who have not seen and have believed."

A WORD FOR CRITICS

Sixth Week of the Year, Tuesday **Mark 8:14-21**

How often the Lord emphasized the evil inherent in gossip. What sin did He condemn more than the sin of slander? Over and over He pardoned sinners. But always He warned them, "Go now, and sin no more."

Only the slanderers, those who sought to find fault with everyone, even the Son of God, could not accept His forgiveness. They had hardened themselves against true contrition, since their whole attention was given to finding evil: they looked for matter to condemn. "Now the Pharisees were watching how they might catch Him in His speech."

Jesus spoke openly to the crowds, warning them of the malice of looking for sin in one's neighbor. "Beware of the leaven of the Pharisees, which is hypocrisy," He said. "There is nothing concealed that will not be disclosed, and nothing hidden that will not be made known. For what I tell you in darkness, speak it in the light; and what you hear whispered, preach it on the housetops" (Mt 10:26, 27).

Surely it is a cheap and ignoble mind that can attempt to think itself better by searching for evil in others. By seeking to find fault in my neighbor, and by rejoicing that I have found it, I myself have lost the most precious of all treasures: that virtue which the Lord proclaimed most beautiful and most valuable: charity.

Is it any wonder that in His inspired psalms, God spoke most of all of that love, and condemned most of all the evil tongue of envy and fault-finding? "Who may live on my holy mountain?" the Lord says, and answers, "One who guides his steps without fault, and treats others justly. One whose words are sincere, and does not slander others, and does not spread rumors about his neighbors" (Ps 15).

Jesus, weaken my habit of criticism till it fades away, and strengthen in me the art of praise.

IN STAGES

Sixth Week of the Year, Wednesday   **Mark 8:22-26**

St. Mark is the only evangelist who recounts this curing of the blind man at Bethsaida. This miracle is similar to the one recorded by Mark in the previous chapter, the cure of the deaf-mute. In both cases Jesus used some material thing, spittle, saliva, to effect the cure. This sort of foreshadows the use of material things in the sacraments, giving them a power beyond the material.

Yet today's recorded miracle of the cure of the blind man has something very special about it. It is the only cure in the Gospels that takes place gradually, in two stages. In all other cases the miraculous healing was instantaneous. It may be that Jesus intended this gradual restoration of sight to be a symbol of the gradual enlightenment that would come to His disciples concerning His teaching.

So it is with our religious life, with our faith. Many times we hardly see at all. We don't understand. We simply have faith—the first dim light, by which we see darkly as through smoked glass. But if we persevere, if we don't become discouraged because of our lack of understanding, we will come to see more clearly. If we are open to the gifts of the Holy Spirit, especially the gifts of knowledge, wisdom and understanding, we will gradually have a better spiritual sight or insight.

This openness to the Spirit's gifts comes from regular prayer, from responding to God's word and call as we hear it in the Scriptures, and as it comes to us in the events of our lives.

No one need suffer from spiritual blindness. The cure is ours for the taking.

How patient You are, O Lord, with our human weakness!

SPIRITUAL ATHLETE

Sixth Week of the Year, Thursday　　　　　**Mark 8:27-33**

"He then began to teach them that the Son of Man had to suffer much."

The athlete who trains his body experiences both pain and pleasure. There is pain, especially in the first exercises of the season, when the muscles that have been idle must resume their work. There is the burden of the daily push and pull, the natural tedium which accompanies oft-repeated exercise. The young contestant must run farther than the weakened body pleases; his limbs will be stiff and sore for a few days. But this, he says, is very little compared with the pleasure of feeling his re-awakened strength, of sensing the new health and vigor as it grows with him. He will soon forget the pains, when each day the weights become easier to lift, the track is easier to run, and every physical effort diminishes.

The joy of the spiritual athlete is no less. Indeed, much of our human joy would be lost, if we had no temptation to conquer. The spiritual life would seem dull indeed if it cost us nothing, if it did not bring us the glory of battle and of victory.

Jesus, the champion of spiritual athletes, began to tell His disciples of the challenges that faced Him. He would have to "suffer much, be rejected by the religious leaders, be put to death." But He also predicted His victory: after His death, He would "rise three days later."

Peter doesn't like the sound of this all-out spiritual challenge. He tries to talk Jesus out of it, like a friend who hates to see his closest companion break his neck, or like a mother who tries to keep her son from playing football for fear of serious injury.

What a surprise to Peter that Jesus is not to be coddled, even by those who love Him best. How Peter must have been shaken by the stern reply of Jesus: "Get out of my sight, enemy. You're not judging by God's standards, but by man's!"

Thank you, Jesus, for instructing us so clearly about God's standards. Your words are a powerful medicine when our challenges are great and the road gets rough. How much courage and strength Your saints have drawn from Your wonderful example.

CROSS AS CRITERION

Sixth Week of the Year, Friday   **Mark 8:34-9:1**

It is interesting to note that this Gospel passage, proclaiming the doctrine of the Cross, comes right after Peter had confessed his faith in Jesus as the Messiah. Jesus having gotten this act of faith from Peter and the other Apostles began telling them of His coming suffering, cross and death. Peter was shocked. He expected a different kingdom in which he would sit at the right hand of Christ, who would be king. "This can't be," Peter said, and he got so upset about it all that Jesus had to reprimand him.

It is shortly after this that Jesus teaches what it will be like to belong to His kingdom. The cross is meant for everyone, not just for Himself and a select few. He makes it very clear that the cross is an essential part of the Christian life. After all, what does it mean when Jesus says, "If a man wishes to come after Me?" It means simply, "If a man wishes to be a Christian."

But why be a Christian—a genuine Christian? If we have faith, listen to the Gospel, "What profit is there to gain the whole world and lose ourselves in the process. What can a man offer in exchange for his life?"

Jesus says, "Are you ashamed of Me and My doctrine? So I'll be ashamed of you, too, when judgment comes." Powerful words! What IS our view on trials, crosses, hardships? Do we see them as splinters of Christ's cross? Are we ready to lose our life in the human sense to gain it for Christ?

The doctrine of Christ teaches that true fulfillment comes by emptying self, not by any conscious effort at fulfillment. We profit most by seeking less. We gain most by giving most.

The doctrine of the cross, because it is actually in practice the way of love, is the criterion of the Christian life. "If a man wishes to come after Me, he must deny his very self, take up his cross and follow in My steps."

Thank you for this invitation to follow You, Lord.

ON THE MOUNTAIN

Sixth Week of the Year, Saturday   **Mark 9:2-13**

Jesus told the three disciples not to tell anyone what they had seen on the mountain until after He had risen from the dead. Now that Jesus has risen, we can talk about it. Jesus went up the mountain with Peter, James and John. There Moses and Elijah came and talked with Jesus. The apostles were struck with awe and bowed down in worship. What is the meaning of all this?

Jesus often went up to a mountain for prayer. The night before He gave us the great promise of the Bread of Life, Jesus was up on the mountain for prayer (Mk 6:46; Jn 6:15). Matthew says, "After sending the people away, Jesus went up a mountain by himself to pray" (14:22).

So often in the events recorded in the Bible, going up a mountainside alone meant close communion with God. One got away from noise and distraction, and there was a special feeling of nearness to God.

Moses went up the mountain to pray and learn God's Will. In Exodus 24:17 we read: "To the Israelites the glory of the Lord was seen as a consuming fire on the mountain-top. But Moses passed into the midst of the cloud as he went up the mountain; and there he stayed forty days and forty nights," reminiscent of Jesus' forty days of prayer and fasting alone in the wilderness.

When Queen Jezabel threatened to kill Elijah within twenty-four hours, he escaped and headed across the desert. When from hunger and thirst he could go no further, God sent him bread that strengthened him for the long journey to a mountain, Mount Horeb, where God spoke to him and told him what to do.

This group—Jesus with Moses and Elijah—was packed with meaning. So Jesus wanted His special three disciples to be there! You know what this was? A terrific prayer meeting. A group come together for prayer, for conversation with the Holy Trinity. In prayer we come to speak with Jesus, with His heavenly Father, with the Holy Spirit, together with His holy ones, Moses, Elijah, the apostles, the saints. Jesus said, "Where two or three are gathered in My Name, I am right there with them."

I DO BELIEVE

Seventh Week of the Year, Monday   **Mark 9:14-29**

Mark in this passage weaves the story of Jesus healing the epileptic boy into three distinct scenes.

First we have the crowd gathered around the disciples who had just failed to expel the demons from the boy. The father tells Jesus about the convulsions and fits the boy goes through, and that his disciples had not been able to help him. Jesus accuses the whole crowd of a lack of faith.

Next Jesus asks that the boy be brought to Him. Again there are terrible convulsions. When the father seems doubtful about Jesus being able to free the boy, Jesus says "Everything is possible to the man who trusts." The father responds with faith: "I do believe. Help my unbelief."

In the final scene Jesus waits for the crowd to gather. He reprimands the unclean spirit. Again there are terrible convulsions until finally the boy appears dead. Jesus takes him by the hand and raises him up. When the disciples ask why they couldn't expel the demon, Jesus tells them they lacked prayer. "This kind can be driven out only by prayer."

Today we too move in a crowd that lacks faith. We live in an era of little faith. In such circumstances it is difficult to oppose evils. Yet if we keep our eyes on Jesus, if we remember those words of His, "Everything is possible to the man who trusts," we will be able to overcome especially if we constantly turn to the Lord and say, "I do believe, help my unbelief."

Jesus' answer to the puzzled disciples about the need for prayer in such situations is meant for us too. Unless we pray regularly, daily, we shall not have the faith and the consequent power of the Holy Spirit to overcome the evils around us. We can all be healers to one degree or another, but only if we are men and women of deep prayer.

**Jesus, I do believe that You alone are the Savior, help
me to grow in prayerful intimacy with You.**

ENCOURAGEMENT

Seventh Week of the Year, Tuesday **Mark 9:30-37**

"Whoever welcomes a child such as this for My sake welcomes Me."

So many people need encouragement; so many good things need development. There was an old saying, "There's so much good in the worst of us, and so much bad in the best of us, that it doesn't behoove the best of us to condemn or criticize the worst of us." That's all very well, and we left it at that, not realizing it's too negative, too unproductive.

The good in the worst of us, and the good in the best of us—they need so much encouragement. They grow cold so easily. They need a fire, many fires built for them. They need rekindling over and over.

We are shameful killers of spirit. We are a good blocking team— terrific on defense, weak on scoring. We kill the good desires, the warm greetings, the helping hand, the thoughtful gesture. The schoolboy blocks his classmate's helping hand and friendly smile by interception, "Teacher's pet!" The mother blocks her child's scoring power and willing heart with, "Get out of here! You're doing it all wrong!"

We're all out blocking and tackling, shooting and killing: business sharpies blowing up honesty, cranky critics stabbing at creativeness, weaklings ridiculing purity, doting parents killing a child's self-reliance with lavish handouts, sour grapes sneering at love, cynics scoffing at faith and hope.

Thaw us out, Jesus, be our fire. Fan us with the wings of good desire. Warm us with the flames of Your encouragement. Bring us fuel against the cold winds of discouragement. Give us a heart like Yours, an open heart. Let us be, like you, "the servant of all."

Lord, our sinful stains efface,
On our drought pour down Your grace,
Guide our weak, uncertain pace.
Bend the stubborn, halt the bold,
Melt the frozen, warm the cold,
Lead the wayward to Your fold.

CHRISTIAN UNITY

Seventh Week of the Year, Wednesday   **Mark 9:38-40**

"No one who works a miracle in My name is likely to speak evil of Me. Anyone who is not against us is for us." With these words Jesus encourages us to seek unity and peace, and to avoid misunderstanding, narrowness, unjust and unhelpful criticism of one another. Was it not pride and envy and personal prejudice that caused to a large extent the divisions among Christians throughout history? Was it not selfishness and greediness and corruption in political and social life that brought disunity among Christians?

Each of us can do very much toward the cause of Christian unity. We must do it in our own families, our own parishes, our own clubs, neighborhoods, cities. We must reverence and practice those virtues which lead to unity and harmony. And we need to take as our pattern of living those beatitudes by which Jesus described His own way of life:

Blessed are the poor in spirit: heaven's wealth shall be at their command.
Blessed are the meek and gentle: theirs shall be the promised land.
Blessed they who suffer sorrow: comfort shall not be denied.
Blessed those who seek for justice: they shall yet be satisfied.
Blessed those who show compassion: heaven's mercy shall be their reward.
Blessed are the pure of conscience: they will see their God and Lord.
Blessed are the reconcilers: God's own children they shall be.
Blessed they who die for justice: heaven is their victory.

(Mt 5:3-10)

"I pray, O Father, that they be united:
The glory that is Yours is theirs to see.
Such love as ours, which makes us One forever,
I ask for those who now believe in Me" (Jn 17).

HARD SAYINGS

Seventh Week of the Year, Thursday   **Mark 9:41-50**

We have here a collection of Jesus' hard sayings, rather loosely connected. Yet they are mostly warnings regarding scandal, causing sin in others, and the causes and occasions of sin in ourselves. A third group of sayings refers to the suffering and persecution the disciples would have to go through.

What Jesus is saying is that we must have our priorities straight. We must have a sense of the value of salvation if we are to avoid putting it in jeopardy, both in others' and in our own lives.

To impress this upon us Jesus uses some very strong images. Better that the scandal giver be plunged in the sea with a millstone around his neck than to let him lead someone astray. Better to get to heaven having lost human members than to die with them and go to hell. Everyone will be salted with fire. The true disciple will be seasoned and strengthened through persecution. When Mark was recording these sayings of Jesus, Christians were probably already being persecuted. Which made these sayings very relevant.

Are we aware of the possibility of our words or acts leading someone into sin? Jesus wants us to take a good hard look at our lives. Are we a steady positive influence on others?

And what about our priorities? We know certain things, certain activities, are an occasion of sin. Do we value our relationship with the Lord enough to avoid these conscientiously?

We do not live in the midst of persecutions. Yet our faith, our salvation, is put in danger by the worldly values we are constantly exposed to. Are we seasoned enough with discipline, with the Word of God to remain loyal disciples in our world?

Many are the troubles of the just man, but out of them all the Lord delivers him (Ps 34:20).

TWO IN ONE FLESH

Seventh Week of the Year, Friday   **Mark 10:1-12**

We have here the teaching of Jesus regarding the indissolubility of marriage. The Pharisees asked Jesus about it to test Him. The Jews had a rather free interpretation of the laws of marriage. According to them men could divorce their wives for quite a number of "valid" reasons. They claimed Moses permitted it. True, in case of adultery, but they had added many reasons or excuses for divorce. And besides, Jesus reminded them, Moses only did so because of their stubbornness. He tells them that the only reason for the exception Moses made was because they couldn't take it. Regardless of their feelings, of the anger He would cause in them, Jesus insists on the principle that "what God has joined together, let no man separate." Valid marriages are indissoluble.

Jesus is very clear, very definite. There can be no misunderstanding what He means. The disciples of Jesus are surprised at this teaching and question Him further to get it absolutely straight. Jesus answers them with a clear statement that if a man and wife had been validly married, they cannot remarry after divorce without committing adultery.

We turn to God and ask Him to show us the beauty of this union. "The two shall become one." With a little reflection we notice in good marriages a closer tie, more oneness between man and wife, than with blood relations.

In the United States the divorce rate is very high. Nearly half of all marriages end in divorce. How contrary to what Jesus teaches. Yet how much anger, resentment, guilt is generated because of this teaching.

Jesus teaches the truth. But Jesus is also compassionate. He definitely has great compassion for the divorced, those in bad marriages, broken families. Have we? Have we ever done anything to show our compassion?

We praise You, Lord, for your teachings, for your compassion and love of the weak, the broken, the sinner.

AS CHILDREN

Seventh Week of the Year, Saturday   Mark 10:13-16

Jesus loved children. He became indignant when the disciples scolded the parents for bringing them to Him. He made sure the children were not kept away. He embraced them, blessed them, placing His hands on them. This is exactly what the parents wanted, they wanted Jesus to at least touch their children.

Was Jesus a mere politician, getting at the heartstrings of the parents through their children? Politicians like to have their picture, holding or kissing a child, spread in the news media.

I think if we read on a sentence or two in the Gospel we immediately see that this was not Jesus' intention. He was rather using the occasion to teach His disciples and us a lesson. There was, of course, a simple matter of love and kindness Christ would show anyone that was brought to Him. But beyond this He was using these children as a symbol for the poor in spirit, for the lowly, within the Christian community. This is another instance of Jesus emphasizing that God loves the lowly, the poor and the afflicted, in contrast to the religious thought of the time which regarded poverty and human affliction as a punishment for personal sins.

Jesus seems to be saying that it is easier for the lowly to understand and accept the reign of God. It is certainly easier for a child to say, "Abba, Father" that is "Pa or Daddy." So if we are to have a child's attitude to God, Our Father, Christ says we should be like children. "I assure you that whoever does not accept the reign of God like a little child shall not take part in it."

We are not to remain children in the sense of remaining childish, immature. We are to have the openness, the humility, the unpretentiousness of most children. Children can be trained. Their characters are pliable, can still be shaped. So we, too, should try to be like wax in the hands of God so that He can shape us ever more perfectly into images of Christ. This is what is meant when we are asked to be like children if we wish to share in the kingdom of God.

Jesus, I surrender to Your Lordship as a child in a mother's arms.

IMPOSSIBLE FOR MAN

Eighth Week of the Year, Monday   **Mark 10:17-27**

Jesus has just given His disciples a stern warning about making one's self an obstacle to love of God. He warns against pride and envy. "Keep yourself small," He says, "by welcoming the little children." He Himself blesses the children "because the kingdom of God belongs to such as these."

Now Jesus warns us also about putting "things" in the way of God's love. The rich young man wants to know how to arrive at his best potential, how to live forever. Jesus reminds him that there is a guidebook, the commandments of God. The young man answers, "These I have always kept."

Jesus looks at the man's fine clothing and expensive jewelry. This young man is quite sincere, but he has not been put to the test. He is well groomed, well fed, well protected from the hardships of life. It is time for him to face reality. Jesus lays it on the man but, says Mark, He presents it with love: "You need something more, friend. You're in danger of letting the kingdom of thingdom get between you and God's kingdom. Go, sell it all! Give it to those who are in real need, and come, follow me. Choose voluntary poverty, complete self-giving; trust completely in God for your earthly needs."

The young man is visibly shaken. Apparently he wasn't asking Jesus to challenge him, but only to approve of him. Jesus has opened the door wide to spiritual growth by leaps and bounds. But His light comes too clearly through that open door. And it shows the man that he is really attached to his possessions. He is chained, hooked, bogged down. He cannot free himself to follow Jesus.

> How free You were, Jesus. How imprisoned was the
> rich man. He walked away quiet and sad. You looked
> at him, Jesus, shaking Your head, and as You turned
> back to Your friends You said, "How hard it is for the
> rich to enter God's kingdom!"

The poor disciples have always thought riches were a blessing from God! "How can anyone be saved then?" they want to know. Jesus answers, "Man does not save himself. But God can do anything."

POSSIBLE WITH GOD

Eighth Week of the Year, Tuesday   **Mark 10:28-31**

This part of Mark's Gospel is consolation and relief, compared with the very hard sayings Jesus has just laid on His followers. We see Jesus here as a shocking radical. When the rich young man approached Jesus, feeling quite proud of himself because he was keeping all the commandments, Jesus set down some demands that have sent shock waves through the whole world and all the way down the centuries.

These shock waves brought forth such power-houses of dedication and reform as St. Benedict, St. Francis of Assisi, St. Dominic, St. Ignatius of Loyola, St. Teresa of Avila, St. Elizabeth Ann Seton, and how many thousands of dedicated members of how many hundreds of religious orders and societies in the Church. These holy men and women have taken literally the words with which Jesus answered the wealthy young man: "There is one thing more you must do. Go and sell what you have and give to the poor. Then come and follow me."

There are no "ifs" about it. The disciple of Jesus is one who is completely detached from everything and everyone. In the words of Jesus, the disciple "has given up home, brothers or sisters, mother or father, children or property" for Jesus and for the Gospel. Jesus is radical indeed! The true disciple of Christ is totally attached to Jesus and to His new kingdom. He has preferred Jesus to all that the world holds dear.

Mark tells us that such a radical demand deeply shocked the disciples. They considered such dedication, even to Jesus, as impossible, and Jesus agreed. He said, "For man this is impossible, but for God all things are possible."

The history of the saints, the great dedicated Christians of every age and place, shows us that God can indeed give His children the power of total dedication. In one of the Eucharistic Prefaces of the Saints, the Church says, "This great company of witnesses spurs us on to victory, to share their prize of everlasting glory."

Jesus, You promised these faithful witnesses a return of "a hundred times" in "this present age," and "in the age to come, everlasting life."

TRUE GREATNESS

Eighth Week of the Year, Wednesday   Mark 10:32-45

Again and again Our Lord prophesies His passion to try to make His Apostles understand the kind of kingdom He came to establish. Now He proceeds deliberately to confront it.

James and John, two of the three favorite Apostles, declare that they are ready to be baptized in the pain and drink the cup that Christ foretells is waiting for them. They are willing to die with Him. On one condition, that He promise them the highest position in His kingdom. Jesus gladly accepts their pledge to suffer with them and simply states that they will share in His bath of pain. But He categorically says that it is not His to grant them the highest place in the kingdom.

Taken on face value this statement seems strange and contrary to His divinity. Why can't Jesus grant two of His favorite Apostles positions of honor? The answer lies in the very fact that He is God. God rewards the good, punishes the wicked. He is merciful but also just.

Just as Christ's greatest claim on our love and honor lies in His complete emptying of self for mankind—His complete service—so also the Apostles were not to glory in any authority that came from sitting at Christ's right side, but their greatest glory would lie in the service to others. Jesus' words are very clear: "Whoever wants to rank first among you must serve the needs of all." So Christ can't grant the first place to just anyone. Only if we live a life of service to others can we expect great rewards both in this life and in the eternal kingdom that is to come.

Give us the grace, O Lord, to live for others.

A NAME AS NO OTHER ·

Eighth Week of the Year, Thursday   **Mark 10:46-52**

The blind man calls on the name of Jesus and receives his sight. What power in the Name of Jesus! He obediently accepted death on a cross, and "because of this God highly exalted Him and gave Him a name above every other name, so that at the name of Jesus every knee must bend in the heavens, on the earth, and under the earth, and every tongue proclaim to the glory of God the Father: Jesus Christ is Lord!" (Ph 2).

This is the name of which St. Peter wrote, "There is no other name in the whole world given to men by which we are to be saved" (Ac 4:12).

The name of Jesus is most dear to every true Christian. The name of Jesus is, in the words of St. Bernard, "honey to the mouth, music to the ear, a shout of gladness in the heart. Behold with the dawning of that name every cloud scatters and clear day returns. Has anyone fallen into sin, and does he run despairingly towards the toils of death? If he but invokes the name of Life, will not life be renewed within him?" (Sermon 15 on the Canticles).

When the blind beggar heard that Jesus was in the crowd, he began to call out, "Jesus, Son of David, have pity on me!" See the loving response of Jesus: he stops and says to the crowd, "Call him over." And the people tell the blind man, "You have nothing to fear from Jesus! Arise! He is calling you!" What an invitation to each of us to call upon the name of Jesus in every need!

Few have written so beautifully on the healing power of the Name of Jesus, as St. Bernard. Meditating on the Canticle's praise of the beloved's name, Bernard says, "Not without reason does the Holy Spirit compare the name of the Bridegroom to oil, when he inspires the bride to say to the Bridegroom: Your Name is as oil poured out. For oil gives light, it nourishes, it anoints. It kindles fire; it renews the flesh; it assuages pain. It is light, food, medicine. See how like to this is the name of the true Bridegroom. It is light when it is preached; it is food in meditation; it is balm and healing when it is invoked for aid."

Blessed be the Name of Jesus!

HOUSE OF PRAYER

Eighth Week of the Year, Friday   **Mark 11:11-26**

The fact that Jesus threw the buyers and sellers from the Temple is not understood correctly if we regard it only as an objection to the practice in the Temple precincts. Actually these matters were rather well controlled by the religious authorities. Generally only transactions necessary to obtain the items for the offerings were tolerated. We only understand the event better if we remember the Old Testament quote, "My house shall be called a house of prayer for all peoples."

Jesus' action is indicative of God's judgment against any and all abuses of the Temple. He seems to point to a failure on the part of the Jewish priests to instruct the people in the meaning of Temple worship.

It is also very significant that the quote from Isaiah says that the house of prayer is for all peoples, not just for the chosen race. This is a messianic prophecy that looks to the Gentiles' taking their rightful place in God's Temple.

We are these Gentiles, most of us. We have been given a place in God's house. His house of prayer has become our home, our house of prayer. We are to feel at home there with Our Father. We are to be as children sitting inthe warmth of our home around Our Father who loves us.

But this privilege requires something of us as Jesus so vividly indicates in the Gospel. If we do not respect the sacredness of our house of prayer, if we make it figuratively a "den of thieves," that is, a worldly place, a place of gossip, a place to daydream, slouch, sleep, then we deserve to be deprived of the warmth and welcome of God's house.

Our churches are houses of prayer, places for conversation with God, our Father, with Christ, our brother and saviour, places for common worship of the Father in union with Christ. All this can be done in a very relaxed and warm manner without losing the reverence due to this House of God.

We thank you, Lord, that we can feel at home in your house.

AUTHORITY HANG-UP

Eighth Week of the Year, Saturday   **Mark 11:27-33**

In this incident we find the top men, the official leaders of the Jews, confront Jesus regarding His authority. He had just entered triumphantly into Jerusalem, had driven the money changers from the temple and was now teaching in the temple precincts. "On what authority are you doing these things?" they asked Him.

Jesus very calmly answers with another question regarding John's Baptism. Was it from God or man? This puts these Jewish leaders into a dilemma. They answer, "We do not know."

Jesus responds that He will not tell them either on what authority He is acting. This statement is the whole point of the story. Since they don't want to admit that John was a messenger of God, neither would they believe if He told them plainly the origin of His authority. His statement is an indirect claim to Messiahship.

Today we would say these Jewish leaders had an authority hang-up. They could not accept any other authority than their own. They were gods onto themselves. Whatever Jesus preached that went against their interpretation of the law, whatever might endanger their authority, they resisted and used it against Him.

We, too, have our problems with authority, with its use or exercise, with its acceptance. Do we use the authority we have regardless of its level, to serve others? Or are we puffed up with it? Do we accept legitimate authority in the Church, in society, in community, in family, as coming from God? Or do we react when our leaders, our superiors, make decisions which affect us adversely? Legitimate authority shares in God's. Are we aware whom we are ultimately opposing?

O God, You alone are the Lord of all creation. All other lords have merely a tiny share of your power.

FRUIT OR THORNS?

Ninth Week of the Year, Monday **Mark 12:1-12**

From Isaiah as from Jesus we hear the story of the chosen vineyard, the garden of God's delight. We hear how the Lord expected to find fruit and found only thorns. "What then shall the Master of that vineyard do?" Jesus asked. Those very people who were producing no fruit answered and condemned themselves out of their own mouth: "He shall take the vineyard away, and give it to others who will yield its fruits in due season."

We, like the chosen people in the desert, "eat the same prophetic food and drink the same prophetic drink and are nourished by the same prophetic rock, the rock that is Christ." Must it be said of us, too, that "with most of them God was not pleased?" (1 Cor 10:4-5).

How much we ourselves feel the slightest ingratitude! Those who have received any favor from us are expected to pay for it dearly. Truly, human ingratitude is painful:

> Blow, blow, thou winter wind,
> Thou art not so unkind
> As man's ingratitude.
> Freeze, freeze, thou bitter sky,
> That dost not bite so nigh
> As benefits forgot. (*As You Like It,* II, 7)

It is good for each of us to feel deeply the ingratitude of friends. For in this pain we shall learn the pain we ourselves have caused. In their thanklessness we see the image of our own ingratitude. In the hurt we feel, we learn the hurt we have caused others.

Whenever again I feel critical of someone who has returned me evil for good, let me say in all truth: "There is the image of myself. There is what I do to You, Lord, day after day. There is my return for the graces You have lavished on me. There go I, my Lord. What I reject in that ungrateful other is what I myself have done too often to count."

UNLESS THE LORD . . .

Ninth Week of the Year, Tuesday   **Mark 12:13-17**

Over and over Jesus confronts the hypocrisy of the Pharisees. And always His comments are honest and straightforward. Even the Pharisees admit this: "Teacher, we know you are a truthful man. . . . You do not act out of human respect but teach God's way of life sincerely." High praise, but unfortunately, wrongly motivated. So Jesus must answer, "Why are you trying to trip me?" Then He wisely answers them, "Give to Caesar what is Caesar's, and to God what is God's."

And what is God's? The very first place, the priority in our life. Even Caesar owes his authority to God, whether he recognizes it or not.

One of the great American founders meeting at the Federal Convention in 1787 to draw up the United States' Constitution was Benjamin Franklin. It was he who urged that the daily proceedings be opened with a prayer. He was so convinced that God governs the affairs of men that he said no empire could rise without God's providence. He quoted from the Bible in the words of Psalm 127, "Unless the Lord build the house, they labor in vain who build it." And so he asked that the assembly would each morning implore the help of God before proceeding to its business.

Think of our national, local, community, family and personal problems today. Do they not result from not giving to God what is God's? The bitterness, prejudice, hatreds and injustices all around us are the outgrowth of pride and greed, the rejection of God's law in our daily living.

It is the Lord, and He only, who can solve these dilemmas, who can teach us the way to go, who speaks most powerfully through His own example. The power to cure our ills is offered to us, the power over evil is given us, but we do not accept it.

We do not give to God what is God's: we do not really let the Lord fill us with His power. We put all kinds of obstacles in His way, just as the Pharisees did. We try to find easy substitutes for Christ, but they do not work. The Saints, who gave to God what is God's, spent hours daily listening to Him, in prayer, in studying the Gospel of Jesus with the inner heart, in following His example carefully.

Lord Jesus, You are the only answer! Why don't we ask the right questions?

INTERFERENCE

Ninth Week of the Year, Wednesday   **Mark 12:18-27**

No matter what approach Jesus took to warn the Pharisees, to make them take an honest look at themselves, to enlighten them before it was too late, they refused to be honest. They seemed only to become more entrenched in their smugness and in their hatred for Him. It is the old story of human narrowness ruining God's plan for our growth and development.

It has been said that all human affairs, given enough time, will go badly. Does this sound pessimistic, or realistic? Human selfishness is all too contagious and invades and weakens the best of us. Jesus accused the Pharisees of ruining their chance to hear the voice of God by intruding their own desires and pet ideas.

Don't we all do that? Don't we make so much noise of our own that we can't hear God? We blame other people for our troubles, when it's really ourselves who are spoiling our chances. We're not happy because we're always interfering with God's blueprint. God is our Creator. He knows what it takes to make us truly human.

So our aim in life must be to take things calmly, listen more and more to what God has to tell us, and make less and less noise of our own. It's *we* ourselves who spoil our happiness.

This is no easy job. Without realizing it, we turn off God. If any of us had a penny for every time we know better than God what this world needs and what we ought to have, we'd be rich. A good prayer for all of us would be this: "O Lord, give me the good sense to make less noise, so that I can tune You in, because that's the only way I'll really learn to live."

> Dead to sin, alive to You!
> Come, Lord Jesus, make us new!
> Light, break out like morning dew,
> Come, new power, make us true!

TRUE LOVE

Ninth Week of the Year, Thursday   **Mark 12:28-34**

Jesus praised the scribe for understanding that love is God's most important commandment. Love of God and love of neighbor—these were the great commandments, Jesus told him. And the man agreed wholeheartedly.

It's not as easy as it sounds. Real love is a great challenge to us Americans, greater than ever before. We have too many material comforts, and that tends to make people selfish. In pioneer days people had to struggle hard and give up much for the basic family and community needs. Children had to work hard on farms to help keep the family alive; families had to give generously of their own time and materials to build churches and community centers. This had its drawbacks, but it was a genuine gift of self, a human response, cooperation for the common needs. And it developed a sense of responsibility.

Today we don't automatically feel this great need for each other. And how many people are lonely and starved for true love! An increasing flood of false literature gives a wrong picture of what human love is. If you don't have shiny teeth and soft hair and rosebud perfume, nobody will love you. We laugh at these ridiculous commercials, but they seep into our thinking. They make us want to *get* instead of *give*. Love then becomes a mere surface attraction which has nothing to do with real love.

What a tragedy if a beautiful home with color TV, two fine cars, a charcoal broiler and a pool table and all the rest, is an unhappy home, because true love is missing. There is no real love which is not open and generous and sacrificing and well-disciplined. God is love, and only those who live in real love can live in God. True love goes out of self to others. If genuine love does not actively grow and flourish in the family, how can it go out to others? Here is the parents' first responsibility: to teach real love to their children, by having it themselves. They must learn love in order to learn of God, for God is love.

> **Together in the love of Christ**
> **Let us rejoice!**
> **United praise the living God**
> **With heart and voice!**

SON OR LORD?

Ninth Week of the Year, Friday   **Mark 12:35-37**

Teaching in the temple, Jesus asks, "How can the scribes claim, the Messiah is David's son?" He quotes the prophecy in which David calls the Messiah his "Lord." Jesus knows it is time to show the people that they are being taught false notions about the Messiah. The religious teachers have been trying to discredit Jesus as a prophet and possible Messiah by setting traps for Him.

The Pharisees tried to compromise Jesus politically by asking Him if it is lawful to pay taxes to the Roman emperor. They tried to embroil Him in religious disputes by raising controversial questions about the resurrection of the dead and the relative importance of commandments. In each case Jesus surprised them by the wisdom of His answers.

He asks, in effect, "How clear are you people about the nature of the Messiah? How much do you know about the one who is to come?" The point is, "How can you set yourselves up as judges of who can be the Messiah and who cannot?" They wanted the Messiah made to their image and likeness, rather than to the image and likeness of God, the One who sends Him, the One who chooses Him and anoints Him for His saving work in the world.

The Pharisees tried their cruel game of making Jesus a laughing stock by setting traps for Him. But the joke—and not a cruel but a loving and generous joke—is on them. God's Messiah is not man's Messiah at all. The big surprise is that the Redeemer is going to be the person of God's choice, not man's choice, for the simple reason that man doesn't really know how to choose wisely.

Man's self-made Messiah is supposed to have huge wealth and political influence. But God's Chosen One is a humble carpenter, a working man, a poor man, who comes not with the noise of trumpets of war and force and revenge. He comes quietly, the Prince of Peace, the Lord of love, the forgiving Father—God's answer to our false standards!

> **Lord Jesus, prepare our small minds and hearts for Your great surprises. Will we not always find You where we least suspect?**

THE WIDOW'S OFFERING

Ninth Week of the Year, Saturday **Mark 12:38-44**

One day Jesus and His disciples were sitting in the temple area near the collection box. In came a parade of very wealthy Pharisees, tossing in their silver coins, holding their hands high so that everyone can see, and letting the silver rattle loudly.

Then quietly came a poor little widow, trying to hide because she has almost nothing to give. She slips in her two pennies. Jesus notices, and He wants His followers to notice, too. "I want you to observe that this poor widow contributed more than all the others who donated to the treasury. They gave from their surplus wealth, but she gave from her poverty, all that she had to live on." They gave what they wouldn't even miss, but she gave her last coins. That's love: that's the heart of giving.

"Giving till it hurts" is done by the poor, not the rich. It's sad, for if the very rich gave as generously as the poor do, no one would be in need; all would have enough to live on. No wonder that Jesus spoke so often and in such strong words about the danger of riches. No wonder He had a preference for the spirit of the poor, and chose to be poor. It was a sign of His wholehearted generosity.

Jesus did not condemn people who had more than others. But He did warn them seriously against selfishness and greediness. He told many stories in which He showed how evil it was to have more and not be willing to share, as in the parable of the rich man and Lazarus, and the fool who built those bigger storehouses and then died.

The majority of Christ's followers were of the poor, because they were more willing to listen to Him. The rich were afraid they might lose their power and influence if they followed the Lord's example. It really means that they were not willing to trust in God. They preferred to trust in their own power and wealth.

Loving always means giving of yourself, not giving something you don't even miss. To love is to give something of your own self: your care and concern, your time, your talents and skills, your attention and interest in the needs of others.

Lord, we are all poor before You. Why should we be afraid to share of what we have received? Do we fail to

**trust You? Don't we know Your return is always more
than our small gift?**

THE HAPPY ONES

Tenth Week of the Year, Monday   **Matthew 5:1-12**

What does it mean to be a saint? Just listen to Christ as He tells
you in today's Gospel passage.

They are the blest ones, who are poor in spirit. They are the blest
ones, who mourn over man's disobedience to God's Law. They are
the blest ones, who are full of mercy to others. They are the blest ones,
who bring peace among friends and relatives. They are the blest ones,
the really happy ones, who suffer for the sake of truth, faith and love.
They are happy and fulfilled in spite of their pain, because they are
always hungry for God and the things of God.

To such people, if we are such people, Christ says, "Be glad and
rejoice, for your reward is great in heaven." Such people will find real
happiness because their lives are centered in God and in their
fellowman for the sake of God. They are not self-centered.

To be a saint means to make a decision for Christ. If we were to
study or read the life of our patron saints, we would be certain to find
that somewhere, sometime in their lives, they made a firm decision for
Christ, to be peace-makers in the name of Christ, to be poor like
Christ, to be humble and honest like Christ.

Have we made such a commitment? Have we made a firm decision
for Christ? What is most important in our lives?

If we still are very much concerned with riches, with our material
needs, if we are turned in on self instead of showing mercy, making
peace, then we are not yet converted to Jesus as true Christians.

Jesus gives us the rules, the prescription for happiness, for
sanctity, in the beatitudes. There is no other way to be converted, to
be really committed to a life of sanctity.

**Those who sow in love and tears and mercy shall reap
in joy and love. The Lord has done great things for us.
We are glad indeed.**

LEADERSHIP

Tenth Week of the Year, Tuesday   **Matthew 5:13-16**

"You are the salt of the earth . . . You are the light of the world . . . Your light must shine before men . . ." In these figures, Jesus encourages leadership in His followers. We must be an inspiration to others, that they "may see goodness" in our actions.

Too many of us leave it up to somebody else to notice that command of Christ. "It's not my job," we say. "I don't have the time or the talent." We're willing to criticize those who do take the time, of course—the pastor, the teachers, the chairmen of parish committees, the readers at Mass. But if we're asked to give of our own talents, we become suddenly impoverished, we have nothing to offer.

Every one of us has much more to offer than we ourselves may dream of. As the Lord told us to learn lessons from the lilies of the fields, the birds of the air, the fig tree, and many more, so I suggest today that we learn a lesson from the bumble bee. He could easily complain that he can't possibly fly, and the laws of aerodynamics will support his claim. The bumble bee's size, weight and clumsy shape in relation to his stubby wingspread are all against him. Scientific tests have shown that he's not supposed to be able to get off the ground.

Since he's ignorant of science, the bumble bee continues to zoom through the air whenever it pleases. And the lesson? No matter how low you rate yourself, no matter how low your friends rate you, you are underestimating your potential. God has given you more energy and more skills than you dream of. And He will provide the graces, once you begin doing what you ought to, and what you really can do.

It sounds like an old cliche: "Where there's a will, there's a way." But it's an old truth. If you really want to respond to the needs of Christ and His Church, if you really want to listen to Christ's call for laborers in His vineyard, if you really want to do your part to spread the Lord's message, you will find a way—in fact, you will find many ways.

"Lord, that I may see—"

MAN-MADE MONOTONY

Tenth Week of the Year, Wednesday   **Matthew 5:17-19**

"What? Fulfill all these commandments? Even the smallest letter of the law? What a bore! What do you take me for?" asks the modern Christian.

Too often this fear of so-called religious boredom is a cloak. The real fear is not the fear of boredom or of "routine." We fear the very vigor of God's demands, the pains of the Christian's endless battle, the strain of developing a Christ-like wisdom and will. The "bored" modern Christian is like a boy who says he does not like football because it is "boring" or requires no skill like other games, when really he inwardly fears getting hurt or being humiliated by stronger and better athletes. How many of our "reasons" are really "excuses."

"In the measure you give, you shall receive," says Jesus. Too many of us who pretend to fear the "boredom" of religion and the "monotony" of praising God—too many of us simply want to do nothing. We falsely term "boring" the very things that would deliver us from the greater boredom we choose. We fear all things that might compel us to do something worthwhile, because these great works demand some sacrifice from us.

The danger we are in is very great. Doing nothing, loving our comfortable way, guarding our ease is a first class form of selfishness. Selfishness is the principal element of sin. Utterly bored with ourselves and afraid of the effort required to rise out of our lethargy, we will turn to some form of sin as a way of getting something done. We call it "getting the fun out of life" and "living only once." In other words, we are so self-centered that when we do rise from sleep, we act in a selfish way.

Those who are great in the eyes of God and man find endless work to be done in praise of God; every creature leads them to Him; every talent is spent for Him; even their rest and relaxation is spent in His loving presence; they have no time for boredom.

> "Praise the Lord, my soul! As long as I live, I will praise God! Of Him my songs shall be, as long as I have life to sing them!" (Ps 146).

GO BE RECONCILED

Tenth Week of the Year, Thursday   **Matthew 5:20-26**

Today's Gospel reading is a short passage taken from our Lord's Sermon on the Mount. He reminds us of our duty to love our neighbor.

There is great need for more charity in the world. In our material age there is a great tendency for each one to get what he can out of life: money, pleasure, honours. We are so individualistic-minded. We are too selfish. This has been the greatest barrier to Christian unity. We may believe that our separated Christian brethren are wrong in their beliefs, but this is no excuse for lack of Christian love. We need charity for all people. Christ died for all, and we must be willing to go out of our way to be especially kind, instead of prejudiced.

Love has many wonderful effects. It increases our energy for good. It gives strength to overcome obstacles, even to perform heroic deeds. Love makes us joyful, cheerful. Nothing can disturb or weary us. Everything we do out of love seems light, for love is our strength, our joy and peace.

Today Christ emphasizes that we should always be on good terms with our neighbor, with everyone. If we aren't, we're not on good terms with God either, and as a result much of the good we do goes to waste.

Let us follow Christ's advice as he tells us, "If you bring your gift to the altar—if you are at prayer or about to attend Holy Mass—and there recall that your brother has anything against you—you're on the outs with someone, you have insulted him—leave your gift at the altar, go first to be reconciled with your brother—make up, pay him his due, apologize—and then come and offer your gift."

The conclusion? Charity in the eyes of God is more important than prayer. Without charity it is no real prayer. St. John says, "If anyone says, 'I love God,' and hates his brother, he is a liar."

Lord, we recognize your insistence on love as the great commandment. We ask your grace that we may truly live it.

IN THE HEART

Tenth Week of the Year, Friday   **Matthew 5:27-32**

Everywhere in the Gospels we see Jesus strike unusually hard blows at hypocrisy, the problem of a clean outside and a corrupt inside. With His sharp discerning mind and His keen understanding of human psychology, Jesus always struck at the core of things. He went to the very center and cause of our troubles.

He says in today's Gospel, "Anyone who looks lustfully at a woman has already committed adultery with her in his thoughts." It's where your heart is that counts!

Evidently the Pharisees, at least at first, were underhanded about their criticism of Jesus. But Jesus was not deceived; He knew their attitude. He said, "Why do you murmur about this in your hearts?" They have not the courage to speak their minds openly, so they try to cover their envy and hatred by saying, "Master, we know you are an honest teacher and fear no man. Tell us, then, is it right for us to pay taxes to Caeser or not?" Jesus at once saw through their words into their hearts, and He answered, "Why do you tempt me, you hypocrites?"

Another time Jesus told his disciples, "These people are dull of heart." Notice that He did not say, "They are dull of brain." He did not complain about the low I.Q. of the crowd. He wished they were not "dull of heart," empty of godly desire, uninterested in purity of heart.

Jesus also told His followers, "No evil comes to you from the outside, but from within. Your mouth speaks from the overflow of your heart!" Again He said, "Where your treasure is, there your heart will be." It is deep in the core of our being, then, that our human goodness and uprightness must dwell. Jesus wants us to be sure that He is not deceived by a false front; He sees into our very hearts and knows the inside motives of our actions. We cannot fool Him with invented excuses. By His very strong statement about "plucking out your eye if it leads you to sin," Jesus is saying that He holds us responsible for what is going on in our minds and our hearts. We must uproot corruption at its very source, and direct our wills to pure desire for God.

Lord Jesus, give me light to know my inner heart, that I may direct it to You.

YES OR NO

Tenth Week of the Year, Saturday **Matthew 5:33-37**

This paragraph of the Sermon on the Mount is introduced, as many of the other passages, with the couplet "You have heard . . . , what I tell you." Jesus said He did not come to abolish the old law, but to fulfill it. In so many cases the law had either been watered down or interpreted in a rigid way if it helped the status of those in authority.

In our present passage Jesus says that the old law was interpreted to say "Do not swear falsely." Actually you should not have to swear at all. Neither is it an excuse to use various substitutes for the divine name in the oath you take. Swearing by heaven, by the earth, by Jerusalem is still a sign that you consider yourself untruthful and mistrusting.

An oath is a reflection of man's sinful state. It shows his tendency to lie, his untrustfulness. And so to try to overcome this and enforce the truth an oath is used. Secondly it shows man's distrust of his fellow man. If we were inclined to trust, to believe others, to take them at their word, oaths would have no place whatsoever.

So an oath is a sign that we accept these evils as a matter of course. We don't expect truthfulness or trust among men. That's what Jesus meant when He said that anything more or less than YES or NO is from the evil one.

Jesus brings us the New Dispensation. He has promised us His Spirit with all His fruits and gifts. In the Christian Life there is to be love, trust, truth. In such a society, in such a community an oath has no place whatsoever. Introducing them into our living will simply bring back the evils of mistrust and falsehood.

Jesus, help us to live in Your kingdom with love and trust, our words always trustworthy.

LOVE'S GREATEST PROOF

Eleventh Week of the Year, Monday   **Matthew 5:38-42**

Christ in His sermon on the Mount urges us to love our enemies. This was a complete surprise to the people of His time. It was completely contrary to the Law of Retaliation as found in the Old Testament. This New Law of Retaliation puts a completely different slant, a Christian stamp, on love.

There have been attempts to interpret these passages as referring to the "evil one," or to "evil things," instead of to those who do evil to us. Christ's words are very clear. He gives four instances or examples of ways in which others could hurt us. First by physical violence. Jesus recommends no retaliation but rather that we suffer it. Secondly He gives an example of legal action. "Should anyone press you into law over your shirt, hand him your coat as well." Christ recommends not only giving what may be illegally taken, but even to go beyond in giving. The third area is one of forced labor. "Should anyone press you into service for one mile, go two with him." Finally, Jesus recommends that we are not to turn our backs on a borrower, be he friend or foe.

Christ then explains why this love of our enemies is so important. He says it is a proof that we are sons of our heavenly Father, who lets the sun shine and the rain fall on both the good and bad, the just and the unjust.

Loving our friends, those whom we naturally love, those who do good to us, is a very easy thing. It proves nothing about our Christian attitude. Tax collectors and pagans do the same to each other. Christ does not say that love of those who are dear to us is not real love. The real proof is in the love of those whom we find repulsive, those who always seem to hurt us, those who never show any appreciation. It is here that we show that our love is firmly based in God.

Lord Jesus, You gave us the best example of love of enemies: "Father, forgive them, for they know not what they do."

NOTHING BUT LOVE

Eleventh Week of the Year, Tuesday   Matthew 5:43-48

"Love your enemies, pray for your persecutors. This will prove that you are sons of your heavenly Father, for his sun rises on the bad and the good."

When Jesus told us to love our enemies, He was deeply psychological in analyzing the problem. Jesus himself would have gone mad if He had not forgiven the Pharisees. They were so hopelessly full of hate and envy.

Jesus couldn't help guessing that they were hatching a plot to kill Him. Their efforts to trap Him and discredit Him were obvious to all. And when they did actually nail Him to the cross, Jesus showed us how to love and forgive. As he hung there in agony, He said, "Father, forgive them!"

Nothing but love in His heart, even at the worst hurt a man could ever suffer: complete rejection and murder. That kind of love, dear friends, healed us, and washed away the worst of our sins! Forgiveness heals! That is what Jesus teaches us from His cross. That overpowering love from the Cross of Jesus is what heals the wounds of the world.

We know that Adam's sin had lost that healthy, happy, healing love. We know the story well enough. Adam and his two little boys, Cain and Abel, were walking one day in the desert, the hot sands burning their feet. Looking over at a fine, shady, wooded area in the distance, Abel asked, "Daddy, why can't we live over there in that nice cool oasis?"

Adam answered, "It's your mother's fault, boy! She ate us out of house and home." There you go, Adam! You can't even forgive your wife. Do you see what sin does? It robs us of love, so that we blame others for our faults, and then refuse to forgive.

But God doesn't give up on us rebels. He sent us His divine Son Jesus, to restore that powerful divine healing love to us. Jesus teaches us, "Love and forgive. In a word, you must be made perfect as your heavenly Father is perfect."

Jesus came to restore us to that original love of Paradise, that love of the heavenly Father that makes Him "rain on the just and unjust alike." What wise psychology, what a precious healing remedy, what a new vision of hope for the world!

Grant it, O Lord!

HONESTY

Eleventh Week of the Year, Wednesday   Matthew 6:1-6, 16-18

Jesus warned us frequently to be on guard against hyprocisy. It is an intolerable dishonesty. One of the clearest signs of a healthy society is the inherent honesty of its people. And the surest preservative of mental health in the individual is his own habitual honesty.

Honesty is rightly called most fundamental, the most primitive and basic of human virtues. It is the very foundation upon which faith and hope are built, and it is the absolute prerequisite of love.

The great ideal today is "authentic personality." What can that mean, if not fundamental honesty in a person? Parents are told by psychiatrists, "Be honest, and you can have faults with impunity. You have your weaknesses, but be strong in honesty and your children will respect you."

The Lord knew well that honesty saves souls. He constantly decried hyprocisy as the great destroyer. Most of His severe warnings were directed at the vice of duplicity. He gave us the key, "You will recognize them by their fruits," and by this we could identify ourselves as well as others. The fruits, not the words or pretences, told the story.

Dishonesty keeps people in the old sinful rut. The problem is never faced—be it alcohol, gambling, infidelity, nagging, jealousy, greed, envy, prejudice, cheating. Without honesty in our total outlook, we will not conquer ourselves.

"Nobody appreciates me, nobody trusts me, nobody listens to me," we complain. Be honest: why? Because of what's wrong with me. Everybody else seems to know. Why don't I? I'm not honest with myself. I don't face the problem: I avoid any form of cure that might hurt. And I'm furious with anyone who might try to help.

Come, O Spirit, Lord of light:
Come, our Hope, set all aright!
Sear our souls with inner sight,
Lure our love to heaven's height!

A PRAYER FOR FORGIVING

Eleventh Week of the Year, Thursday   **Matthew 6:7-15**

"If you forgive the faults of others, your heavenly Father will forgive you yours. If you do not forgive others, neither will your Father forgive you."

Jesus says here that a great obstacle to being healed by Him is lack of forgiveness. To be healed spiritually, mentally, emotionally, even physically in some cases, we need to forgive, really forgive. It is so essential, but at times not easy. So let's pray to the Lord for the gift of forgiveness, a grace we need from Him:

Father, I thank You for Your Son Jesus, who accepted so much pain and suffering for me. As He hung nailed to the cross He said, "Father, forgive them." He prayed for those who had caused Him all this pain, and He forgave them everything.

Jesus, You taught us to forgive, not seven times, but seventy times seven. And You forgave every sinner who came to you. Lord, I find it hard to forgive certain people who have hurt me. The wound seems to be very deep. Jesus, where I am unable to forgive, put Your Spirit of forgiveness into my heart. I am not yet perfect, so I find it very hard to forget injuries. But you, dear Jesus, the perfectly obedient Son, obedient unto death, and forgiving unto death, fill my heart with Your powerful love. Your perfect generosity, Jesus, is a forgiving love, a love that washes away every sin, however great.

Jesus, wherever I cannot forgive, come into my heart, change me, fill me with Your forgiving love. Jesus, You take my hand, You place it into the hand of those who have hurt me. You love them for me, and thus You will teach me to forgive in Your Name.

To be saved in Your Name is to learn to forgive in Your Name. I remember, Jesus, how You answered Your disciples' question, "Who then can be saved?" You said, "With man it is impossible, but with

God all things are possible." When I find it nearly impossible to forgive and to keep forgiving, I will place the problem in Your hands, my Lord and my God. For with God all things are possible. Thank you, loving Jesus, for teaching me how to forgive.

HAPPINESS IS—

Eleventh Week of the Year, Friday   **Matthew 6:19-23**

Happiness is—going to the mail box and finding no bills that need to be paid. How we all long to be "at peace with the financial world," by having more money than we ever need to shell out. Then some wise guy wonders, "If that's what brings peace and happiness, why are the richest people the most restless?"

Some pious soul may remark, "Spiritual joy, inner happiness of mind, is finding all our debts paid to God and neighbor." But when shall we ever find all those debts paid? Is there a time when we can say, I've done enough?

Nothing in this world can ever completely satisfy us. We keep thinking, "If I could just have this one thing yet, I'd be happy." But the wishes are never finished, nor should they ever be. All things in this world are not enough to make anyone perfectly happy. Experience bears this out. Observe it in yourself and in others.

Therefore, Jesus said, "Don't store up earthly treasures. Moths and rust corrode; thieves break in and steal." Nothing merely human will ever satisfy you.

St. Augustine was one of the most brilliant minds in history. He had a surplus of talent. He searched for happiness everywhere—in friends, in position, in carnal pleasures, in intellectual pursuits. All eventually disappointed him. It took him many years, but at last he faced the truth. He wrote, "O rich man, if you do not have God, what have you? O poor man, if you have God, what more do you need?"

Augustine spoke from the deepest soul of his experience when he said, "The human heart remains restless, Lord, until it rest in You." Nothing else is big enough.

I love You, Lord, my strength, my guide, my burning light,
A beacon and a hope, my refuge, my delight!
O Lord, Redeemer blest, I praise You through the night!
Billows of death arise, deep flows the dismal tide,
The grave entraps my feet, dark clouds around me glide,
In my distress I call, "O Lord, be at my side,
Show me where to go, for You know." (Ps 18).

FATHER

Eleventh Week of the Year, Saturday   **Matthew 6:24-34**

How often Jesus told us that we have a knowing and loving Father. He went so far as to say, don't worry about what you'll eat or drink or wear, "for your Father knows that you need all these things. But seek first the kingdom of God and his justice, and all the rest will be given you besides."

I may remember learning in my earliest school days that God is the "supreme being" and the "pure spirit" and the "almighty creator." But I've never got it clear—in real life—that God is my Father, truly my Father in the most real and beautiful sense of that word. God knows me and loves me completely, everything that I am and all that I need, far better than I know myself.

Jesus insisted that "one" is my Father, "who is in heaven." He came to assure us that our Father loves us, even as Jesus loves us. (Jn 17:23). The Son came to reveal His Father: "You know neither me nor my Father," He told the Pharisees. "If you knew me, you would then know my Father also. . . . He who sent me is true, and the things I heard from Him, I tell the world."

In the love the Father and Jesus have for me, I will find life. "For the Father loves the Son, and shows Him all that He Himself does. And greater works than these He will show Him, for your amazement. For just as the Father raises the dead and gives them life, so also the Son gives life to whom He chooses."

Into this life and love, Jesus has received us: "As the Father has loved me, I also have loved you. Live on in my love" (Jn 15:9).

Heavenly Father, your care for us is greater than any on earth; Your care for each one of us is complete and intimate and personal.

**Our sins you have covered with fatherly care,
Restore us to life, Lord, we pray.
Don't let us forget, we are nothing alone,
We need your strong arm day by day.**

YOUR VERDICT

Twelfth Week of the Year, Monday   **Matthew 7:1-5**

Jesus says, "Your verdict on others will be the verdict passed on you. The measure with which you measure will be used to measure you." If this be the case, and the Lord is known for keeping His promises, we had better pass judgment on others with care. If we expect a merciful judgment from God, then we had better judge our fellow men with the love, the forgiveness, and the understanding that we expect from God.

If we reflect on what is lost by rash and unjust criticism of others, we see why Jesus spoke so strongly on this subject. Gossip often grows out of envy, jealousy, revenge and prejudice. Consider what is lost when our judgments come from such sources:

1) charity is lost—the main virtue that God demands of us. Jesus said you must do good even to those who hate you. What, then, if we don't even do good to our friends?

2) self-control is lost. St. James in his famous letter says you cannot even come near to perfect if your tongue is not in control. By the glib use of our tongues in passing judgments, we lose that self-discipline which is essential to Christian growth.

3) your desire for good is hindered. The gossiper not only discourages others from doing good, but destroys his own capacity for good. You cannot be looking for good and evil at the same time.

4) you waste much time. All the time spent in fault-finding and rash judgment should have been spent in helping your neighbor, in

developing a love for them to bring about concrete Christian and charitable action.

If, on the other hand, your judgments are kind and considerate, see the good you can do. Your praise is an encouragement to others; it will definitely help make them better. It is an encouragement to yourself; when you are looking for good in others, you are well on the way to finding it in yourself. You are giving, rather than taking: thus you are helping wonderfully to build up the people of God.

Lord, teach me to forgive rather than condemn; to praise rather than judge.

MISSING THE MARK

Twelfth Week of the Year, Tuesday   Matthew 7:6, 12, 14

Jesus says, "The gate that leads to damnation is wide, the road is clear, and many choose to travel it. But how narrow is the gate that leads to life, how rough the road, and how few there are who find it!"

In effect Jesus is saying, "Do you know what sin is? Sin is missing the mark." That is what the Greek verb for sin, *hamartano*, means: to be off the target, to be a poor shot, to miss the goal.

A sinner is a poor marksman; he keeps missing the target. To make a field goal on the football field, you have to aim for the "straight and narrow," that limited space between the goal posts. You must hit that narrow space to score. You can kick anywhere else on the field, even into the bleachers, to miss it. The length of your kick might be impressive, but if you miss that limited target you don't score.

A sinner is a poor kicker; he keeps missing the goal, that target which Jesus calls "the narrow gate." And that missing the goal, sin, brings about fear, guilt, depression, even paranoia. Many mental disorders are spiritual disorders. They should not be part of normal, healthy Christian life.

God sent his Son Jesus to us, to restore for us the power of hitting the target, of aiming successfully toward the goal, of finding what life really means. Only God is perfect Love. He could only trust His own Son to be right on target, to restore that normal love to our lives. God the Son, the One we can trust, took all our evils, all our bad marksmanship, on His own shoulders, died to them on the cross, buried these evils in the grave, and rose to new life: the victorious new life which He now holds out to us.

> Through forty days, O Lord, You prayed,
> Prepared to teach and save;
> On You all sins of men were laid,
> For them Your life You gave.
> Teach us to watch and pray with You
> Through pain and trials, Lord,
> Till we in all we say and do
> May share in Your reward.

FALSE PROPHETS

Twelfth Week of the Year, Wednesday   Matthew 7:15-20

"Be on your guard against false prophets." These words, "false prophets," as well as "wolves in sheep's clothing" and "by their deeds you will know them," have become Christian cliches over the centuries. The modern translators have used some different words, but the ideas are the same.

Each stage of history has had its false prophets. Who are they today? How are we to recognize them? Especially in this age of creative thinking, fresh expression of Christian teaching, it can become a bit of a problem. Eminent men, dedicated Christians hold strongly to opposite views on everything from celibacy for the clergy to the ideal age for confirmation.

How do we know the false prophets from the true? Christ says, "By their deeds—by their fruits—you will know them." What deeds? By their fidelity to the teachings of Christ in the Gospels, for God is revealed to us in Christ and only in Him do we have a sure way to the Father.

If we try to have a "sound eye and ear for the Gospel," knowing it through reading and prayer, with the help of the Spirit we will grow in the ability to discern the sentimentality which turns Christ's teaching into a sort of easy love ethic without discipline or sacrifice. We will be able to recognize the permissiveness which clouds the difference between right and wrong as well as the hair-splitting legalism which holds the letter of the law in greater respect than the spirit.

Nothing will serve us better than this seeking of the guidance of the Spirit. When we are hard pressed to find the security and certainty we look for, let us depend on the Spirit of God to bring us His fruits. St. Paul has listed these fruits of the Spirit: joy, love, peace, patience, kindness, generosity, fidelity. Where you find these you can be sure there is no false prophet present.

"By their fruits you will know them." Your fruits, O Holy Spirit, are the test of a true prophet.

HEARERS AND DOERS

Twelfth Week of the Year, Thursday   Matthew 7:21-29

We have here in this passage the final words of the Sermon on the Mount. The sermon does not drag on to a final end. It comes to a powerful climax and ends.

Jesus tells us not to deceive ourselves nor to try to deceive Him. Don't think that just proclaiming Him Lord in word without substantiating it with deeds in doing the Father's will, will get you into the kingdom. Even if you have received some charismatic gifts of prophecy or healing, this alone is no guarantee of sanctity. St. Paul says the same thing, that without love it is all worth nothing.

Merely hearing and understanding the message of Jesus is not enough of a response. We must also be doers of the Word. Jesus makes it clear that He is giving us a serious challenge. Failure in doing the Word will be like building a house on sand. We'll end with a catastrophe, complete ruin.

The real test is in doing the Father's will. Jesus claims and accepts as an acquaintance and as friend only him who obeys, who does the Father's will, who puts the Word into practice. If we don't He will say "I never knew you. Out of my sight, you evildoers."

Strong words! Yes, but notice how the crowd accepted them. They were spellbound at His teaching because He taught with authority and not like the Scribes.

We have a lesson here from the crowd. Do we accept those leaders in the Church who teach, who speak with authority? Or are we more inclined to accept watered-down teachings, those who are less challenging to us?

> You said, "He who obeys the commandments he has from Me is the man who loves Me . . . I too will love him and reveal myself to him." Thank you, Jesus.

LITTLE THINGS

Twelfth Week of the Year, Friday   **Matthew 8:1-4**

Notice that the leper in the Gospel, who came to beg Christ for a cure, not only came to Him, "he came and did Him homage." Perhaps it was just a bow or genuflection, something small in a way, but Christ in return gave the leper his health, a big reward for a small favor, for a small sign of respect.

So, too, many of God's gifts to us depend on what we give to God. For actual kernels, for little scraps of time or energy or effort Christ makes precious rewards. "A cup of water given in my name shall not be without its reward."

What are some of these little things, these little signs of love, these little scraps for which we receive such big returns from Christ?

There is the little item of morning prayer. It takes just a little scrap of time and effort, but it makes the entire day worthwhile.

A chapter read from the Bible once in a while, even everyday, takes only a few minutes, but a kernel of time. You'll be surprised how richly God will reward it.

A kind word, a kind deed, is another kernel we place in the

outstretched hand of God. He wants it from us to prove our generosity before He returns that kindness a hundredfold. As reward He promised nothing less than the kingdom of heaven. "Come you blessed of My Father, possess the kingdom of heaven. I was hungry and you gave Me to eat; I was thirsty and you gave Me to drink; sick and you visited Me."

Think of it! Heaven for visiting a sick person, for giving a bite to the hungry, a cup of water to the thirsty!

The leper in today's Gospel gave Christ a little special attention. Look at his reward. What are we giving to God: a little prayer, a little Bible reading, a visit to the sick, a kind word? On it depends God's generosity to us.

Happy is he who is faithful in little things, the Lord's reward to him will be great.

SAY BUT THE WORD

Twelfth Week of the Year, Saturday   **Matthew 8:5-17**

This beautiful incident of the centurion's great faith in Jesus points to the future conversion of the Gentiles. Jesus makes it very clear that He is impressed by this faith. But even before the Centurion proves his faith Jesus shows that He is willing to come and cure the servant boy. He has compassion for all, whether they are Jew or Gentile. Is our kindness, our readiness to help just as unprejudiced? Or do we have a little list of those who don't fall within our love?

The faith of the Centurion is unlimited, without conditions. "I am not worthy to have you under my roof. Just give an order and my boy will get better." He believed that Jesus could cure at a distance, without a visit or personal contact. This is the big point of the story. It shows that he believed Jesus to have divine power over all nature.

The Gospel says that Jesus was amazed at the Centurion s faith. He used it as the occasion to teach the crowd. First He says this is more faith than He has found among the Jew, the chosen of God. But unless the chosen children of Abraham start believing, the kingdom will be taken away from them and given to such Gentiles as this Centurion.

We are Christians. We have been chosen to receive the Word, to receive the gifts of faith and love. We belong to God's people. Why is it that we aren't better witnesses to Christ and His good news? Why don't unbelievers point to us and say, "There's something special about those Christians, we'll have to look into it?" Just belonging to the Church is no guarantee of our faith, of our membership in the kingdom. The simple uneducated new convert can completely put us to shame with his unconditional faith.

Jesus, You bore or infirmities, endured our sufferings. We trust in You. Heal us of our weak faith.

THE DAILY CROSS

Thirteenth Week of the Year, Monday　　　　**Matthew 8:18-22**

As the Gospel tells us, Jesus had "nowhere to lay His head."

Born in the cold damp of a stable-cave, He had to flee from a cruel dictator before He was two years old. He suffered what His parents suffered in the strange land of Egypt, for He knew, or at least He felt their loneliness.

He experienced what it means to be poor and unwanted, without friends, without this world's securities. He returned with His parents to Galilee penniless, with the poorest of homes to live in. He learned at a very young age what hard labor means. How often do we stop to think that the greater part of His life was not spent in working wonders, but in quiet, honest, tedious labor? And then we say we cannot imitate Him?

He must have been among the hardest working men of His town: carpentry was an all day job. At any hour He would be called to help a farmer fix his plow, his yoke, his tools, his buildings. His was heavy work with very little pay. His townspeople considered His station humble, and were indignant to see Him appear in public as a leader. When He began preaching and teaching, He was not deceived about glory or human honors. He experienced constant criticism, opposition, the hatred of religious people who should have welcomed Him the most. And I say His Cross is beyond the scope of my life? What of His other burdens? We know from the Gospels that He suffered fatigue, sleepless nights, nights often spent in prayer after He had exhausted Himself healing the sick and instructing the people. He experienced every ingratitude and every unjust treatment. It is hard to think of any human cross that He did not carry before me.

If I could remember how You lived, Jesus, perhaps my burdens would feel much lighter, and my life would become much holier and much happier.

FEAR NOT

Thirteenth Week of the Year, Tuesday   **Matthew 8:23-27**

"Where is your courage? How little faith you have!" With these words Our Lord chides His disciples. But they are also directed to us. He also chides us about being fearful about so many things. It is a very good lesson He wants to teach us. So often we are anxious about so many things without much confidence in God's goodness and power.

We need no proof that fear is very widespread. The poor are afraid that they cannot make ends meet. The rich are afraid they may lose their wealth in the stock market. The less educated are afraid of conversation with the more educated lest they be put to shame. The educated often are afraid of losing social position and prestige. Then you have the superstitious who are afraid of all kinds of nonsense from black cats to walking under ladders.

People without religion or faith are fearful of the uncertainties of life and especially of death. But it is very sad and surprsing to find people with faith, religious people, with vain empty fears.

They are like the disciples in the Gospel today. Although Our Lord Himself was right there with them in the boat when they were caught in the storm, they still cried out in utter dread, "Lord save us!

We are lost!" Jesus in His goodness calmed the sea, but He reproached them for their lack of faith and for their fear in spite of His presence. "Where is your courage? How little faith you have!"

The same rebuke Jesus addresses to us for our petty dreads and foolish fears. We forget that He is ever present in our lives. And so we fear for our health, we are afraid for our children, for our homes.

There are, of course, healthy fears or rather healthy concerns. We should take necessary precautions for our lives, our families, for our moral well-being and for the spiritual welfare of our dear ones. We should have a healthy dread of sin.

But there are so many foolish fears that hinder our work, our happiness and our spiritual life. These are the fears for which Our Lord chides us and asks us to simply remember His constant presence in our lives.

In You, O Lord, I trust. I shall never fear.

OUT WITH YOU!

Thirteenth Week of the Year, Wednesday   Matthew 8:28-34

Jesus had just calmed the storm on Lake Genesareth and now came to the Gadarene territory on the other side of the lake. Having shown His healing power over illnesses and His power over the elements, He now shows that His healing power is complete. He can overcome even the worst evils of life.

The two men coming out of the tombs are described as so horribly possessed by the demons that no one is safe in their presence. The power of Jesus, however, is immediately felt by the demons. They request to be sent into the herd of swine. How appropriate! The swine are considered a very dirty animal. You can expect demons to associate with the unclean, the impure, the perverted.

It just takes a word from Jeşus: "Out with you!" The exorcisms of Jesus show us that we can have His protection from evil if we wish it. But even more, they tell us that Jesus also wants to free us from the fear of demons by showing us that they have no real power. A simple word subdues them. We can overcome them simply by using the name of Jesus. There is power in that name.

An interesting point about this story is the fact that the Gadarenes were not impressed. We have here a miracle that failed to inspire faith. The Gospel simply mentions it and makes no further comment. The Gadarenes did not believe, they were only afraid.

How about us? Isn't it true that many times in our lives the hand of God is at work, there is just no other explanation. God shows us His power and His love. Are we impressed? Does it strengthen our faith, our love, our trust in the Lord? Or are we cold? Or lukewarm?

Hear, O God, my voice in my lament; from the dread enemy preserve my life (Ps 64:1).

POWER OVER SIN

Thirteenth Week of the Year, Thursday   **Matthew 9:1-8**

All through Our Lord's public life He was constantly looking for occasions to teach His message and mission to mankind. On many occasions He showed His divinity by manifesting His power over the ills of the body. But many times He also showed His power and His concern over the ills of the soul at the same time.

Jesus used every opportunity to show His followers that He possessed divine power over sin. He wanted them to know that He could forgive sins on His own right.

One such occasion is recorded in today's Gospel. A paralyzed man was brought to Him. Jesus saw the faith of the man and of those who brought him, and immediately said, "Have courage, son, your sins are forgiven."

At this the Scribes judged Jesus to be blaspheming. Jesus knew what they were thinking and asked them, "Why do you harbor evil thoughts? Which is less trouble to say, 'Your sins are forgiven' or 'Stand up and walk?' To help you realize that the Son of Man has authority on earth to forgive sins"—He then said to the paralyzed man—"Stand up! Roll up your mat and go home."

Jesus shows them that if He has the divine power to heal the man instantly, He surely also has the power to forgive sins. Both require divine power.

It is certainly consoling to know that Christ had this power of forgiveness and that He gave this power to Peter and the other Apostles and their successors. On the first Easter Sunday he appeared to the Apostles and spoke to them: "Peace be with you; as the Father has sent Me so I also send you." Then He breathed on them and said: "Receive the Holy Spirit. If you forgive men's sins, they are forgiven them." From that day on down to this very day the Church has exercised this wonderful power through her sacramental ministers.

We should ask ourselves if we really appreciate this great sacrament of forgiveness. Do we consider it another instance of Our Lord exercising His power of spiritual healing?

Give thanks to the Lord for he is good, His mercy endures forever.

FOLLOW ME

Thirteenth Week of the Year, Friday   **Matthew 9:9-13**

The call of Matthew is very unusual and interesting. It gives us a lot of insight into the ways of God. Matthew was a tax collector; among the Jews a moral reprobate. The Romans farmed out the taxes to bidders. Whoever got the bid on a certain region collected whatever he could to the very limit, to make as much profit as possible. In a sense they were traitors to their own people. Such a man was Matthew.

All this makes it so much more surprising how quickly he responded to the call of Christ to follow Him. The Gospel simply says, "Matthew got up and followed Him." He followed Christ with the same promptness as the fishermen.

Christ certainly must have had an attractive and dynamic personality to bring about such a change in a man like Matthew: from the tax collector's table to Apostleship!

Such Apostles are still needed today more than ever. Christ is still approaching all kinds of Matthews at their various occupations with His call. It can come at various ages, it can be heard quietly in the secrets of our hearts, or it can come more openly.

The very fact that today, more than ever, many young people want to do something worthwhile with their lives, shows that they have open hearts. They have a desire to serve—to give themselves for the betterment of the human race. Somehow or other we must help them also hear Christ's call to serve. A vocation to the priesthood and religious life is a dedication to service, to give one's life completely to others, as Christ did.

This takes generosity but what joy this generosity will bring. It takes generosity on the part of parents to give their son or daughter but again what joy it brings. By losing son or daughter they regain them a hundredfold.

If we hear Christ's words, "Follow Me," we should rise up immediately, as Matthew did, and follow Christ to a life of service to God and man.

"Here I am Lord, send me" (Is 6:8).

NEW WINE

Thirteenth Week of the Year, Saturday   Matthew 9:14-17

John the Baptist, and his disciples lived a very ascetical life. He came to call people to repentance, to do penance for sin. It was very appropriate that they should fast. These disciples, however, were puzzled why Jesus' disciples did not fast.

Jesus in His answer uses very figurative language, but the meaning is clear. Fasting is a sign of mourning, of grief, of penance. Certainly, then, it is out of place at a wedding. While Jesus, the groom, is with His own, there should be joy, there should be an atmosphere of freedom and love.

Fasting is good. But it must be done freely and appropriately as to time, place and manner. Fasting must not be an end in itself.

Jesus goes on to speak about the whole new way of life that He is introducing. He makes it clear that He is not just inserting a few new ideas, new interpretations on the Old Law. You shouldn't patch new cloth onto an old garment. You shouldn't put new wine into old wine skins. In the same way His message must not be confused with the Old Law. His Gospel, His Good News is news, it is all new. Jesus came to put us into an entirely new relationship with God, a relationship of friendship and love and not of fear.

We, too, have been called to a new life. Through Baptism we are reborn. Maybe God has given us a renewed spirit in our faith, a new relationship of love with Him. Why do we hang on to the old? Why do we try to reconcile our old ways, our selfish and earthly interests, with the Lord's call to this new life? We must die to that old self and not try to compromise.

Jesus, by the power of Your Spirit make our Baptism come alive. Make all things new as we live under the law of love.

HIS TOUCH TODAY

Fourteenth Week of the Year, Monday   **Matthew 9:18-26**

We find two miracles narrated in the Gospel today. There is something very similar in these two incidents. It has to do with the touch of Christ and faith in this touch. A synagogue leader came up to Christ, did Him reverence, and said, "My daughter has just died. Please come and lay your hand on her and she will come back to life." He simply believes that if Jesus comes and touches her she will rise again. He sees with faith that Christ has power over life and death. His faith in Christ's touch is rewarded, for when He arrives at the house He takes the girl by the hand and she arises.

The woman suffering for years from hemorrhages shows equally great faith in the touch of Christ. "If only I can touch His cloak," she thought, "I shall get well." Again it was her great faith that cured her. "Courage, daughter! Your faith has restored you to health." This was Christ's response to her faith in His touch.

We see in the decisive actions of Jesus that He wanted to touch these people personally and bring them grace and mercy. Elsewhere in the Gospels we read, "The sick were brought to Him and He touched them all."

This is why Our Lord came, that as our faith reaches up to touch Him, so His power and His goodness may reach out to touch us.

In His lifetime Jesus came in contact with men of faith by His physical presence, His words, His actions. He wished and He planned to continue this presence by words and actions. In the sacraments Jesus continues to touch us; by words and actions, as often as we reach out to Him with faith.

In the Holy Eucharist Christ is here to touch us bodily, to nourish us and make us holy. In penance His words are here to forgive and heal us. We hear them through the priest and we are assured. In His Church the power of Christ, His words, His actions continue to touch us.

We thank You, Lord, for your constant presence and personal touch in the sacraments.

SEVEN NEW DEMONS

Fourteenth Week of the Year, Tuesday   **Matthew 9:32-38**

Jesus casts out one demon and at once seven more appear: jealous Pharisees. And isn't it always like that? You get rid of one problem, and seven more are waiting for you right behind it. As the scientist and the doctor discover a vaccine to conquer one virus, seven new mutations appear. As Jesus said on another occasion, "One devil driven out goes on to find seven others for the next invasion." Such is mankind's problem: ever conquering one enemy to find seven more.

"His heart was moved with pity at the sight of the crowds." Matthew had observed the compassion and understanding of Jesus. The harvest was great, but the laborers were too few. There was always too much work left to do. Is it any different today?

While physical labor can be taken over by machinery, what about the human things that need to be done? It was the empty, lonely, unhappy and meaningless lives of men that concerned Jesus. In the impoverished societies, the work that remains to be done is staggering. Millions and millions of people suffer an existence that is less than human. In the wealthier societies like ours, there are deeper forms of loneliness and unhappiness and emptiness that must be conquered.

Patience with these problems does not mean inactivity. Some people *sit* and wait: nothing changes, nothing improves. Some others work feverishly and rush headlong into every new project, and the merry-go-round stops with bigger troubles than when it started. If only we could do both in unity and balance: work and wait.

Both patience and determined effort must be our pattern for every problem. That is the pattern clearly set by Christ. We have many struggles on a worldwide scale: population, starvation, standard of living, tyranny, aggression and war. We have many other problems right at home. Great effort and hard labor are needed. But every effort for justice, order, peace, and freedom requires intelligent patience. We need much wisdom and love; we need to work and to wait.

> Wake us up, O Lord, awake us,
> Let Your call, O Lord, remake us,
> Let Your power overtake us!

SHARE YOUR GIFTS

**Fourteenth Week of the Year, Wednesday		Matthew 10:1-7**

Jesus summons His twelve disciples, gives them power over unclean Spirits and all manner of diseases and tells them to go out and proclaim the Good News: "The reign of God is at hand." For this reason they are called "Apostles." They are the ones who are sent out on mission.

We are all Apostles or missionaries in some respects. We all are to bear witness to the reign of God, to the Good News. We have received the message of Christ, we have been given the gift of faith. Now we must share it.

Jesus tells the Apostles, "The gift you have received, give as a gift." Give without expecting anything in return except your bare necessities.

What gifts had the apostles received? Faith in the message,—"The reign of God is here"—authority over demons, power to heal the sick, to raise the dead. These gifts they were to use for the good of others without any advantage to themselves.

We, too, have received gifts from the Lord which He wants us to share. What are some of these gifts? We all enjoy the gift of life, the energy of our bodies, our senses. We have received various gifts of grace: faith, hope, love, probably some gifts of the Spirit. All these we must be willing to share with others at opportune times without expecting any return. Do you have time on your hands? Visit the elderly and bring them some of the joy you have received. Read to them, pray with them. There are so many ways in which you can share the gifts you have received.

How is it best to give? How will the gift be received most graciously and with love? Jesus tells us to go without trappings, without any big show. Travel light if you want to be a true disciple of the Lord. When the gift comes with a lot of trappings or show, it is hard to receive. It does not come in love.

Help us, Lord, to give freely of ourselves and our gifts.

EXPECT REJECTION

Fourteenth Week of the Year, Thursday   **Matthew 10:7-15**

Jesus advises, "If anyone does not receive you or listen to what you have to say, leave that town or house." The Lord tells us to expect rejection in bringing the Good News. Sometimes that rejection can take rather violent forms, as we know.

An interesting example of this is found in the diary of St. Athanasius, fourth century bishop of Alexandria, Egypt. One

Saturday night he and his people were having a late Vigil Service in his cathedral. (These late night Bible Vigils made better Christians than our late, late TV shows.) Near midnight there was a loud noise outside the church doors, and Athanasius suspected what was happening. The heretical Arian party—political as well as heretical—had surrounded the church and were going to attack the Catholics inside and take Athanasius prisoner.

As the attackers began breaking down the cathedral door, Athanasius intoned the beautiful psalm, "Give thanks to the Lord of lords, for His mercy endures forever." He continued to lead each verse and the people roared the answer, "His mercy endures forever." Undaunted, the invaders made their way down the aisle toward the altar, where Athanasius stood leading the psalm. At the center of the church the people surrounded the Arians and a hot riot began. During the fray someone knocked out Athanasius, and his friends carried him out to safety while the battle raged on.

This remarkable escape was followed by a few months of hiding, after which Athanasius, champion of orthodoxy, returned to his post to lead his people toward the final peace. In his preaching, this saint had insisted upon the divinity of Christ, and the rejection of this doctrine by Arians degenerated into a violent political struggle. Athanasius had to take the advice of Jesus, "if they persecute you in one city, flee to another" (Mt 10:23).

> Lord, if we are "knocked out" at times, or chased from city to city, or perhaps just ridiculed for our faith, who are we to complain? The "rejection syndrome" places us in the company of some very interesting saints—including You, the Saint of Saints.

THE CROOKED ROAD TO GLORY

Fourteenth Week of the Year, Friday   **Matthew 10:16-23**

Jesus never hesitated to predict that His Church and His true followers would undergo severe trials. The weak-kneed would see only a dark future. But always, Jesus came through with a great note of optimism, an assurance of deep interior joy gained through these sufferings. "Whoever holds out to the end will be saved."

Can we really be optimists by habit? Can there be a bright fire of happiness deep inside all the time, even when everything is going wrong? Most of us, if we've lived long enough, remember feeling so dark and dismal that we could light up a room just by leaving it. There seems to be so much about us that isn't destined to a glorious future. Yet, that's the whole fact of our lives: we are to pass into glory with Christ! Through sorrow and death we are to reach resurrection and eternal happiness. If life doesn't mean that, what does it mean?

Our trouble, naturally, is with the present state of affairs: we are in the stage of suffering and dying with Christ. That's never been very easy. But was it easy for Christ?

If anything comes through clear in the life of Jesus, it's the daily failures. He didn't succeed in beating Herod out of his crown, but had to run off to Egypt. Later on Jesus often had to beat a hasty retreat. There were always temple police around, wanting to arrest Him. He hadn't been a booming success as a carpenter at Nazareth, either. He didn't get any richer than any other working men. He didn't even seem to be a successful teacher, if you are to count His friends at the end when He needed them, or if you are to consider the enthusiasm His people had for defending Him in several courtrooms.

But He gave His life in this way, to teach us what all of life really means. A strange mystery, but that's the way God chose to live it. Can we trust His infinite wisdom? Can we follow this very crooked road to final glory and happiness? Who are we, really, to argue the matter with God?

Lord, increase our faith!

AFRAID AND NOT AFRAID

Fourteenth Week of the Year, Saturday   **Matthew 10:24-33**

In His teaching Jesus brought out many an interesting paradox.

So in today's Gospel He says, "Do *not* be afraid," and then He says, "*Do* be afraid." Do not be afraid of your audience; have no fear of what people will say; don't fear even those who would kill you, says Jesus. But do be afraid of him who could send your *soul* into the fire! Be afraid of what goes on in your heart: be afraid of your weaker self, and of the evil one who can team up with that weaker self to destroy you.

Have you ever noticed how people can become great and noble when faced with the question of life and death; in times of sudden tragedy or disaster, as in a flood when a wall of water starts rushing in and they are faced with immediate danger of death? Not just one, but many people, young and old, have been on their way to safety but went back, risking their lives to help someone else. Many have died trying to save others. In the face of death, of meeting God, suddenly all the old hatreds and prejudices go, and people become unselfish, thoughtful, loving, self-giving. The closer we feel to God, the better we are. It does something for us—changes us for the better.

So Jesus says, "Yes, be afraid of God: be concerned about what God thinks of you, but don't worry about the gossips for they talk without thinking anyway."

Yet at the very time that Jesus says "Be afraid of God" He also says, "Don't be afraid of God: He is your loving Father; He will take care of you—so completely that He has the hair on your head counted!"

So we have to strike a good balance between fear and love. When love is real, there is surely less to fear. If love is real, we are not afraid, we don't fear being found out, we are honest with the one we truly love. And yet, we *are* afraid: afraid to hurt the one we love, afraid of becoming selfish or dishonest or unfaithful. True love has a fear in it: a fear "that some day I might take my beloved for granted."

Lord, let us be concerned, even afraid of what goes on in our inner heart: it is there that love must be real if it is to survive.

TOTAL COMMITMENT

Fifteenth Week of the Year, Monday   Matthew 10:34-11:1

Some of Our Lord's words in this Gospel passage are shocking. He says that He came not to spread peace, but division. The Prince of Peace says that He came to bring divisions, to set people at odds. Strange. But Our Lord can't help this. If a man goes all out for Christ and the rest of his family doesn't, it is no fault of Christ.

Christ demands total commitment, "Whoever loves father or mother, son or daughter more than Me is not worthy of Me. He who seeks only himself brings himself to ruin." Christ makes it clear that self-seeking is the opposite of real self-fulfillment, "Whereas he who brings himself to nought for Me," Christ says, "discovers who he is." Such a one has no identity problem. He knows himself, knows his place.

Our Lord's words make it clear that He does not want any wishy-washy application of His doctrine of love. He confronts people with a clear cut choice, either for or against Him. Even close family ties are no excuse for not following Christ.

Are we authentic, genuine Christians? Do we understand that Christ's doctrine of love may cause divisions among our closest friends? Are we courageous enough to confront others with the Gospel message? Are we willing to live lives that may be a reproach to someone dear to us? Christianity is not for slackers. It demands commitment, it demands service, unstinting service, to our fellow men, especially to the poor and oppressed.

But herein is also our reward, our fulfillment, our true discovery of self. We have this on Christ's own words. "I promise you that whoever gives a cup of cold water to one of these lowly ones will not want for his reward."

I say to the Lord, "My Lord are you: apart from You I have no good" (Ps 16:2).

WONDERS WITHOUT FAITH

Fifteenth Week of the Year, Tuesday **Matthew 11:20-24**

Jesus is very human. He is disappointed with the towns of Galilee where He had spent so much time preaching and performing miracles. He had shown them His love and compassion by the many healings He had worked. Yet they failed to accept Him. Certainly the works showing His divine power and authority should have moved them to faith. True, they came to Him in large crowds, the Gospels continuously tell us, but they must have remained unmoved by His preaching, His proclamation of the Kingdom. They came merely to see what they could get out of Him by way of his miraculous powers, a cure, a demon expelled. It would save them medical expenses and other inconveniences.

The Gospels seem to indicate that Jesus found very few true followers in Galilee in spite of all His favors shown to that province. Even though these towns of Galilee were favored with special graces, temporal and spiritual, they failed to respond. Jesus now predicts that it will not go well with them because of this lack of faith.

Who of us would dare say that he hasn't been similarly favored. Perhaps not with physical signs and wonders, but with many gifts of graces as well as gifts of nature. We have a body with a measure of health, we have senses, we have a mind to think, energy to work. We have the gift of faith, we have God's Word, we have the freedom to worship and pray, the privilege to hear God's voice in our hearts in prayer. We are blessed to live in this country of plenty and freedom.

What is our response? Do we give God the credit? Is He Lord of everything in our lives? Do we use our gifts in faith to share them with others? Are we concerned that many do not enjoy the gifts we have. Does it really disturb us in Christian love? It should. It should shock us into sharing our gifts in whatever way possible.

Jesus, thank You for Your gifts. May You never be disappointed in me.

TO MEREST CHILDREN

Fifteenth Week of the Year, Wednesday **Matthew 11:25-27**

What a beautiful prayer of thanksgiving to the Father is the Gospel today! Jesus thanks the Father for His disciples and for the understanding that has been given to them, who were intellectually mere children. "What you have hidden from the learned and clever you have revealed to the merest children."

Jesus here is contrasting the little ones, the disciples, with the educated and the wise, in particular, the Scribes and the Pharisees. He acknowledges that it was the Father's will that only the uneducated had accepted His message so far. Only a few peasants, fishermen and working people had followed Him because of His teaching and not merely because of His miracles. This, Jesus says, is the work of the Father. The good news is not grasped by wisdom and reason; it is only known through revelation and faith. Not that revelation was denied the wise and educated in the Jewish community. Jesus clearly proclaimed the good news, the revelation of His kingdom to all, and substantiated it with miracles. But only the simple had accepted it and received the insight given by the Father.

In a very real sense Jewish wisdom and learning, which mainly amounted to a thorough knowledge of the old law, was a genuine obstacle to understanding Jesus' message of the new law. The stronger the attachment to the law, the less open they were to change, to the new law, the new covenant.

We also must be sure to always have an open mind to the message that comes to us from the Gospels, as they are revealed to us through the Church, through events in our lives, through charismatic and prophetic preachers and public figures. Today we live in a world of rapid change in all areas. We must be open to new ways of applying the Gospel message to our lives. We must be open to accept new ways which others may be living the Gospel message. Let us graciously thank the Father for whatever insight He gives us to the message of Jesus.

"Unless you become like little children, you shall not enter the Kingdom of God" (Mt 18:3).

DONE CAN BE UNDONE

Fifteenth Week of the Year, Thursday   Matthew 11:28-30

In the madness of despair over her guilt, Lady Macbeth is heard muttering, "What, will these hands ne'er be clean? . . . Here's the smell of the blood still . . . What's done cannot be undone." She has lost hope in the possibility of deliverance from her sin. She sees her soul a ruin beyond repair, and in her depression she commits suicide.

Wherever Jesus went in His public life, wherever He worked miracles to heal suffering, His first concern was always, "Take heart, your sins are forgiven." His whole attitude, His words and actions said, "I read your heart; I know your regret and sorrow. But rejoice, I have come to find what was lost; I have come to rebuild what has fallen to ruin. What's done is done, but I shall undo it, and I shall give you many opportunities to undo it with Me and because of Me. Every good word, every gesture of love, every thought of faith and sorrow, every self-denial and generous deed shall repair what was done."

"Come to me, all you who are weary and find life burdensome, and I will refresh you." What's done is done, but it can indeed be undone! Christian repentance is the very opposite of despair. It is full of hope and joy. It knows how to blend remorse with joyous response to God's forgiveness.

It was to repair the fallen house, to open the closed heart, to guide our feet in the way of peace, that Christ the Redeemer came. He brought us forgiveness, inspiration, and grace to undo what was done.

> **The Lord rose up to save me,**
> **His strong support he gave me,**
> **His mercy set me free:**
> **O Lord, I know You love me,**
> **Your guiding hand above me,**
> **In fortune or calamity.**

FEAR OF THE CRITICS

Fifteenth Week of the Year, Friday   **Matthew 12:1-8**

Throughout His public life, Jesus is hounded by protesting Pharisees. Am I afraid of criticism? Do I hesitate to do what is right because of what "important" people might say? For what did the Pharisees criticize Jesus? Nearly everything! For having friends who were "not in good standing." It mattered little to them that Jesus had come to save not the just but sinners—that is, those who know they are sinners.

They criticized Jesus for letting a "sinful woman" anoint His feet. They criticized Jesus for eating and drinking, for accepting invitations to dine with "sinners," for forgiving an adulteress, for breaking the law by healing the sick on the Sabbath, for letting His hungry disciples pick corn on the Sabbath. In the end, they accused Him of causing sedition and revolution, of blaspheming and declaring that He was the Son of God!

When His disciples informed Jesus that the Pharisees took offense at His words, because they were words of power and justice, Jesus gave His answer to the Pharisees of all times: "Every plant that my heavenly Father has not planted will be uprooted. Let them alone; they are blind guides of blind men. And if one blind man guides another, both fall into the pit" (Mt 15:14).

Lord Jesus, make me understand how foolish it is to live by mere human judgments. If others accuse me with good reason, let me be honest enough to admit the truth. But if ever I make human praise the end and standard of what I do, I am a traitor to You and to myself.

Remove the sackcloth from the wasted frame,
Let glory round the weakened shoulder spread his cloak,
And praise your Savior—Justice is His Name!—
Whose tender mercies never fail His humble folk

                                        (Is 61:3)

WE NEED HIM

Fifteenth Week of the Year, Saturday   Matthew 12:14-21

In the Gospel we see Jesus dealing with two kinds of people: 1) the Pharisees, who think they don't need Jesus, and even hate Him: "The Pharisees began to plot against Jesus to find a way to destroy Him." 2) the outcasts, the so-called "sinners" who know they need Jesus and want Him: "Many people followed Him and He cured them all."

Jesus when speaking of the joy in heaven over repentant sinners says, "I came for those who know they need my healing power, not for those who are 'so good' that they don't need me." So Jesus says it is not "the healthy" but the infirm who need the doctor. He came so that the ailing and failing might enjoy new life and new strength.

Too often in the past we Christians have not made use of the healing power of Jesus. But He wants us to do so! Everywhere in the Gospels we see Jesus either in the act of healing someone, or just on His way to go and heal someone, or just returning from having healed someone. The sick were brought to Jesus "and He healed them all." The people knew that Jesus was a powerful prophet on whom the power of God rested. He healed the crippled and blind, the insane, the depressed and disturbed, and the repentant sinners. He made saints out of sinners—what they knew was great spiritual power!

We see in the Gospels that Jesus wanted His followers to do the same. He said to the apostles, "cure the sick, raise the dead, heal lepers, expel devils" (Mt 10:8). Jesus wants His Church to do this work of healing—through the Sacraments, through prayer for healing, through communities of faith.

But this may require a greater faith and trust than we have had, and a much closer relationship to Jesus, so that living in Him and with Him daily, we can experience His great power in our lives and in those around us.

> **The prophet Hosea says, "Let's strive to know the Lord," and he adds, "He will come to us like the rain" (6:3). The dry ground needs the rain, and the farmer welcomes the rain because he knows he must have it. Is this the way we welcome you, Lord? Do we feel the**

same desperate need for You? If not, we do not know
You.

NO GREATER SIGN

Sixteenth Week of the Year, Monday   Matthew 12:38-42

"Teacher, we want to see you work some signs." A shallow
question, the product of shallow minds. "Entertain us, Master. Just
now we haven't anything better to do." To a very superficial request,
the Lord's answer is far from superficial. His people are ignoring
Christ's real mission, but Christ has not forgotten it. They shall not
have their shallow curiosity satisfied, but for whoever is seriously
looking for a sign from God, they shall have one that will astound the
world and shock all history. It will be the Sign of the prophet Jonah, a
man who converted not his own people, but foreigners, sincere men
who accepted faith when it was given to them.

In this "Sign of Jonah" Jesus predicted two events: His own
glorious Resurrection, and the conversion of a new race, a new
people, who would listen to Him when His own people had closed
their ears. These foreign people, accepting the Savior with joy, would
be on hand to judge those chosen people who had rejected Him. What
greater sign could the Pharisees have wanted?

What greater sign did the Pharisees need? Was not the very sign of
their envy and hatred, their unbelief and their prejudice—was not this
a sign that Jesus was a true prophet of God? For so had the chosen
people treated all their prophets. Isaiah and Jeremiah, the greatest of
their prophets, had been put to death by their own people.

They would be given a sign for all the world to see: they would
deliver Jesus up to a most shameful death, and His friends would
bury Him, thinking it was the end, another sad farewell to a great
prophet.

As Jonah reappeared the third day, so now here would be a sign to
outdo all signs of God's approval. Jesus would rise in glory and in
that Resurrection all nations could find salvation. What greater sign
of God's goodness and mercy and love?

"Roll back the grave-stone, comrades, the Lord has broken out!
He's here to keep His promise: let glory sing and shout!"

WHO DARES CLIMB?

Sixteenth Week of the Year, Tuesday   Matthew 12:46-50

"Whoever does the will of my heavenly Father is brother and
sister and mother to me."

Some day I hope to see the gates of heaven roll back to receive me.
Remembering that heaven is full of saints, I should take notice of
what stuff saints are made. I marvel at how pure their intentions were.
And sometimes I even tell myself, how I wish I could do great things
in God; and then a small temptation comes along, and I know again
that I can't even do small things in God. I console myself by thinking,
"God can't expect that much of me. There are too many other people
like me—proud, selfish, critical, stubborn, envious, gossipy, unfair,
unkind. Yet all these people must expect to get to heaven as I do. God
can't be so demanding."

Yet I'm bothered by the kind of people I'm afraid I'll find in
heaven. Won't I feel a bit embarrassed among them? Those ancient
saints who fled to the desert, who died all kinds of cruel deaths rather
than disobey the smallest of God's laws?

Perhaps I had better move on to my contemporaries for
consolation. The Roman martyrs have so little comfort to offer. But
here is more trouble for me than ever! Millions of men and women,
boys, girls, all ages, from all countries, and all of them far too good
for me. Which of them enjoyed my comfortable life? Which of them
was so honored and befriended? They will surely make me uneasy,
because they all fought against the gods of this world, and found the
true God. What I have, they would have despised—money, honors,
pleasures, comforts, vain ambitions. They spent themselves for one
thing: the glory of God. That is what today's saints are doing.

I look about me in this strange heaven, bewildered at the great,
strong, courageous heroes of God. I shudder at the things they have
done. Is it in *this* heaven, among *these* people, that I expect a reserved

seat? If it is, then I must pay the price—some day, somewhere, some way, I must pay the price.

Jesus, give me the courage to answer Your call to this great company!

FALLING SEED

Sixteenth Week of the Year, Wednesday **Matthew 13:1-9**

The seed is the word of God, said Jesus. And it falls on different kinds of ground. Some ground is good, some is too thorny or too rocky. And such ground doesn't give the seed a chance.

God speaks to us in many ways. That seed is falling on us every day, by whatever happens to us. For God intends all of it, you know. What kind of ground do you give His seed?

Let me give you an example from true life. A young couple just had their first child. Unfortunately, the little boy was born terribly deformed, without either of his arms: just two stumps at the shoulders. The child's father went into black despair, cursing God and fate and his doctor for having let the child live. The father saw only the dark side.

Naturally, bird-happy optimism would seem out of place, too. You could hardly expect the parents to smile happily and say, "Well, at least he'll never become a pick-pocket."

But the mother's attitude is worthy of note. She looked at her child and said, "Poor little fellow. He's going to need a lot of help. Thank God we're able to give it to him." This is the Christian attitude: facing the reality with hope, with courage and with faith. She is letting the seed fall on good ground.

If the child's father has any faith, if there is even a little of Christ's love in him, he will come to love that child for what he is. He will deeply regret having wished him dead because of something he happened to be missing.

Christ loves us in spite of what we don't have, in spite of how little we are. He is not blind to our sinfulness and weakness, but He continues to hold out opportunity for us. He continues to let the heavenly seed fall on us, waiting and hoping that we will learn to prepare the ground.

> "Let justice fall like gentle rain from out the sky,
> And open, Earth, to wisdom from the Lord on high!"

PARABLES' PURPOSE

Sixteenth Week of the Year, Thursday   Matthew 13:10-17

Jesus was a great preacher. He spoke the language of the people. He used stories, made comparisons, used examples, all from the everyday life of the people He was speaking to.

Yet sometimes He used parables that were a bit puzzling. He liked to use language that would make the good listener think.

So when the disciples asked Him why He spoke to the people in parables, His answer shows that He wanted His listeners to hear with open hearts. The parables open up the mysteries of the kingdom of God to believers, those who are open. But to those who are not open to Jesus' message they become vagaries without meaning. Jesus says that those whose hearts are closed will not understand.

The important thing is a personal response. If there is no openness Jesus' message is not even heard. If there is no response to the message heard, it will not remain. Faith is indeed a gift, but it does not take away our responsibility to open our hearts to the Word and to respond to the Word when heard.

Scripture can be puzzling, vague, if we just read with shallow mind and heart. It must be read in a prayerful way, with an openness that may receive whatever the Spirit wants to reveal to us.

Spiritual food, spiritual knowledge is not like physical food. The more you partake of it, the hungrier you become. The more you open up, the more spiritual insight you receive. While just an occasional reading of the Scripture will leave us cold and without relish.

As we read Scripture, as we hear God's Word, we must open our hearts to whatever He wants to say. And when we have heard, when the message is clear, we must act. Otherwise it will be taken from us. The message of the Christian life will stay in us only if we live that life to the full. We have been given that message, loud and clear, as well as in parables. What has been our response?

Lord, Jesus, I open my heart to Your Word, to hear it as well as to live it.

SOIL AND SEED

Sixteenth Week of the Year, Friday   **Matthew 13:18-23**

"Mark well, then, the parable of the sower." With these words today's Gospel passage begins the interpretation of the famous parable. It is first of all made very clear that the seed represents the message about God's reign, His will, His commandments. The ground or soil represents the various types of members in the Church, those who have heard the message of Christ, who know God's will, who are aware of His commandments and have accepted them in various degrees. But this acceptance, this faith is not always persevering.

Today let us ask ourselves what kind of ground this message of God, especially His commandments, falls on in our own lives.

Sometimes we may feel God's commandments are unreasonable, outmoded, old fashioned, not for our enlightened age. It is then, the parable says, that the evil one approaches us to steal away what was sown in our minds by God's word.

Do we stick to God's word through thick and thin, in adversity as well as in prosperity? Or are we like the rocky patches of ground? Do we joyfully live it when easy and agreeable, but shirk it when it means carrying the cross with Christ? As the Gospels says, "When some setback or persecution involving the message occurs, he soon falters."

Perhaps we keep God's precepts quite regularly. But when it comes to money and living in ease and comfort we lose our sights. The lure of money may choke out the message. We see sins of injustice as simply good business. We look at our ease and our comfortable living as absolute necessities of life, and so reason that we have very little to give to the support of the Church, the Missions; very little to give to the uplifting of the poor and oppressed.

O Lord, let me not be barren, rocky weed-filled ground, but good soil on which the seed of Your word may yield a hundredfold.

A PRAYER FOR PATIENCE

Sixteenth Week of the Year, Saturday   Matthew 13:24-30

"Pull up the weeds and you might take the wheat along with them. Let them grow together until harvest." Let's talk to Jesus about today's parable. Let's make it a "Prayer for Patience."

Lord Jesus, You know that patience comes very hard for me. I need to talk to You about this over and over. I do know how long You have endured my sinfulness. And You know how impatient I have been with others. Perhaps I don't really understand Your patience with my neighbor, Lord.

In the parable of the wheat and weeds You enlighten me on Your divine patience, Lord. You sowed good seed in Your people's hearts. The field You speak of is our life in this world. Since Adam's sin, the evil one, Satan, has sown an abundant crop of weeds in us, too.

You are the Harvester, Jesus, and You allow both the wheat and the weeds to grow until the time of harvest, the time of separating good crop from the useless, the time of judgment. And that day of reckoning is in Your hands, not mine. I cannot see clearly into the heart of my neighbor, so I cannot be his or her judge.

I can trust in You, Lord, the just judge, the reader of minds and hearts, the Patient One. You see the truth, Jesus, but You wait. As You have waited all my life for my repentance, can I not wait all my life for my neighbor's repentance? Whence comes my haste to convert my neighbor before the time Your Providence knows well, Lord?

Did You not say in a parable that the Lord said to His unforgiving servant, "I forgave all your debts. Should you not have forgiven your fellow-servant just as I forgave you?" Lord Jesus, I know well how patient and long-suffering You have been with me. I know how You endure me with boundless love. Lord, let that knowledge teach me love and patience toward my brothers and sisters. Let my prayer of love win Your grace and help for them. Amen.

THE LEAVEN OF GRACE

Seventeenth Week of the Year Monday,   **Matthew 13:31-35**

I'm quite sure that most of us have an alarm clock; and how we need them! Tell this watchman when you must get up, and he counts the seconds till that time and then wakes you from sleep. He merely gives the signal. He can't lift you out of bed.

Here we have a bit of a picture of the yeast talked about in the Gospel today, the leaven of the kingdom of God which is grace, the real leaven in a Christian's life. Actual grace may touch us any moment of the day, like a soft summer breeze, or like the rush of a storm cloud and the force of thunder. Or it may again come through a word spoken by a friend, a glance, a picture.

What is this wonderful leaven called grace? Actual grace is a help from God to live as true Christians. We receive it many times a day. It is an unmerited interior help which God gives us to strengthen us, when strength is needed, to warn us when caution is dictated, to give us joy, courage, hope beyond the human.

It is God's alarm clock ringing in us. But it does more than the alarm; it not only tells us to get up, but also gives us a boost, it helps us to rise from sin, to rise above the mere natural.

St. Paul, writing to the Philippians, says, "It is God who works in you both to will and to accomplish." That is actual grace. It not only inspires us to the good, but helps us to accomplish it. We will desire what is good only if our minds are enlightened. We must first know what is good. So we must not shut out the grace of knowledge. We must be open to the light, willing to do good reading, to think, to pray. We must keep the blinds open.

Yet even when we have been enlightened to know right from

wrong we need the leaven of grace to raise us up to doing the right. God gives us this help, this strength, the drive and the desire to do what He wants. We all get these urgings in our inmost being, but too often we pay no attention to them.

"If I settle at the farthest limits of the sea, even Your hand shall guide me" (Ps 139:9, 10).

WHEAT AND WEEDS

Seventeenth Week of the Year, Tuesday   Matthew 13:35-43

Many of Christ's parables of the Kingdom of Heaven concern the problem of good and evil, and how God wants them both to be in our lives, but eventually they must be separated. In this parable the wheat is to be saved: it has the only value. The weeds are to be burned. The harvest time is the time of decision, the time of judgment, when good must be separated from evil.

Can we take an extremely simple view of this: the wheat are good people, the weeds are the bad? Is this in line with most of our experience? Do we find the all-good and the all-bad? Or do we rather see in ourselves, each of us, that we are both—wheat and weeds, good and evil. And sooner or later, before we can enjoy true happiness and the reward of heaven, all the evil must be cast off and burned?

Yes, each of us unfortunately is growing a double crop, some good wheat mixed with some pretty awful weeds. And the weeds must be burned away before the wheat is good enough to be stored for future happiness. That is why God sends us suffering; that is why we must sacrifice, deny ourselves, make up for our neglect. Weeds grow in a neglected garden. So the weeds of which Christ speaks are those evils that grow in a neglected soul.

One other reality we see: many of us, unhappily, do not complete this weeding out process before God calls us and tells us, "Your time is up." That is why we believe in a purgatory, a place of purification. We find it reasonable to hope for a way in which the rest of our weeds can be burned away, so that only the good wheat is left. Perfect happiness is for perfect people, so in heaven no evil can remain.

Hence the urgent need for good works on our part: to accomplish as much of this purification as we can on earth. God made us to help one another. Remember to be generous, kind, and unselfish. Remember to pray for you neighbor: the life you save may be your own!

**Lord, as we return to You,
Heal our hearts, our lives renew.**

I FOUND IT!

Seventeenth Week of the Year, Wednesday   Matthew 13:44-46

In this little parable, Jesus says He knows something we don't know. He calls that something a "buried treasure."

Look at the parable: the man is out plowing his field when suddenly—klunk! He says, "Since klunks have rarely blessed my life, I shall investigate this klunk!" He stops and digs it up. Surprise! He runs all the way home to his wife and he excitedly announces, "Honey! I found it! I found it!"

She eyes him suspiciously. "How much is it going to cost?"

He says, "I'll sell everything for it! Everything!"

She says, "You have flipped out! Did you get hooked by one of those free trips?"

Jesus is saying to us here, "If you knew what I know, you'd make the Kingdom of God the priority in your life!"

"Oooh, Lord! That means—I make it *first!*"

The Lord answers, "You do, and you'll be amazed at what happens! Some may stumble on this treasure quite suddenly and get zapped by it, like St. Paul, while others may have searched for it for years, but both must give up everything to have that treasure and keep it. Because," Jesus says, "that treasure takes care of all your problems—whether political, social, economic, psychological or marital—all problems."

I answer, "Lord—do you mean—that treasure is a cure-all?"

"Yes!" He says, "Because, brother or sister, when God finishes establishing His Kingdom in you, you have *changed!*"

"Lord, are you trying to get me into heaven?"

"No," says the Lord. "I am trying to get heaven into you! I establish My Kingdom in you in order to establish My Kingdom through you. So kick out the old sins, expand your spiritual capacity, adjust your life radically, till the Kingdom of God is the very first thing in your life, so that when anyone bumps into you, the treasure spills out."

Jesus, Your treasure conquers sin, self, and Satan, so that we may rise in victory with You.

WORTHWHILE OR USELESS

Seventeenth Week of the Year, Thursday   · **Matthew 13:47-53**

The parable of the dragnet thrown into the lake is the last in Matthew's parable discourse. It is similar to the parable of the weeds which we find earlier in this chapter thirteen.

The reign of God is likened to a net full of all sorts of things, all sorts of fish, those edible and those not. All that are worthwhile, good-eating fish, are kept. The rest, the useless, are thrown away. So the reign of God here on earth, whether taken as the whole Church or a smaller section, a parish or a community, gathers all sorts. It harbors them until judgment time when the good will be separated forever from the evil.

As individuals we belong to the kingdom. We are a part of the Church, of a parish, of a community. Which side are we on? Are we worthwhile members? There can be no middle ground. Either we are committed Christians or we are useless, a drag on the kingdom.

The parables of the dragnet and the weeds make it quite clear that there can be no complete peace in this life. Jesus says very clearly that this is possible only at the judgment. Yet He said, "Blessed are the peacemakers." We are not excused from trying to bring more people to a true commitment to Christ, to become worthwhile members.

Have we understood all this? If our answer is "yes," Jesus says we should be able to reconcile the old with the new. We should be able to see that in God's Kingdom everything of true value has its place, whether Old Testament or New, whether traditional in the Church or new insights. Are our minds and hearts open to the worthwhile, wherever it is found? Or are we inclined to discredit anything just because it is new, or just because it is old?

Your love, O Lord, extends to all in the kingdom. Even the worthless You give the grace to change.

NEED OF FAITH

Seventeenth Week of the Year, Friday   Matthew 13:54-58

"And he did not work many miracles there because of their lack of faith." So ends the passage of today's Gospel. The people of Nazareth felt that since they knew Jesus as a fellow townsman, as an ordinary carpenter's son, these things they heard about Him couldn't be true. They knew better.

In the same way there is a tendency today to belittle faith, to accept only what can be understood or scientifically proven. Man in his scientific advancement has come to think of himself as self-sufficient. He thinks he does not need God, or any help from above. So he needs no faith.

This is a very foolish conclusion to come to when you think of all the trouble in the world today: armed conflict; the incongruity of over half of the people in the world practically starving while the rest live in luxury.

Man is not supreme. His mind is quite limited. In all these centuries man hasn't figured out ways in which to avoid wars, how to feed the starving, how to bring harmony among nations. We need God's help. We need faith; we need divine wisdom and understanding.

It is only through the gift of faith that we can get a glimpse of that wisdom of God. Without a deep and living faith we are blind, we can't see the obvious solutions to world and domestic problems. But how do we get to see, how can we be cured of this blindness? Simply by an initial act of faith. "Lord, that we may see. Give us clearer vision, enlighten our human knowledge, our minds, with divine wisdom."

Faith will make us live, really live, more aware of God's continuous presence and influence in the world and in our lives. Faith will open the door to wonders, the wonders of God in the world around us, in our neighbor and in ourselves.

"I have come to the world as its light, to keep anyone who believes in me from remaining in the dark" (Jn 12:46).

SHAKEN BY THE WIND

Seventeenth Week of the Year, Saturday   Matthew 14:1-12

We have here a kind of a flashback in Matthew's narrative. As in Mark's Gospel (6:17-29), Matthew relates the death of John the Baptist as a kind of a parenthesis in the story of Jesus.

We know what a strong man of virtue John was. He was not afraid to confront the powerful with their wrong doings. Being accused of living in adultery by John, Herod had desired to kill him, but was afraid, because of the people who favored the Baptist. He did, however, unjustly put him into prison.

Herod was a weak man. He was afraid. At the height of passion and pleasure he was imprudent. He promised Herodias' daughter, Salome, anything she might ask for, and confirmed it with an oath in the presence of all his guests. This foolishness put him in a deep dilemma. He was afraid and had misgivings. What would the people say? But he was even more ashamed to go back on his foolish word, his drunken oath, because of his guests. Human respect in the bad sense of this phrase was the trigger that killed John the Baptist.

We have here the ultimate examples of the strong man and the weak character. John stands up for what he believes in regardless of the consequences. Herod is the reed blown this way and that by every wind of the popular mood.

The world makes every effort to shake the disciples of Christ. It has become very unpopular to live up to true Christian morals. The new morality of convenience is in. Only the strong will survive, and live up to the teachings of Christ. But we must not despair. Even though we know we are weak, we can be strong with the strength of Christ and the power of His Spirit.

**O Lord, help us to listen attentively to Your prophets,
and not be swayed by every popular mood.**

SHARING

Eighteenth Week of the Year, Monday   **Matthew 14:13-21**

The crowds followed Jesus on foot from everywhere, because He had something to give them, and He shared it with them willingly. Spiritually Jesus shared His divine wisdom with the people. We are told that "He spoke with power," and "the people listened to Him gladly." Jesus felt deep sympathy for their needs. "His heart was moved with pity, and He cured their sick." Then, as this Gospel recalls, He fed the hungry with great generosity, from the five loaves and a couple of fish.

The feeding of the thousands with bread, of course, is continued in the Eucharist which Jesus gave us. Again, it grows out of His desire to share with us. The living Bread is the sign of our love shared with Christ and shared with one another.

In the impressive story of Sir Launfal, we see a young, selfish soldier who does not understand this Christian spirit of sharing. He despises beggars who come to His gate for a little food or warmth. He leaves home, then, a knight in shining armor headed for the Holy Land, searching for the precious relic, the Holy Chalice or Holy Grail.

When he returns after many years, defeated, sick, weak, and ragged, he tries to get into his own castle. His servants do not recognize him, and throw him into the snow as a beggar. Now when a needy man comes up to him, how changed Sir Launfal is! His long fruitless search and his sufferings have taught him to share. He gives the man his last bread and a cup of water. Suddenly he sees that the man is Christ, and the Lord tells Launfal:

> "The Holy Supper is kept indeed
> In what we share with another's need;
> Not what we give but what we share—
> For the gift without the giver is bare;
> Who gives *Himself* with his alms feeds three—
> Himself, his hungering neighbor, and Me."

We cannot think of You breaking bread, Jesus, whether in the wilderness or at the Supper, without thinking of Your overwhelming generosity. You took bread for one purpose: to share with all of us, and to teach us to share with others.

TOO LITTLE FAITH

Eighteenth Week of the Year, Tuesday   **Matthew 14:22-36**

Jesus had just fed the five thousand the evening before and had gone off alone to pray. He had sent His disciples by boat across to the other side of Lake Genesareth.

Strong winds came up during the night tossing the boat about in the waves. In the midst of the storm the disciples were astonished to see Jesus come walking towards them on the waters. It is easy to see how amazed they were. They had hardly gotten over their shock at the miracle of the loaves.

And so they were terrified and thought it was a ghost that was coming towards them. But Jesus reassured them, "Don't be afraid. It is I."

Peter, his old impetuous self, challenged Him. "If it's really you, let me also walk on the waters." And the Lord said, "Come."

Peter got out of the boat and began to walk on the water, but when the high waves came at him he got scared and began to sink. The Lord took him by the hand and saved him from drowning, but at the same time rebuked him. "How little faith you have." There are many lessons we can draw from this Gospel passage. After much action, a busy day, at least after a busy week, we need prayer. Our Lord did it. He went off alone to pray.

On the stormy seas of life we should have faith that Christ is always near. When the sea became stormy, here was Jesus walking on the waters. It should give us confidence, joy and peace to be aware of Christ's nearness, His goodness, His mercy, His divine power over the storms of life.

Faith is the foundation of everything in our Christian life. If we have to ask ourselves, "why did you falter?" We know the answer is always, at least in part, "because we had too little faith."

Your presence, Lord, is my constant strength.

POSITIVE OR NEGATIVE?

Eighteenth Week of the Year, Wednesday   **Matthew 15:21-28**

Did you ever wonder whether you're a positive or a negative Christian? It makes a big difference. If you're a positive Christian, you leave this world a better place because of your positive good influence on others. If a negative Christian, you leave this world more miserable, more damaged by sin than it was before you came.

There are many tests by which we can find out if we are a plus or a minus as a Christian. One way is by the attitude we take toward the actions of others. For instance, what is your attitude toward Jesus in this passage of the Gospel? Do you feel negative about what Jesus did? Are you embarrassed about Jesus' being so rude or so cold toward this Canaanite woman?

Or do you feel positive about Jesus here? Do you ask, "What did Jesus know, that I *don't* know, that made Him test this pagan woman? Did Jesus know there was a treasure house of faith and humility inside this great woman, so that He could reveal it to us best by testing her?" In reality, that is certainly what happened. Jesus put her to the test, and her faith, her humility, her perseverance is beautiful.

These were all qualities of prayer and qualities of life that Jesus was constantly teaching. What better way could He teach us than by holding out a live example to us? The Canaanite woman of faith is woman's answer to the man of faith, the Roman officer. This man, too, Jesus held up to us as an example of great faith: "I have not found such great faith in the house of Israel."

What does Jesus teach us by the example of the Canaanite woman? Several things: 1) Don't give up if your prayer isn't answered at once. 2) God puts you to the test, to bring out the best in you. 3) Don't threaten God or make demands with your prayer. Trust in His love for you, as this woman did. Trust that God loves you fully as much as He loves the people who have their prayers answered. It may just be that the Lord sees you need real growth in faith and courage, in patience and perseverance. Trust that God sees you may need these virtues more than the other favors you asked for.

WHY THE CROSS?

Eighteenth Week of the Year, Thursday   Matthew 16:13-23

After drawing an act of faith from Peter and promising to establish His Church with him as the rock and foundation, Jesus tells Peter and the other disciples about His coming passion, death and resurrection. Peter immediately answers that no such thing must happen. He does not understand. Jesus tells him not to judge merely by man's standards but by God's.

The cross has been a stumbling block not only to Peter but to mankind in general throughout the centuries. The question is so often asked: why suffering? Why the cross? Why did Christ have to become the Man of Sorrow so that we might become the children of God?

Suffering and death remains a mystery, but we do see some light in nature. We see here that strange truth, that paradox, that death produces life. A seed must die to produce a new plant. A mother undergoes the pangs of childbirth to bring about new life. Ultimately we can't reach eternal life without first dying to this life.

Christ's death makes eternal life possible for us. But we must first share in His death by a dying to self. Jesus is very clear about this, "If a man wishes to come after Me, he must deny his very self, take up his cross and begin to follow in my footsteps." No hedging here. The words are clear and emphatic. Everywhere in the Scriptures we can read that our union with Christ is conditioned by our conformity with Him in His sufferings on this earth.

St. Paul writes to the Romans: "If we have died with Christ, we believe that we are also to live with Him . . . if we have been united with Him through likeness to His death, so shall we be through a like resurrection." The reason we suffer with Christ is that we may be glorified with Him.

Without the cross there is no glory, without death, no resurrection. Without Good Friday there never would have been an Easter Sunday. So also does our Easter, our resurrection to new life, both here and hereafter, depend on how we accept our earthly Good Friday.

> O Jesus, if I must suffer and die with You, I believe that
> I will also live with You.

BROKEN ARCS

Eighteenth Week of the Year, Friday   **Matthew 16:24-28**

"Whoever would save his life will lose it, but whoever loses his life for my sake will find it." Suffering and misfortune are in God's purpose a "first life" to prepare us for a second. The first life, which we know as our earthly years in this world, is a school.

We learn to desire heaven by being without it for a time. We appreciate heat when we come inside after being out in the cold. We value light after being left in the darkness. A summer of drought has taught us to appreciate rain. Yes, even our mistakes have taught us the value of being right, of having a clear conscience.

When we begin our second, eternal life, the injustices of this world have taught us the perfect justice of heaven. All on earth that left us dissatisfied, aching, hoping, crying out—all this, writes Robert Browning, shall be corrected:

There shall never be one lost good! What was, shall live as before;
The evil is null, is naught, is silence implying sound;
What was good shall be good, with, for evil, so much good more;
On the earth the broken arcs; in the heaven a perfect round.

All we have willed or hoped or dreamed of good shall exist;
Not its semblance, but itself; no beauty, nor good nor power
Whose voice has gone forth, but each survives for the melodist
When eternity affirms the conception of an hour.

The high that proved too high, the heroic for earth too hard,
The passion that left the ground to lose itself in the sky,
Are music sent up to God by the lover and the bard.
Enough that he heard it once; we shall hear it by and by.

And what is our failure here but a triumph's evidence.
For the fullness of the days? Have we withered or agonized?
Why else was the pause prolonged but that singing might issue thence?
Why rushed the discords in, but that harmony should be prized?
(Abt Vogler II, 69-80)

Lord, teach us to lose our life on earth for Your sake, that we may find our real life, both on earth and in heaven.

LET GOD BE GOD

Eighteenth Week of the Year, Saturday   **Matthew 17:14-20**

Earlier in Matthew's Gospel (10:5-8) we heard how Jesus sent out His apostles to preach the kingdom of God, to heal the sick, drive out demons, and even raise the dead. Now (in chapter 17) the apostles find they cannot heal the epileptic boy. They are frankly surprised— and embarrassed. They ask Jesus privately, "Why couldn't *we* drive that demon out?"

Jesus answers, "Because you have so little faith. With even a little faith you could move a mountain!"

What happened? A likely explanation (especially if you compare this with Luke 10:17-20) is that the disciples have let their healings go to their heads. They have pulled the plug on God. It was by God's power they were healing; they began by letting God work through them. But there's always the danger of thinking it's *me*, rather than God, that's doing the great things around here. They had probably fallen into that trap.

Jesus warned us against such an attitude. When the disciples came back from one of their preaching and teaching tours, they told Jesus, "Lord, even the devils beat it at our command!"

Jesus answered, "Yes, but don't let those same devils catch you from behind. I saw Satan fall like lightning from heaven. Pride is a big, wide trap. Don't be glad that you have some special power, but be glad your names are written in heaven." That is, be glad that God loves you and chooses to show His love for your brothers and sisters through you. But don't forget: the power around here is God! That's what faith really means—keeping plugged into God; seeing the reality—God is always in command.

My work is worth only what I let God do in me. My life will be what I open myself to let the Lord do. I must be sure that I let God be God! That's faith, and that's the power that works wonders.

> **The folly of God is wiser than men,**
> **The weakness of God is stronger than men,**
> **Consider our calling, my brothers:**
> **To which of us do great riches belong?**
> **Not many are wise, not many are strong,**
> **Our gifts do not shadow another's.** (1 Cor 1:26-27)

INTEGRITY

Nineteenth Week of the Year, Monday   Matthew 17:22-27

When we meditate on the last days of Christ's earthly life, we try to conceive what He must have felt. He was innocent, more innocent than an army of saints; His trial was among the most unjust ever seen on this earth; His enemies were totally blind and willfully ignorant. Had He been "of this world," Jesus could have gone free. The Pharisees didn't ask much, really. They only asked that Jesus keep silent and do nothing. "Be witness, Lord, that I do not seal my lips," writes the prophet (Ps 40).

They only wanted Jesus to say nothing about them and their vices. He could have appeased their anger—simply by not carrying out His mission—"To carry out Your law, Lord, is my desire."

If only Jesus had compromised—compromised truth and justice! For His own safety, He could have let them be. "Lord, Your just dealings are no secret hidden away in my heart."

For a few peaceful years, Jesus could have given in. He could easily have escaped death and suffering, and yet restored us to grace by His very incarnation. To such a temptation He did not yield—"I am coming to fulfill what is written of me."

There is some doubt about us, His followers. Each of us has some great temptation in life. It may not be a temptation to rescue our one and only human life—but it is some great trial, something that demands a definite choice. On one hand is a safe, easy, comfortable life; on the other, the struggle of fulfilling our real purpose in life.

You rightly expect me to overcome that great temptation, Lord. You accomplished Your purpose; I must accomplish mine. Give me no peace, until I am truly at work conquering my great weakness. So I will find my peace in You.

RETURN TO INNOCENCE

Nineteenth Week of the Year, Tuesday Matthew 18:1-5, 10, 12-14

Throughout the Gospels, we see a very special quality in Jesus: a very great tenderness toward children, toward the poor, and toward repentant sinners. He tells us that these are specially close to God, so He loves them most specially. "Whoever welcomes one such child for my sake welcomes me."

The best way to examine the quality of our love, to see how genuine and how Christian it is, is to examine our love for "the little ones," for children, for the poor, for those who seem least endowed in a worldly sense.

See how the Son of God Himself chose to come into this world. Not in a marble palace, not in a wealthy or important family, not in a gold cradle with satin pillows and silk coverlets. There were no rich, noble ladies there to coo over Him, and there were no reporters to cover the story. No, He chose poverty and simplicity, a cold, dark cave for sheep. He chose the poorest of parents, a poor cradle, poor food, no comforts, no publicity. And who were His first friends? Not emperors or governors. A king was in fact His worst enemy: Herod. The friends of Jesus were ignorant, impoverished shepherds who smelled no better than their sheep.

He loved the children because they were honest, innocent, open-hearted, and pure. He loved the harlots and publicans who were called sinners by the Pharisees, because these simple people were truly repentant. They were of good heart, they desired a return to innocence, they listened and responded willingly to God's mercy.

These are the truly humble: those who are small in their own eyes. They have not become hypocrites, unjust, proud, vain, or dishonest. They are the humble, whom Jesus loved, and to whom He promised, "The humble will be exalted." For only such people are open to receive the graces of God. Only these have the spiritual wisdom to ask God's forgiveness, and to reverence those other "little ones" whom God loves.

Come, Lord Jesus, come and stay.
Come, Our Light, and lead the way.

CONCERN AND CORRECTION

Nineteenth Week of the Year, Wednesday   **Matthew 18:15-20**

Having expressed His concern for the straying sheep in a parable, Jesus now gives us one way in which a member who has strayed must be sought out. It is by fraternal correction.

We must never despise any of our brothers and sisters who have wandered away or fallen. They are still a part of us, members of the Body of Christ. In loving concern we are to approach them with correction and support. If we can accomplish it quietly and privately, well and good. If not, we should go to them with several witnesses to show them that the community is concerned and wants them to repent and come back.

Maybe we have a friend or acquaintance who is drifting away. We're concerned and worried. We don't know what to do. Jesus tells us to pray for guidance and approach that friend lovingly with correction. Let him or her know your concern, your love. Don't be afraid of losing a friend—you are trying to save one. Tell him others in the community are also concerned. If that friend doesn't believe, bring along a few members as witnesses.

Here Jesus gives a beautiful picture of community and of community love and concern. He immediately follows with a powerful statement about the power of community prayer. He says that if even two or three join their voices to pray, the Father will listen and grant their prayer. Why? Because Jesus promises to be there, too, to join in that prayer.

What a powerful promise! Do we sometimes lose faith in our prayers? Seek out a brother or sister or two and unite in fervent prayer, confident that the Lord will keep His word. He will be there and the Father will listen.

Jesus, help us love our brothers and sisters enough to risk losing their friendship through correction.

SEVENTY TIMES SEVEN

Nineteenth Week of the Year, Thursday   **Matthew 18:21-19:1**

God is merciful, He will forgive even the greatest sin we might have fallen into. However forgiveness also demands a few things on our part. There are a few very important conditions that we must fulfill. The Gospel describes these to us in a vivid story.

The man who owed much to his master, the king, and could not pay, begged for mercy, promising in due time to pay all. The king, moved to compassion, forgave him the whole debt. But after having received such kindness at the hands of the king, this man demanded payment from his fellow servant to the last penny. Since he could not pay he had him thrown into jail. When the king heard this he called back the servant whose debt he had forgiven, rebuked him severely, and put him into jail until he would pay up. Our Lord then goes on to say, "So also will my heavenly Father treat you, unless each of you forgives his brother with all his heart."

Powerful words! Clear as crystal. Our forgiveness from God depends on our forgiveness of our neighbor. Our Lord taught us the same thing in the Our Father, and we repeat it every day. "Forgive us our trespasses as we forgive those who trespass against us." Do we really mean it? We are to ask God to forgive us only insofar as we forgive our fellow man. It doesn't matter how or how severely they have offended us, our forgiveness from God depends on whether we forgive any offense against us.

So these are the two conditions: that we humbly ask forgiveness from God, and that we forgive our neighbor any offense he commits against us. This lesson is so prominent in Our Lord's teaching that we just can't miss it. There is no love of God without love of neighbor — no forgiveness from God without forgiveness of our neighbor.

Such mutual love and forgiveness in our families, at work, in all our associations, is the greatest assurance of God's forgiveness, as well as of happiness and understanding in families and communities.

Jesus Christ, Son of God, have mercy on us, sinners.

MARRIED LOVE

Nineteenth Week of the Year, Friday   **Matthew 19:3-12**

"For this reason a man shall leave his father and mother and cling to his wife, and the two shall become as one." Any union of two persons can only remain so by the power of Christian love. We can never become too busy to pay attention to that love, and see to it that it grows and develops. The union of husband and wife needs love most of all.

A wife who is too busy with too many other things may become the nagging wife, driving her husband to depression. A husband too busy with things outside his home may become the neglectful husband, driving his wife to unhappiness. When we are too busy to love one another, we are dangerously busy, and all our work is time wasted.

The worst evil in marriage is that husband and wife lose sight of the good qualities in each other. As soon as you lose a deep appreciation of the good in your partner, you are on the road to bitterness and even hatred. A good definition of hell has been given. It is this: Living together without love.

If such a problem arises in a Christian home, let us hope to God that at least one of the two, husband or wife, will do something about it. Once we are fully aware that the problem exists, we have made good progress toward the solution. If the family cannot solve it together with one another, outside counsel must be called in. It is essential that the problem be met. A home without true charity as its rule is a hell on earth, and cannot in any sense be called a Catholic home.

Let us, above all, never be responsible for destroying our partner by discouragement. People think the big elements in marriage are sex and children. A far more important element, however, is the quality of love in the marriage. A marriage can be destroyed by nagging, bitter talk, quarreling, fault-finding, excessive criticism.

To be united in love, husband and wife, parents and children must learn to meet one another more than halfway. There must be more giving than taking. There must be a cheerful acceptance of one another and a desire to see one another happy.

"God is Love, and whoever lives in love lives in God and God lives in him" (1 Jn 4:16).

CHILDHOOD

Nineteenth Sunday of the Year, Saturday   **Matthew 19:13-15**

Not all the beauties of the mountains, rivers, lakes, valleys and forests, nor the marvels produced by the handiwork of man can be compared with the loveliness of an innocent soul.

As we grow older, we grow familiar with the cynical distrust of the godless, the bitter selfishness of the materialist, the nervous anxiety of money-makers, the cut-throat battles for power and influence—and we forget. Who shall save us from these falsehoods and the temptation of despair they inevitably bring? If we ourselves would try, we might not be believed, though we are professed Christians. With good reason we would be suspect, for our own records are not unblemished, our own deeds are no favorable witness.

But the honesty, the blameless joy, the guileless confidence of a child has the power to return us to the simple truths of life. The most hardened of men, the most vicious, hateful, cynical of human beings can hardly reject the love of a little child.

The Lord said it was His delight to be with the children of men. We remember that Jesus rebuked His apostles for holding back the children from Him, and He said, "Let the little ones come to me, for of these is the kingdom of heaven made."

When I fail to recognize my neighbor as the child of God that he is, or when I myself fail to be interiorly a child of God, I make of myself the inhuman monster of which Shakespeare speaks and concludes, "How sharper than a serpent's tooth it is to have a thankless child."

Of children Dickens wrote, "I love these little people; and it is not a slight thing when they, who are so fresh from God, love us."

"Call not that man wretched," wrote Southey, "who, whatever ills he suffers, has a child to love." "Children are God's apostles," wrote

James Russell Lowell, "sent forth, day by day, to preach of love, and hope and peace."

Jesus, let us see Your love and Your goodness in the joy of the children.

A MIXED BLESSING

Twentieth Week of the Year, Monday   **Matthew 19:16-22**

How often in the Gospels we read of Jesus' warning against the dangers of riches. He again used for this same purpose the occasion of the man coming to Him and asking what he must do to share in everlasting life. Jesus tells him outright that besides the commandments there is one more thing he must do, sell what he has, give to the poor and then follow Him. He promises him treasure in heaven.

Jesus' contemporaries considered riches a sign of divine favor. Jesus denies this categorically and shows that wealth can even be a hindrance to accept the Gospel message. Since this was such a new idea at the time, His disciples were completely amazed and overwhelmed. To them it meant that if not even the rich can be saved, then who can? But Jesus says that for man it is impossible, that is, man can't understand this at all, but not for God. God's values are different from man's. Riches mean very little with God. It is not what man HAS that counts with God, but what he IS.

This does not mean that material things, wealth in this sense, are evil in themselves. They are good things created by God for good purposes. Jesus simply teaches us that we must be poor in spirit, not attached to wealth, if we wish to follow Him. Money, property, power—all these things—must take second place to Christ. They must be subordinate to our allegiance to Christ: they must be used for good, to share with the poor, to help spread the kingdom of God on earth, to relieve the sufferings of mankind.

It remains true that it is harder for the rich man to be poor in spirit than for the man of ordinary or meager means. Being rich is a very mixed blessing. Being poor can be a great blessing. It all depends on our attitude toward wealth and its place and its proper use in God's kingdom on earth.

Lord, Jesus, teach us how to live poor in spirit amid all the riches of this world.

LOVE AND WEALTH

Twentieth Week of the Year, Tuesday **Matthew 19:23-30**

Christ's description of the danger of affluence was penetrating: like seed among thorns, materialists are "stifled by the cares and riches and pleasures of life, and they do not mature." Materialists never mature; they remain ridiculously small. Their desires and their love cannot expand. Enslaved by a thousand needs—for the latest fashions, for a sumptuous house with two or more expensive cars, for a television set on every floor, another new freezer, costly cocktails and lavish parties—the soul is progressively choked.

Unfortunately love does not thrive where material wealth abounds, because one must empty himself to love purely. Greed and envy constantly threaten love; wealth makes its demands mercilessly. It corrodes and corrupts.

The "rich in spirit" ignore Christian efforts to secure justice for the oppressed, relief for the suffering, or help for the poor, because this work is uncomfortable. They will "give to charitable causes" if it requires no personal sacrifice. They agree in theory that "everyone ought to have a chance," and the "equal rights is a good idea, if rebels are kept in check," but they never read the handwriting on the wall. "Who speaks of emptiness and danger in living for money, pleasure, popularity and power? Only kill-joys and cracked preachers talk like that! Envy makes them scowl and howl and point fingers. Give *them* a chance, and they'll grab all the good things of life with both hands!"

What about Christ, who had everything and emptied Himself? What about the saints—the martyrs and apostles and comtemplatives and voluntary poor of every age—who left all to follow Him and serve their fellow men? Are these the crackpots because they alone knew how to love?

Your promises, O God, are true and faultless,
Like silver tried and freed from stain and weakness.
Keep us, O Lord, from sin, though rich men stumble
And high thrones tumble (Ps 12).

ARE YOU ENVIOUS?

Twentieth Week of the Year, Wednesday   Matthew 20:1-16

The parable of today's Gospel appears only in Matthew. It therefore belongs to the early Jewish Christian tradition. The Jewish converts were probably envious that the Gentiles who were admitted late were put on an equal standing with the Jews in the early Church. The admission of the Gentiles was one of the early controversies in the Apostolic Church. It turned out to be its major problem. Ultimately the controversy was resolved very much in the manner indicated by today's parable.

Envy is certainly a very basic problem that can create all manner of trouble both in the community and in the individual.

The vineyard workers, especially those who had worked the longer hours show this fundamental weakness, this selfishness, basis of all sin.

The goodness, generosity and openness of our heavenly Father are evident in the parable. So also can we see, reflected in some of the workers, our own envy, selfishness, our lack of response to God's generosity. You notice it was their faulty response to the owner's generosity that let to divisions among the workers, to envy, to complaining. Isn't the same true of us? Selfishness and envy lead to divisions in the community, in the family. They bring sins against charity, prejudices, lack of communication.

"Could it be," the owner in the Gospel says, "that you are envious because I am generous?" Are we envious of the gifts of God to others? Shouldn't we rejoice with our brothers and sisters if God has been good to them? Why do we always want everything for ourselves and not for others, especially those for whom we don't have a liking?

Our response to God's generosity should be the same: generosity.

Generosity in our service to God and neighbor, all our fellowmen, including those who may have hurt us, those who seem to make it hard for us to love them.

Bless the Lord, O my soul! O Lord, My God, You are generous and good! Let me not be envious of your gifts to others.

AN INVITATION

Twentieth Week of the Year, Thursday   Matthew 22:1-14

Jesus in today's Gospel says the kingdom of God is like a marriage, a union between two parties, God and us. God sent prophets to invite His people. But they were ignored and even killed. The Gospel parable is a history of the chosen people. In spite of the many calls, few of them responded. But the parable is also a personal history of each of us. God invites, but how often we refuse.

We even go so far as to fear God's invitation, foolishly imagining that He will "spoil our fun." We forget that He is our Creator, our Designer and our loving Father. He knows the difference between the fun that leads to real happiness and the fun that leads to bitterness and despair.

If God's invitation is listened to and responded to, our destiny is safe, our future is glorious, our life is in order. We can examine history and see it for ourselves. If people have truly responded, they have rejoiced to feel the power of God work in their lives. But if they have closed the way to God, then often they fear His power. It is fear of the unknown.

There's the story of a lady on her first trans-Atlantic jet flight. The plane hit a storm and was floundering in air pockets. The lady got very upset and asked the stewardess, "Oh, are we going to crash?"

The stewardess tried to calm her down, saying, "Don't be afraid. We're all in the hands of God."

The lady replied, "Oh, is it that bad?"

Once we accept the Lord's invitation, and truly come to know

Him, we'll never say that. We'll say, "Oh, it's that good." It's only bad
when we forget that we are always in the hands of God.

**Lord, keep us always in Your powerful, loving hands,
and there will always be order and peace in our lives.**

HEART AND MIND

Twentieth Week of the Year, Friday   Matthew 22:34-40

Jesus said to him, "You shall love the Lord your God with your
whole heart, with your whole soul, and with all your mind. This is the
first and greatest commandment. The second is like it: you shall love
your neighbor as yourself."

Our competitive society puts too much emphasis on the head
without the heart. Those who use their head devilishly well, to the
point of trampling down their neighbor, are considered a "success."
They "get ahead," but neglecting the "heart" and "soul" Jesus speaks
of, they never find any happiness that is real.

Almost all of us can speak about the importance of love in life,
and yet real love is so hard to find. Take an example: some time ago a
group of teachers sent out a questionnaire to more than two thousand
employers. As a service to students who would soon be seeking their
first job, they asked, "Would you look up the last three persons
dismissed from your company, and indicate why you let them go?"

The business firms responded with the same answer in two out of
every three cases, regardless of the type of work or what part of the
country. The reason for dismissal: "They could not get along with
other people." Which seems to be saying, they broke the commandment, "Love your neighbor as yourself."

Of course, Jesus never said, "You must love your neighbor so that
you can keep your job." But He did tell us that we must forgive and we
must love even those who hate us, if we are to be worthy children of
our heavenly Father.

One reason why many find it difficult to love their neighbor is,
they don't know what real love is. They have never experienced it.

They are drowning in a flood of false values and false advertising, so that they have a totally wrong picture of love. They try to fill the emptiness inside with things, but they are starved for true love.

Lord, make us aware that the secret of living lies not in having things. It is not even in using one's head— although we need a head. It is head and heart together in a harmony that only You can give us, because God is Love. Only when we find God do we find real love.

THE GREATEST WILL SERVE

Twentieth Week of the Year, Saturday   **Matthew 23:1-12**

Chapter 23 of Matthew's Gospel is entirely taken up with the hypocrisy and vanity of the scribes and Pharisees. In the opening lines Jesus tells the crowds to obey them as leaders, to do what they tell them, but not to follow their example.

We must distinguish the word we hear from the person who speaks it. We should accept what is good, whatever its source. Yet if we are to have any influence for good, our actions and our lives must be examples of what we speak. Parents cannot expect children to accept their advice if their very own lives proclaim the opposite. Honesty of life is the best teacher.

Jesus accuses the Pharisees of performing their works just to be seen, to be given honor at banquets and festivals. Their acts were not done out of love for God. They wanted the glory themselves. They were not interested in giving glory to God. Theirs was a mere formalism in religion.

Surely it is good to give a good example. It is good that others are inspired by our lives. Jesus told us not to hide our light under a basket, but to let it shine out. But this does not mean that the only reason we act well is to be seen, to be honored, to be respected. Our first intention must be to do the will of the Father, to give Him honor and glory. "Seek first the Kingdom of God and His justice."

The accusations Jesus makes against the Pharisees are not all out of date. Do we ever perform just to be seen? Do we wear clothes mainly so others can admire us? Do we ever seek the best seats? Or are we really aware that, as Jesus says, "The greatest among you will be the one who serves the rest," who is willing to take the last place, who works behind the scenes?

**Jesus, meek and humble of heart,
Make our hearts like unto Thine.**

USING HIS NAME

Twenty-first Week of the Year, Monday   **Matthew 23:13-22**

The hair-splitting Pharisees were concerned about just how to swear—by the temple or by its gold, by the altar or by the gifts on it. Brushing away this non-sensical nit-picking, Jesus goes to the heart of the matter. Whoever swears by altar or temple, swears by God who lives there. He cannot but condemn their narrow negativism.

Are we not involved in similar hair-splitting and negativism in our view of "swearing" and the misuse of God's name? There is no doubt that cursing and swearing as habits are crude and uncivilized. It is often a matter of poor vocabulary and a laziness that will not use accurate language. In such persons, language becomes mindless and meaningless, a mere habit of excessive emotion.

There is another extreme. Some people never misuse the name of the Lord because God is so far from their minds that they wouldn't think of using His name in vain. The saints used God's name very often, daily, hourly, habitually—but certainly not in vain. They used His name with great success and deep meaning. One who really loves God is often using His name, but with love and gratitude.

When Johnny loves Rosy, everything makes him think of Rosy, everything reminds him of Rosy. In fact, life *becomes* Rosy! So it is for the true Christian: everything reminds him of God. Everything we look at should bring us closer to God, make us thank Him more, make us desire His presence.

A lack of reverence is a lack of love. Jesus seemed to indicate by

His objection to the Pharisaical rule book, that they had made God and the things of God so dull and impersonal, that people could no longer approach Him. "You shut the doors of the Kingdom of God in men's faces," by your formalistic, hair-splitting, fraudulent approach to religion. They had built their own false gods, forgetting the true God, the kind, loving, merciful Father, whom Jesus knew.

Lord, may Your Name never be far from my lips—but never in vain.

CLEAN INSIDE

Twenty-first Week of the Year, Tuesday   Matthew 23:23-26

Today's Gospel reading contains two invectives against the Scribes and Pharisees for their hypocrisy. He first attacks the teaching of these men. "Woe to you Scribes and Pharisees, you frauds! You pay tithes on mint and herbs and seeds while neglecting the weightier matters of law, justice, mercy and good faith." The reference is to rigor in regard to such trivial matters of herbs and mints while such weightier matters as justice and mercy are neglected. Jesus adds a touch of ridicule with the example of straining out the gnat and swallowing the camel.

Legalism can get so lost in little details that it forgets to ask the most important questions, questions of fairness, justice, decency, charity. No law should ever make us be unjust or act against charity.

The second invective has to do with the traditional ceremonial cleansings and washings of Jewish tradition and law. Jesus is not condemning these ceremonies. But He does condemn the fanaticism with which they were sometimes adhered to without much reference to their meaning and symbolism. The cup, the vessels, here are metaphors for the person. The condemnation is aimed at the concern for external correctness without much concern for the interior disposition it was to symbolize and help bring about.

Jesus says, "First clean the inside of the cup so that its outside may be clean." He means, of course, that if our interior dispositions are good, wholesome, truly Christian and Gospel oriented, then our exterior, our lives, our actions, our contacts with our fellow men will also be truly Christian.

There is little good in being exteriorly correct, polite, civil, unless our interior thoughts are the origin and basis for these acts. Otherwise it is all hypocrisy and we are no better than the Scribes and Pharisees. Honesty with self is not only good mental health. It is also Christian in every sense of the word.

O Lord, You see into the heart, You know our inmost thoughts and designs. Cleanse us of all that is not of You.

WOE TO WHITE-WASHERS

Twenty-first Week of the Year, Wednesday   Matthew 23:27-32

This passage includes the last two of the seven woes Jesus speaks against the Pharisees for their hypocrisy and vanity. In all the woes Jesus calls them "frauds."

Jesus is usually very gentle and forgiving with sinners. Why this sudden change with the sin of hypocrisy? He evidently saw in them very little inclination to admitting guilt, little desire for true sorrow. He realized that the only approach in their case was the use of strong invectives. Probably Jesus foresaw a need in us and in all who came after Him. He wanted to show us the rottenness of this vice.

So the Lord calls the Pharisees white-washed tombs, beautiful to look at on the outside, but full of filth and "dead men's bones" on the inside. Tombs are white-washed even today in Palestine, a practice that dates back to the time of Christ and earlier. In the Old Testament, contact with death caused uncleanness. The white-washing helped to identify the tombs and keep away anyone who might accidentally touch them and become unclean.

In our way of speaking, white-washing means covering up. Regarding the Pharisees, Jesus says that their law-observance was a cover-up for a line that was not at all in line with the Law and its spirit.

How often we are inclined to cover up our failings, even our sins. We try to hide our faults so as to appear righteous to others. Yet all the time we know we are dishonest, we are afraid of being found out. We live without peace.

How much better to admit our mistakes, to ask forgiveness for our offenses, and be healed. We need healing and forgiveness from each other and from Christ. But only by honest openness can we expect to receive it.

Jesus, I ask Your mercy and forgiveness.
Heal me of all dishonesty and the anxiety that it brings.

BE PREPARED

Twenty-first Week of the Year, Thursday   **Matthew 24:42-51**

"If the owner of the house knew when the thief was coming he would keep a watchful eye.... You must be prepared in the same way. The Son of Man is coming at the time you least expect."

Jesus uses an unusual image in speaking of Himself here—that of a thief coming in the night. The point is, the "thief" cannot surprise us if we are prepared and watchful. A few sentences later Jesus says the "thief" who would catch the unprepared householder off guard is really the "Master" returning home, interested in what His servants are doing. Happy those servants who are found trustworthy; unhappy those who are caught unprepared and have wasted the time alloted them.

The solution? Don't let the Son of Man walk in on you as a stranger, as one whose coming you have not expected or awaited.

Were we to ask Jesus, "How can we be really prepared?", would He not answer, "Watch and pray?" If we get to know Jesus well in that daily prayer time we set aside, why, He will never catch us by surprise. For we can say, "I just talked to You today, Lord. I just had You in my home. In fact, I have made room for You every day. Welcome back, longtime Friend!"

If we have faced the Lord honestly, by regular daily time spent with Him, we have allowed Him to prepare us for His final coming.

We have given ourselves time to remove the obstacles to a joyous reunion.

> One favor yet is all I ask the Lord,
> To dwell within His temple all my days,
> To see His beauty often I implored,
> Within His house sing my endless praise!
> Around me, Lord, Your lavish love has flowed,
> Upon a rock of strength You lift me high;
> O Lord, protect my soul in Your abode,
> Into the shelter of Your tent I fly. (Ps 27).

A FEARFUL JOY

Twenty-first Week of the Year, Friday   Matthew 25:1-13

In the parable of the ten bridesmaids, Jesus continues speaking on the theme of preparedness. Like the "thief in the night," the bridegroom does not come at the time expected, and only the wise maidens have taken extra oil for their lamps. Only the wise ones are prepared to meet their Lord.

When can we say, "Now I am ready for the Lord?" How do we know when we have "enough oil in our lamps" for that final day of meeting Him?

The great Catholic scholar of Anglo-Saxon England, St. Bede the Venerable, was known and loved widely for his remarkably gentle disposition, his total dedication to Christ, his outstanding humility. All his various talents—teaching, preaching translating, writing— were completely given to God. Such a man, we would think, is totally prepared for the Lord's coming.

Yet on his death-bed, this gentle, humble saint exlaimed, "It is a fearful thing to fall into the hands of the living God!" What had he to fear? A man of exceptional innocence and total dedication—how could he call it "fearful" to stand before Jesus, the rewarder of good works? His "trouble" was that in living close to Jesus, he came to see something of what God is. He came to understand something of

God's infinite holiness, His supreme perfection, and the boundless distance between man and God. His very joy at God's excellence caused him to fear. "How shall I, puny and limited as I am, ever be worthy to face my loving Creator? How shall I ever make a fitting return of love and devotion to my wonderful Redeemer?"

> **O Christ, our great eternal King,**
> **You are alone the Father's Son!**
> **You came as man to save mankind,**
> **as Virgin's Son salvation won.**
> **When You destroyed the sting of death,**
> **You opened life to faithful men;**
> **Now at the Father's side You reign:**
> **to judge us You shall come again.**
> **We ask You now for grace and aid:**
> **You shed Your Blood to make us whole;**
> **We beg to join Your saints in love;**
> **Your blessing on each faithful soul.** (from the Te Deum)

GOD'S GIFTS

Twenty-first Week of the Year, Saturday,   **Matthew 25:14-30**

In the parable of the silver pieces, Jesus warns us that we must of our own will use the gifts of God wisely, if we are to enter the kingdom of heaven. In this parable, as in so many others, He insists that it is God's property we are using, and it remains God's property. He has given a variety of talents and the good things of life to His creatures, things of greater and lesser values, to greater and lesser degrees. This the parable expresses in terms of money, over which each servant is merely the administrator. The Master strictly charges them to use his goods wisely and bear abundant fruit.

When their time is up and the Master returns, he demands an account from each. Those who have allowed God's work to be done through them are rewarded. They shall be judges and leaders in God's kingdom. "Well done!" he says, "Since you were reliable in a small matter, I will put you in charge of greater affairs. Come, share your Master's joy."

It is a strong reminder that we cannot take God's gifts and use them only for our own pleasure. The good things of life are not merely our own, to do with as we please. They must be used well in the service of God and our neighbor. This is another parable in which Jesus warns us about the abuse of riches. Unless we develop a deep charity, a spirit of sharing, a generosity with what God has given us, we shall meet the fate of the foolish man who put his silver pieces in the ground, and did not use them for the glory of God.

Only those who make a lot of room for God and their neighbor, using the good things God has given, only these will be worthy of any reward.

Lord, make our feet to walk the surest way,
Lord, make our words to give Your love away,
Lord, make our time be only Yours today!

FICKLENESS OF MEN

Twenty-second Week of the Year, Monday **Luke 4:16-30**

We are told by Scripture scholars that today's Gospel passage records at least two, possibly three accounts of Jesus' preaching in Nazareth and the reactions of his fellow townspeople. He had already gained quite a reputation throughout the rest of Galilee. His initial reception in Nazareth was also favorable. No doubt they immediately expected some miracles as they had heard He performed elsewhere.

It seems when He came again and read from Isaiah the passage referring to the Mission of the Messiah and applied it to himself they found it hard to bear. They finally ganged up on him and wanted to push him over the cliff to his death.

Why this change in their attitude towards Him? For one thing, He told them they really weren't looking for the Messiah in Him, but simply for some miracles out of curiosity or personal interests. He told them point-blank that they were not accepting Him even as a prophet simply because He was only a hometown boy.

Another thing that may have aggravated them was his insistence that the good news was for the poor and the oppressed, people they had traditionally considered simply cursed by God for whatever reason. Only the well-to-do were blessed by God.

What a consolation and a lesson for us. We are poor, often oppressed, but we are most beloved of the Father. We belong to a Church whose mission is mainly to the poor, the deprived, the needy. Does that mean it is not for the rich? No, they too, are poor in many ways, often lonely, anxious, lacking peace. Christ came to bring peace, healing, joy to all who lack any of these fruits of the Spirit.

We can be instruments of this good news. We must be instruments of this good news, if we are truly followers of Jesus.

Jesus, You were not accepted in your own town. So let us not be upset if we are not always kindly received when we bring Your good news.

OF DEMONS

Twenty-second Week of the Year, Tuesday   **Luke 4:31-37**

You cannot read the Gospels without being impressed by the constant presence of demons who oppose Christ as He begins to announce the good news that those who repent will be saved. The modern reader of the Gospel is a little embarrassed by all these devils. His secularized culture and his complete attention to the material world make him doubtful. Is there really a force as strong and real and personal as Satan?

If we're observant at all, we see the reality of persons who have great power to do evil, to ruin what was good, to confuse and destroy. The forces of evil are great. Some people are embarrassed and restless when you talk about the devil because they are weak of faith. When you are not drawing on God's power in your daily life, you are afraid to admit that another power—the power of evil—is very real and is taking over in your life.

But we see around us now what we always see where faith in the true God has weakened. We see people go for all kinds of substitutes, some of them indeed weird. We find strange new cults, a lot of spiritism, and actual devil worship. There is also a lot of interest in astrology. Many have a very firm faith in these things. They read their horoscope devoutly before they dare make a move. What blind faith in a higher power—unfortunately, the wrong one.

We find all kinds of superstitions among faithless people: the rabbit's foot, the four-leaf clover, the fortune teller, the palm-reader—all forms of looking for that higher power that rules your life. If we take these claims to a higher power as a substitute for faith and trust in the Lord, we are incredibly foolish. As St. Paul says, we have then exchanged the true God for a lie! That lie is Satan's game: he is the father of liars, the prince of deceivers, the enemy of truth. Jesus faced the temptation of deceit by reminding Satan of the first commandment, "I am the Lord your God. You are not to have strange gods before me."

The Gospel message is: Only Jesus in the power of God's Word conquers evil.

Jesus, open our eyes to the truth: God's power is always superior to Satan. We draw upon Your strength in our life. You alone bring us the victory!

PRAYER FOR HEALING

Twenty-second Week of the Year, Wednesday   Luke 4:38-44

"All who had people sick with a variety of diseases took them to Him, and He laid hands on each of them and cured them."

Father in heaven, to heal us of our pain and suffering, You sent us Your only Son, Jesus, to be our Savior, our divine Doctor and Healer.

Jesus, when You were a young man beginning Your public life

among Your people, You became known at once as the God-sent physician who healed all the sick.

People knew, Jesus, that You healed the suffering and the handicapped who were brought to You. You placed Your hands on the sick, the blind, the lame, the mentally tormented, and they were all healed. You praised these people for their faith in You, for their trust in Your goodness, Your power, and Your love for them.

Jesus, we know You are right here with us today, here in this room. And you love each of us, as You loved each of Your people then. We are Your disciples, Lord, and we are eager to listen to Your word. We believe in You, and we ask You to increase our faith. We are listening to Your advice that we must forgive one another from our hearts, to be healed by You in mind and body. We ask You, Jesus, to take all bitterness and resentment out of our hearts. Help us right now, Lord, to forgive each and everyone who may have hurt us in any way. We ask pardon of those whom we have hurt. We ask You, kind and forgivng Jesus, to remove from us all obstacles to Your healing power.

Loving Jesus, take away all our narrowness and selfishness, so that we can open our hearts wide to receive Your refreshing grace. Whenever we receive You, Jesus, in Holy Communion, let Your powerful presence work wonders of healing in us. Heal us, Jesus, of those wounds we don't even recognize. Heal us of all that is making us unhappy, or anxious, or worried, or depressed, or lonely, or bitter.

Let your wonderful presence turn our sorrows into great joy. Give us the deep peace and trust of Your saints. Fill every part of us with Your healing and saving power.

HE CARES

Twenty-second Week of the Year, Thursday   **Luke 5:1-11**

If you combine Matthew's Gospel report of the calling of Simon, with Luke's report, you get an early version of Dale Carnegie. Without ever having read "How to Win Friends and Influence People," Jesus showed how He appreciated persons in a genuine human way. Since He had decided to make a group of fishermen His first co-workers, He wanted to show His personal interest in them and His ability to understand them.

Jesus cares about these men. He knows their luck is down; they've been fishing all night and caught nothing, and their living depends on success in fishing. Watch Jesus: He borrows their boat, so that He will only be "returning a favor" when He hauls in the fish for them. He gives them a real *lift* by a huge catch of fish. This will make up for weeks of bad luck, and will cheer them up. Then He wins them over by explaining how He needs them for His work as much as they needed Him for theirs. He shares rather than dominates. The whole scene is a beautiful indirect exchange of compliments, appreciation of one another. An art we're too likely to forget in these days of disagreements and competition and generation gaps.

We might recall that between Christ and His apostles there was a real generation gap, a big one. They were young, but they had the old view, while He had the new view in religion, traditions, and politics. These fishermen were hardly innovators or intellectuals, but Christ surely was. The differences came out often: they understood Him so little. Yet He could work with them, because He had come to save, not to condemn. He had the love and patience needed. An important quality in all great men: the ability to appreciate the good in people you may well disagree with and perhaps find hard to tolerate. But what is the definition of a true friend? "Someone who knows you very well—but likes you anyway."

> Jesus, You accept us all, just as we are. Can we do less—and be Christians?

RENEWAL

Twenty-second Week of the Year, Friday   **Luke 5:33-39**

It is rather obvious that Jesus frequently clashed with the Pharisees, because His view of life seemed new and radical to them.

They took themselves as representing the old tradition, and He brought things new and fresh, insights they had never heard of, ideas that were young and alive, and they were frightened. They had become smug in the old rut, and His teachings were shaking the old rut considerably. His answers forced people to think, and His actions rocked the very foundations of the old ingrained habits. His common sense about the strict Sabbath observance, for instance, angered them. His preference for charity above the Sabbath rules threatened them.

Jesus was so superior to them, they could not understand. He did not want His disciples glum and gloomy as the Pharisees, because He had brought the joy and peace of a new freedom, a happy friendship with God, a victory over sin and death.

The news Jesus had come to bring was anything but sad or depressing. He brought the joy of a complete renewal, a rebirth, a change of heart for man, and an outpouring of God's mercy and forgiveness, a renewed earth by the fire of the Holy Spirit.

Everything new and fresh and young should remind us of this renewal of the earth. The little child being baptized is new and fresh in the living waters of Christ. The fresh season of spring is like the new dawn of Christ's resurrection. He rose early in the morning, and the new day of eternal life was born. The new spring leaves and the freshly opened blossoms partake in the new glory of the risen Lord.

New discoveries remind us of the great new discovery of God, which we made in the coming of His beloved Son. All the sights and sounds of new life, of young trees and the child-like joy of the bird's morning song, the fresh spring rain falling, the clean laughter of young children—all are God's messages of renewal, of the new beginning always offered to us, of our eternal youth in His resurrection.

Lord God, enlighten our minds and open our hearts, so that Your new gifts and renewed graces may always find room in us.

DON'T BE PICKY

Twenty-second Week of the Year, Saturday   **Luke 6:1-5**

This is the third time in the year this gospel story appears, since it is found almost verbatim in all three synoptic gospels. Luke's account here is very short yet right to the point. He describes in a very simple manner the plucking of a few heads of grain, shelling them by rubbing them together with hands and then eating the small handful of kernels. Any of us who have a little country background have seen farmers do this or have done it ourselves. A very small insignificant act.

Yet the Pharisees are scandalized. All they can think of is the law, the law of Sabbath rest which was interpreted to include preparing food as one of the forbidden works.

Jesus answers their human accusations by referring to the story of David and his men eating the forbidden bread because they were hungry. He answers the human objection with the divinely inspired Scriptures.

We find it rather repulsive, small, on the part of the Pharisees to bring up such an objection. It is really picky, terribly petty, to make an issue out of plucking and shelling a few grains of wheat while walking through the field, be it on the Sabbath day or not.

But are we certain we are not petty, picky, over meticulous in our own way sometimes to the extent of being difficult to others, making their lives miserable? Are we reasonably aware of human differences, that what is important to some is of very little consequence to another? And unless it is a matter of really important principles, the law of love supercedes all. This is what Jesus is teaching us here.

Maybe objectively we are right with regard to this or that matter, the way the Liturgy ought to be conducted, how the sick ought to be treated professionally and pastorally, but can we make exceptions for special people, special circumstances where love asks it?

**O God, You are a God of kindness, mercy and love.
Make us like You in our love for each other.**

LOVE WHEN IT HURTS

Twenty-third Week of the Year, Monday   Luke 6:6-11

The Gospel passage gives us a good lesson in the spirit in which God's laws are to be kept. The Scribes and Pharisees were ready to find a charge against Jesus if He cured the man with the withered hand on the Sabbath. Jesus said, "I ask you, is it lawful to do good on the Sabbath—or evil? To preserve life—or destroy it?" Then He cured the man though it was the Sabbath day.

God's law should never be used as an excuse for not doing good. Sticking to a rule is no excuse for failing in charity. One other time the Pharisees excused themselves from honoring parents because they said they were giving this honor to God instead. Christ's comment was "Hypocrites; these people pay me lip service, but their hearts are far from Me." No, we can't honor Christ and at the same time not honor our parents.

Today we hear much talk about love of neighbor, sincerity, genuineness, authenticity. Could Christ make the same accusation against us? Accuse us of talk, talk, talk; but there is no real living love, no honesty, no sincerity?

Talk is cheap, easy. It doesn't take sacrifice. Real love-in-action does. To love we must give, give ourselves. It may be hard sometimes to deny ourselves, but it is the only way to real, genuine, sincere love. Otherwise we are definitely hypocrites.

You can talk all you want about what should be done to help the poor and starving of the world, but you only prove your genuine Christian love by giving till it hurts. No self-deception then, especially if you do it without fanfare, without any publicity.

If we want to get anywhere in really keeping God's laws we must learn that love is the Number one commandment. And we have to be honest and sincere with ourselves. We have to love and act out of love even when it hurts, when it makes us unpopular with authorities perhaps, like Christ with the Pharisees. Love must be the first criterion in the observance of all laws.

"You are my friends if you do the things that I command . . . love one another (Jn 15:14, 17).

THE GOSPEL MESSAGE

Twenty-third Week of the Year, Tuesday   Luke 6:12-19

This short passage from Luke's Gospel seems to contain a
summary of the whole Good News. It tells us:

1) Jesus lives in communion with God. He is not a "self-
sufficient" or "self-made" man, but a God-made man, who draws His
power from God.

2) After a night of prayer, Jesus chooses His twelve apostles from
the larger number of followers. Yet, not all will be faithful to Him:
there is Judas, the betrayer.

3) Jesus comes down from the mountain of prayer to the level of
everyday needs. The people who follow Him come from everywhere:
Gentiles as well as Israelites. They have come for two reasons: a) to
hear His teaching, b) to be healed of their ills.

4) Jesus has power over Satan and defeats him: "those with
unclean spirits were cured."

5) The people want to touch Jesus, because power goes out from
Him to heal everyone. Jesus has come as universal Savior and Healer.
He has "the personal touch" in the very best sense of that word. (He
establishes a Church to continue that personal touch.)

Notice how Luke's summary of the Gospel message here speaks to
our life:

1) Regular prayer time is essential. We need to draw power from
God for our daily life. Otherwise we will be overpowered by the
paganism around us, that "world" which Jesus warned us would
"hate us" as it hated Him before us.

2) We need to hear the words of Jesus, as the people did. Regular
reading of the Word of God, and a thoughtful listening to Him.

3) We can conquer Satan in our life by making Jesus our only
Lord. Jesus, and only Jesus, drives the evil spirits out of our life.

4) We must frequently touch Jesus to be healed. Jesus touched all
the people who came to Him for healing, and His powerful touch was
always effective, wherever the people accepted Him. He has given us
ways to touch Him. In the Sacraments of Holy Eucharist and
Reconciliation we touch Jesus in order to be healed. Remember the
Lord's words when He healed someone: "Your faith has saved you."

Jesus, be my only Lord. I trust in You completely, that I may be healed!

REJOICE, YOU POOR

Twenty-third Week of the Year, Wednesday   Luke 6:20-26

The discourse of Jesus which St. Luke records in today's Gospel passage and the rest of Chapter six characterizes the Christian as one to be known for his poverty, for his caution against the dangers of wealth. "Blest are you poor, you who hunger and weep, but woe to you rich, you who are full and who laugh now."

Jesus on various occasions had strong words about how riches, or how the attachment to things of this world, could make it hard for us. The rich young man who wanted to be perfect was told to sell what he had, give it to the poor, and then he could follow Christ perfectly. But it was too much to give up. He went away sad.

Frankly what Jesus is telling us is that riches make it hard to grow in virtue. To be poor makes it easier to lead a good life, if with our poverty we are poor in spirit, and not envious of the rich.

Jesus counsels poverty for everyone who wants to really grow in virtue and holiness.

We are living in an era of what is referred to as one which emphasizes incarnational theology—that since Christ became man, all things men do, all things men have must be good. This is true; we look at the world and all that is in it as basically good in themselves, that the world and all things in it must be restored in Christ.

All well and good, but if anything we have draws us away from being just, kind, considerate, prayerful, then it is not good for us. We can easily become too desirous of luxuries, ease, comfort and anything money can buy. We begin to consider many of these things as necessities of life to the neglect of the poor and other causes which our money ought to support.

Jesus in the Gospels teaches us that it is better for us to be poor than rich. It is easier for us; we are more free that way, since we are much less attached. We have less to worry about.

O Lord, great is Your world and all that is in it. May it all praise You and be a sign of Your love for the poor.

CHRISTIAN PATIENCE

Twenty-third Week of the Year, Thursday   Luke 6:27-38

"Love your enemies; do good to those who hate you."

In his treatise on Psalm 54, St. Augustine says, "Never think that the wicked are in this world for nothing, or that God does no good with them. Every wicked man lives either to amend his life or to exercise the good men. But let us not hate them, though they continue to persecute us, for we do not know whether they will persevere to the end in their wickedness. And many times, when you imagine that you are hating your enemy, it is your brother you hate, without knowing it."

What might have happened to St. Paul, had the Christians hated him instead of praying for him, and bearing patiently his persecution? What might have happened to St. Augustine, had his mother despaired of him, had not St. Ambrose shown his Christian patience? St. Augustine knew of what he spoke. Of St. Ambrose he says, "All unknowingly I was brought by God to him, that knowing I should be brought by him to God. That man of God received me like a father, and as bishop welcomed my coming. From the very first I loved him not only as a teacher of the truth, which I had utterly despaired of finding in Your Church, but also for his kindness towards me. I attended carefully what he preached to the people, not with the right intention, but only to judge whether his eloquence was equal to his fame" (*Confessions*, Book V).

Augustine, a man once so unworthy, became a great saint. With Christian patience, his mother, St. Monica, prayed for his conversion. St. Ambrose added to hers the forgiving love of Christ.

Lord Jesus, only You can tell us how many millions of unexpected conversions have been won by Your friends—by their prayerful, Christian love and patience.

KNOW IT ALL?

Twenty-third Week of the Year, Friday   Luke 6:39-42

"Do not judge, and you will not be judged. Do not condemn, and you will not be condemned . . . Why look at the speck in your brother's eye when you miss the plank in your own?" These words are part of the Lord's instructions on the necessity of charity. He returns to this theme constantly.

He does not mean that mutual esteem must be blind to sin or the dangers of sin. But He does say, "Let us take a critical look at ourselves, before we wax eloquent in the evaluation of others." Certain questions must repeatedly come to mind: is my criticism of others really constructive and creative, or is it simply the old-time sledge-hammer of narrow-minded envy? Is my impatience with others really apostolic? Is it mature judgment? Are my zeal and its results really superior to that "sad generation of has-beens," or is the surface beginning to wear, and the new brand of conformism already exposed? Don't I commit the very faults I condemn?

We cannot afford to forget, what is new and streamlined and my own idea is not thereby faultless. Best results will always come through honest self-criticism and open-minded charity. Reform begins within. Without real self-knowledge and mutual respect, revolt is meaningless or worse.

The Lord Himself, who alone had reason for pride, predicted that only the humble would be exalted. How often we've heard people say, "One thing I've always noticed about really great men. They always seem to be very humble men, too. No arrogance, no superiority complex, no attitude of know-it-all." Quite understandable! For who sees better how little we humans really know than the genius, the master of his field?

Genuine wisdom is always accompanied by vast reverence for God, for fellow men, for the world. The world's truly greatest have learned to "fear God" and to "honor all men."

> **Have mercy, gracious Lord, Your blessing give,**
> **And flood us with the glory of Your face;**
> **Bathed in that light let all Your creatures live,**
> **May all the earth search out Your saving grace.**

BEAR FRUIT

Twenty-third Week of the Year, Saturday   **Luke 6:43-49**

Today Jesus concludes a long teaching He has been giving. To review what has happened in the Gospel this week: after a night in prayer, Jesus chooses His twelve apostles. Then He heals many people in a large crowd. He follows this with a special instruction for His followers, beginning with beatitudes and woes. Beatitudes: blessed are the poor, the hungry, the weeping, the persecuted. Woes: but woe to the rich, the filled, those of the easy life, the popular. The beatitudes and woes are another impressive view of Christ's doctrine that the last shall be first and the first shall be last.

Jesus then follows with His most often repeated teaching: love your enemies, be unselfish, do not set yourself up as judge of others, be generous and forgiving.

At the end of this teaching Jesus concludes (6:43-49), "Bear fruit from this instruction! If my words are in your heart, your fruit will be good. And remember, it is not enough to say, 'Lord, Lord.' You need to build your life on the solid foundation of obedience to the Lord's word. Otherwise your Christian life will wash away in the floods of this world."

Who builds the house without laying a foundation? The one who hears God's word but does not live by it. Who is the person that digs deep and lays solid footings? The one who listens carefully to Jesus and obeys His word.

> **Who comes, O Lord, to pitch his tent with You?**
> **Who on the holy mount of God is fit to dwell?**
> **The man of justice, who is thoughtful of the truth,**
> **Of fellow men he has no evil thing to tell.**
> **He finds no joy in flaying neighbor with reproach,**
> **But rather, those who honor God he honors well.**
> **Through pain or loss he keeps his pledged and promised word,**
> **He takes no bribes, for innocence he cannot sell.**
> **Injustice to a fellow man he cannot bear:**
> **Unmoved he stands, O Lord, as guarded citadel (Ps 15).**

I AM NOT WORTHY

Twenty-fourth Week of the Year, Monday   **Luke 7:1-10**

Outwardly, the man was a pagan, an officer in a foreign army. The presence of his kind in this land of clannish, narrow-minded people was anything but welcome. He represented the invaders, the oppressors, the foreign government which did not understand these people's traditions and customs and attitudes and their very special religion.

Normally this officer would have been hated. But this one was loved. The Pharisees—usually haughty and critical—actually begged Jesus to hear this man's request, for he had done much for their nation, even building them a synagogue in which to worship their true God.

Then the man himself sent word to Jesus, revealing his character and spirit. "Lord, do not trouble yourself, for I am not worthy to have you enter my house. That is why I did not presume to come to you myself. Just give the order and my servant will be cured" (Lk 7:6-7).

By putting the Roman officer's words into our mouths when we approach the table of the Lord, the Church has made this pagan the examplar of the Christian's approach to Christ. The humility, the reverence, the deep faith of the man come through clear and strong.

Jesus praised the deep, manly faith of the officer, and remarked that He had not found so much faith among the chosen people. Faith is a firm trust in God, in His power and goodness, in His love for you. Faith accepts God's wisdom and His providence. Faith opens our eyes and ears to God and His love, to God and His purpose in everything.

O God, Your way is holy: what god is like the Lord?
What other gods work wonders that they might be adored?
All nature feels Your sure hand, Your love and truth we know.
The waters see and tremble, the skies are strong in voice,
White lightnings clear Your pathway and in Your Name rejoice!
(Ps 77)

JESUS IN US

Twenty-fourth Week of the Year, Tuesday   **Luke 7:11-17**

St. Luke, the writer of today's Gospel incident, was a medical doctor. In the true spirit of his profession, he was a man who was very sensitive to people's sufferings. That is why he gives more attention to the plight of the widowed Mother, who lost her only son, than to the miracle of calling her son back to life.

Luke describes the situation; how her only son died at an early age. And at that time there were no widow's pensions, no insurance policies, no social welfare, no nice jobs for women. Life could be very harsh for a lonely middle-aged woman.

Our Lord was quick to realize the tragedy of the situation. He was moved to pity for the woman and told her not to weep. Then He gave life to the young man, her only son.

The message of the Gospel? Certainly it is the compassion and understanding of Christ shown to someone in need. Henceforth for that widow the reality of God's love could never be mere theory. She had experienced it in a real way.

And today—how is God's love made real today? No other way than through us, who are Christ's Body. To the sick, to the aged, to the poor, to anyone in need—Christ's love becomes real only through our compassion, our kindness, our help to their need.

We should ask ourselves how aware we are of the needs of others around us. Their needs may not be great—they may only need a kind word or a smile—they may simply need to be listened to with patience and understanding. But at that very moment our presence might just mean for them the experience of Christ's love, and that is what counts.

My hands and my feet, O Jesus, are Your hands and Your feet in all the acts I do as a member of Your Body.

TREACHEROUS TONGUES

Twenty-fourth Week of the Year, Wednesday   Luke 7:31-35

Suppose I call up an old friend one day, and after the usual small talk I ask him (or her) what he's doing for a living. "I make my living on minor injuries," he says.

"I suppose you operate a kind of first-aid station?" I ask, unsuspecting.

"No, I don't repair the injuries. I give them," he replies, undisturbed.

"You *give* them?" I am puzzled, but only for a moment. "You vaccinate people? You give allergy shots? You feed people intravenously?"

Now he is laughing at what he calls my ignorance. "The fact is," says he, "I carry a good number of pins and needles with me wherever I go, and when I come across someone I know, I take a good swift jab at him. I get a great kick out of the injuries I can inflict daily. It's a daily free-time hobby, and I live well on it."

With that he hangs up the phone, and I am left to wonder. If he wasn't fooling me, that's one friend I can do without. I don't think I'll be seeing more of him—but how can it be? Yes, it can be, and it is! How many of us live—and think we live well—on the injuries we do to others.

So Jesus wrestles with the Pharisees' treacherous tongues. No matter what He does, no matter what John the Baptist does, it's wrong, it's evil in Pharisaic eyes and on Pharisaic tongues. The shame of making a fat living by injuring others! Yet that is what too many of us attempt with our tongues.

Slander, writes Shakespeare, is like a knife

> Whose edge is sharper than the sword, whose tongue
> Outvenoms all the worms of Nile, whose breath
> Rides on the posting winds and both belie
> All corners of the world: Kings, queens and states,
> Maids, matrons, nay the secrets of the grave
> This viperous slander enters.
>
> *(Cymbeline*, III, 4)

Jesus, Lord of love and self-giving, it is clear in the Gospels that You didn't please everyone. The sharp tongues were wagging busily. How can I please everyone, then? Let me not on that account give up striving to please YOU, Lord. You set me that example by Your constancy in pleasing your heavenly Father.

WHOSE TEST?

Twenty-fourth Week of the Year, Thursday   Luke 7:36-50

"A certain Pharisee invited Jesus to dine with him." We read elsewhere in the Gospels that the Pharisees invited Jesus to their homes so that they could watch Him closely, so that they could put Him to the test, so they could pass judgment on Him. Here Simon the Pharisee sits in judgment on Jesus—so he thinks! He says to himself, "If this man were a prophet, he would know who and what sort of woman this is that touches him—that she is a sinner."

What irony that such men can presume to sit in judgment over the Eternal Judge of all the living and dead. It is not Jesus who is being tested and judged; it is those around him. People like Simon, who at that very moment is failing the test. People like the "sinful woman," who at the same moment is passing the test beautifully. For the universal Judge, the Son of God, here declares to the woman, "Your sins are forgiven. Your faith has been your salvation."

By failing the Lord's test, Simon the Pharisee is a warning to us. He shows us how it is not enough to be physically close to Jesus, it is not enough to be called a Christian, or to do God the overwhelming favor of appearing in His church. Simon sits right next to Jesus, yet that great blessing is lost on him spiritually.

By contrast, the poor woman is a great consolation to us. She shows us how to benefit no end in approaching Jesus. She scores at the top of the class because she knows herself clearly, honestly, and humbly. She knows Jesus in the same way, and approaches Jesus with love and worship and repentance, and she places all her trust in Him. She is not bothered by the arrogant judgment of the big-wigs at the dinner. She instinctively understands that the true judgment of her case belongs to Jesus, and knows whose side God is on. She responds well to the movements of God's grace in her life. Jesus declares, "Her many sins are forgiven because of her great love."

Lord, the next time I want to pass judgment on someone, let me remember who is really being tested, and who is the one, true, worthy, all-knowing Judge.

THE FAITHFUL WOMEN

Twenty-fourth Week of the Year, Friday   **Luke 8:1-3**

We see in Luke's Gospel that, unlike the Rabbis of His time, Jesus has women as disciples. They are, in fact, His most devoted followers. Luke tells us how faithful to Jesus these first Christian women are.

Women disciples sympathized with Jesus and followed Him, weeping for Him as He carried His cross to execution. (Lk 23:27) Both Luke and John tell us of women who stood with Mary His mother at the cross of Jesus and assisted in His burial. Mark mentions this, too. All four evangelists tell us that these women were the first to see the Risen Jesus on Easter Sunday morning, the reward of their persevering devotion to Jesus.

We find special emphasis on the faithful qualities of the Christian women in Luke's writings—his Gospel and his Acts of the Apostles. Luke illustrates in his books what Paul tells the Galatians (3:28): "There is no longer slave or free, male or female; we are all one in Christ Jesus."

Luke always parallels an account of a man with that of a woman. Gabriel appears to Zechariah and to Mary, and Mary comes out the uncontested winner of that one. Elizabeth also has more faith than her husband Zechariah. The faithful old man Simeon is paralleled by the holy prophetess Anna. Jesus heals the sick servant of the Roman officer, but He raises from the dead the only son of the widow of Naim.

Jesus praises the charity of the Good Samaritan, but he

immediately follows it by praise of the devotion of Mary, the sister of Martha (Lk 10). Luke reminds us frequently that men and women are equal, and equally endowed with God's gifts.

The women of today's Gospel were cured of their infirmities because they wanted to be cured. We follow their response to Jesus and their spiritual progress in the Gospel. From assisting Jesus out of their means, generosity, they go to sharing in the sufferings of Jesus' sacrifice, and so they share in His glorious resurrection, and become the first preachers of the Good News: the Lord is risen. He has passed through death to glory.

BEARING FRUIT

Twenty-fourth Week of the Year, Saturday   **Luke 8:4-15**

We are told in the Gospel today that loving God and neighbor means two things: to hear the Word of God and to keep it.

Many Jews in the time of Christ were farmers; they understood about planting, good soil, watering, growing crops. And so Christ said that spreading God's Word was just like that, like planting seeds. You've got to do it at the right time, in the right place, in the right way.

He said that some people just don't want to hear God's Word at a certain time, or place, or way. And that is why God's Word doesn't help them. That's why they don't bear fruit.

But for those who really want God's Word, it opens up new worlds. It gives them courage to carry on, enlightens their thoughts and words, brings love to their actions.

Christ's own words are: "The seed on good ground are those who hear the word in a spirit of openness, retain it, and bear fruit through perseverance."

"Bear fruit through perseverance." That's the really important part. It's rather easy to be part of a crowd listening to God's Word about love and justice, the rights of others, our duties in life. But to carry them out in perseverance, in our daily lives, day after day, that is another thing.

Or again, some of us may be a bit choosy. We like to hear the nice words about love and reward and unity. But when Christ speaks to us about the sins we commit, the injustices we do, or about the punishments these sins deserve, we don't want to hear that kind of Word of God at all. We are not consistent. We just look for the easy side of things.

Unless we accept God's message in its entirety we really are not listening. Unless we put into practice the whole of God's law to the best of our ability we really are not bearing fruit through perseverance.

Lord, I open my heart up to You as a field, ready to receive from You the seed of Your word.

BE A LIGHT

Twenty-fifth Week of the Year, Monday   **Luke 8:16-18**

The parable of the lamp in Luke's Gospel today evidently refers to the lamp that was left burning in the entrance of Hellenistic houses so that it would give light to those entering. The immediate application is quite clear. The lamp is to give its light to the Gentiles who are also coming into the kingdom.

The Jews were not to keep the light of faith just for themselves. They were not to hide it so that no one else would see it. but rather put it on a lamp stand, that is, make it known, easily accessible to all peoples.

We, too, have been given the light of faith. The parable applies just as well to us. Does our faith shine through in our lives so that it can easily be seen by others who may not have been so favored? Does our Christian life and love attract others to see the influence of our faith in our lives?

We know that actions speak louder than words. We know the power of good example. Today's Gospel parable tells us that we are obliged to give good example, to have the light of our Christian lives shine brightly. How marvelous if through our good example, through our living faith, another may be brought to faith in Christ.

"Do not put your light under a bushel basket or under a bed. Put it on a lamp stand so that whoever comes can see it."

O Lord, I do want my life to be a witness to your good news. Help me to be a living Gospel that can be seen by all.

CHRISTIAN MAXIMUM

Twenty-fifth Week of the Year, Tuesday   Luke 8:19-21

In the new life, the Christian life which Jesus came to bring us, you have the whole spectrum, the whole scale from zero to a hundred. On the bottom of the scale you have the irreducible minimum, about five or six spiritual heart-beats per minute, so little faith that you can't see it without a microscope. Less than that, you have no life: you have cardiac arrest.

Then on the top of the scale, you have the spiritual maximum. Next to Jesus, Mary is the Christian maximum. She has it all: she is completely filled with the kingdom of God. Mary is so overflowing with the Spirit of God that there is no room for sin in her life.

Now St. Luke says that one day Jesus was told, "Your mother and your brothers wish to see you." Jesus answered, "My mother and my brothers are those who hear the word of God and act upon it."

That's one of the most liberal, democratic statements ever made! Jesus says, "It's not being related by human blood that counts. What counts is this: being related to God in the Spirit, in godly love, in being near to God your Father by a love relationship." In this statement Jesus was not in any way taking honor from Mary His mother. In fact, He wanted to make sure we would honor her for the most important reason. Not because she was His mother, but because she was so close to God by her love, because she opened her heart completely to God's Will, because she was filled with the Holy Spirit, because she was full of faith and trust in the Lord.

So when we honor Mary, we say to her what Elizabeth said, when Mary came into her house: (Lk 1:42-45) "Blessed are you among women, and blessed is the fruit of your womb. But who am I that the mother of my Lord should come to me? Blessed is she who trusted that the Lord's words to her would be fulfilled."

And like Mary, we praise the Lord for His work in her life: "My being proclaims the greatness of the Lord; my spirit finds joy in God my savior" (Lk 1:46-47).

CONFRONTED WITH GOSPEL

Twenty-fifth Week of the Year, Wednesday   **Luke 9:1-6**

The Gospel today is about the mission of the twelve. Jesus sends out His twelve into the world to make people face life, make decisions about themselves and the world they live in, and to make them look at their values.

These Apostles, who are to live in poverty—"take nothing for the journey"—to give them more authority to speak, are to push people a little, to confront them, to require them to make choices that are in line with the Gospel of Jesus. They are to preach repentance. And that means, not just sorrow for sins, but putting one's whole life in order. What do I want my life to be? What basic life-decision has to be made about my career, my job, my relationship with my family, about the upbringing of my children?

Jesus often demanded of people that they make choices like that. He said: "He who is not with Me is against Me. It is either God or Mammon. If you wish to follow Me you must deny self and take up the cross." A choice must be made.

In practical terms this might mean answering questions such as: How would I accept the news that I, or a dear one, have cancer? Would I give in to depression? Would I make it hard for my family? Or would I take the opportunity to use the remaining time well, give an example of cheerfulness and humble acceptance of God's will?

How would I accept being fired from my job? Anger and resentment? Jealousy and envy? Or with charitable understanding and courage look into and accept a new future with confidence in my God-given ability and God's providence?

It is all a matter of values. What do I really want my life to stand for? The Apostles went out to confront people with such decisions. The Gospel today and those who preach the Gospel still confront us today. What is our response?

> **You have told us, Lord, that whatever we sow, that we will also reap. Help us to sow only the seeds of the Gospel.**

WHO IS THIS JESUS?

Twenty-fifth Week of the Year, Thursday   **Luke 9:7-9**

It is very interesting how Luke with three short verses fills in the interval when the apostles were out on their missionary journey, preaching and healing. News about Jesus and His disciples had spread more and more. Even Herod the tetrarch, ruler of Galilee, heard about all that was happening and he was perplexed. He didn't know Jesus. He hadn't seen Him. He only heard what some of the people were saying: John has come back to life; Elijah has appeared; one of the old prophets has risen.

Herod couldn't understand. One thing he was sure of—it wasn't John—he himself had beheaded John. But this Jesus? He wondered what He was like and he became curious. He wanted to see Him.

Herod, as we see throughout the Gospels, was a shallow man. He had no backbone. He was weak. Here Luke tells us he wanted to see Jesus out of mere curiosity. He wasn't interested in seeing whether there was here a true prophet, perhaps even the Messiah.

What is *our* interest in Jesus like? Is it shallow, merely a curiosity to know Him historically? Do we seek to know Him as Savior, as Lord, as the Son of God? What does Jesus mean to us in our everyday lives? Is Jesus real to us, not only as the Risen Lord in heaven, but in the Eucharist, in the Gospels, in the Church, in people? What would we answer if Herod asked us, "Who is this man, about whom I have heard all these reports?"

Jesus, I want to come to know You more and more as my personal Lord and Savior.

DYING WITH CHRIST

Twenty-fifth Week of the Year, Friday   **Luke 9:18-22**

"The Son of Man must first endure many sufferings, be rejected by the elders, the high priests and the Scribes, and be put to death, and then be raised up on the third day." Christ here predicts His passion and death, in which He poured out His blood for our redemption.

Among all peoples suffering, dying for others, pouring out one's life-blood is taken as a sign of generous self-giving. In the darkest hour of World War II when Churchill told his people he had nothing to offer them but "blood, sweat and tears," he used an image all the world understood. To the Jews blood had a special significance. It reminded them of an animal victim offered in order to procure release from the sentence of death. Their escape from Egypt was a memory branded on their consciousness. And this escape was a direct result of the killing of the Egyptians first born, when the Jews were saved because of the blood on the door posts.

The letter to the Hebrews makes this forceful statement: "Without the shedding of blood there is no forgiveness." And it goes on to say that the blood of Christ, offered up unblemished to God cleanses our conscience from dead works to worship the living God. This blood of Christ cleanses us, not exteriorly, but interiorly. It not only cleanses, it redeems us.

But this is not a one way street. The New Testament, like the Old, is a covenant, an agreement. We must do our part, too. We must respond to God's call to share in the paschal mystery. We must interiorly unite ourselves to Christ in His suffering. We must open our hearts to the redeeming blood of Christ. We must be one with Christ in self-giving, in a life of unselfishness and charity, regardless of what the cost may be in blood, sweat and tears.

If we have died with You O Christ, we believe that we
shall also live together with You.

A GREAT FUGUE

Twenty-fifth Week of the Year, Saturday   Luke 9:43-45

"The disciples failed to understand: the meaning was so concealed
from them that they did not grasp it at all."
Our lives are like a great fugue. A humorous commentator was
once asked, "What is a fugue?" He answered, "It is a musical number
in which the voices enter one by one, and the audience leaves, two by
two." Thus we can say that God's will in our life is like a great fugue:
his divine plan unfolds, one event after another. To the inexperienced
ear, a "fugue" appears to be musical confusion. And so to the
inexperienced, worldly, thoughtless Christian, God's wisdom is
confusion.

But to the expert musician a fugue is to the ear what a gorgeous
Persian rug is to the eye; so to the man or woman of faith, God's
wisdom is a work of unspeakable beauty. As God's voices "enter, one
by one," how many Christians, like the unappreciative audience,
walk out on God, "two by two." Their ideals may have been high, but
when God tries to teach them the wisdom of the saints, they fail Him.
They cannot match the reality to the ideal.

The limited joys and painful sorrows that one after another slip in
and out of our lives in apparent disarray—what meaning have they?
Are they not the threads of His infinitely beautiful pattern, are they
not His weaving, a weaving far beyond our sight and hearing?

Lord, let me never fail to hear and appreciate the "great
fugue" You are composing out of my life. It may be a
mystery to me now, but if I accept Your Word, I will
come to experience the unlimited beauty of Your work.

When all worn out, You sat beside the shaded well,
A stranger came and filled Your cup, as John can tell,

But You gave her the living waters—oh surprise!
One cup she gave, and fountains sprang before her eyes! (Jn 4).

HUMILITY

Twenty-sixth Week of the Year, Monday   Luke 9:46-50

How often Our Lord speaks of the value of humility, of how the humble will be exalted, the least will the the greatest. In the Gospel today the disciples of the Lord discussed as to which of them was the greatest. Jesus knew their thoughts and took a little child and placed it beside Him. He meant the child to be a symbol of the simplicity, humility and unpretentiousness that He wanted them to have. And He said, "The least one among you is the greatest." That is, the one who is least in the eyes of men often is the greatest in the eyes of God if he truly accepts his status and condition.

It has been said for ages that humility is simply the truth. That is true, but it is not enough. Indeed humility contains the knowledge about our qualities and that all the good in us is from God. But even to know this won't make us humble. Our conduct, our actions and speech might not at all correspond to that knowledge. We might act as if all the credit were coming to us. For example, we might know and realize that the fact that we are more handsome than others is a gift to us from God. We didn't deserve it. Still we might act as if we deserved special honor and adulation. Or we may do better work than some others. Our ability is from God. We know this, yet we make sure that everybody hears about how wonderful we work, otherwise we think our efforts are in vain. That is not humility. It is pride.

To be humble, in short, we must be satisfied with whatever God has given us in life. We realize our dependence on Him and our true relations with our fellow men and we shape our conduct accordingly.

This does not mean we shouldn't use our God-given qualities to better ourselves. Even this use, this effort is a gift from God. Humility does not lead us to deny the good in us. That is false humility. We are to admit both the good and the bad in us. We are to be honest.

Humility keeps us in the right place where alone we can be happy.

Jesus, meek and humble of heart, make our hearts like unto Thine.

REJECTED

Twenty-sixth Week of the Year, Tuesday   Luke 9:51-56

Jesus "firmly resolved to proceed toward Jerusalem." Twice in this chapter of his Gospel, Luke tells us that Jesus predicted how His people would reject Him and kill Him. They will reject their own Savior out of envy, prejudice, closed minds, an unwillingness to change and be converted. The Gospels tell us this often enough.

Jesus knows why He is going to Jerusalem, and what will happen to Him there. He has already asked His followers to carry that cross with Him.

Now He goes to a Samaritan town, and these foreigners reject Him, too. His own capital, Jerusalem, has already turned a deaf ear, and now the enemies of Jerusalem reject Jesus, too—because He is going to Jerusalem. He certainly knows what it means to be refused, turned down, unaccepted. But He never gets resentful or bitter about it.

Notice how the disciples want to respond by punishing the rejecters. Jesus says, "No." He reprimands them for having an attitude of resentment and revenge.

But the Lord also just stood beside a child and said, "Whoever welcomes a child in my name welcomes me" (Lk 9:48). The implication is, whoever rejects the most insignificant person, like this little child, is also rejecting me, just as the people of Samaria and Jerusalem are rejecting me. This is why St. Paul tells us to accept one another in Christ. That small, humble person you accept is Jesus.

Jesus says, "Whoever welcomes this little one welcomes me." So Jesus takes the side of the poorest, the most miserable and defenseless, those who don't have the money or the power to defend themselves against being rejected. We see Jesus here, going from town to town, to see if anyone will accept Him. How tragic was the case of those who did not welcome Jesus. How much they lost! Then you and I are haunted by the words of Jesus in our own life: "Whoever welcomes these little ones welcomes me. For the least one among you is the greatest."

> **Jesus, don't let me forget the message before I meet one of those little ones again!**

COST OF DISCIPLESHIP

Twenty-sixth Week of the Year, Wednesday   **Luke 9:57-62**

Jesus had a way with Him in stirring His disciples to thought. He speaks here of the requirements for discipleship and some of the language is quite strong. But there is an occasional play on words which stirs the imagination and makes one question the meaning. "Let the dead bury the dead." The meaning of course, is to let the spiritually dead bury the physically dead. Our work is with the living; our message is a message of life, new life.

Another thing that Jesus emphasizes is the difficulty of discipleship. "The foxes have lairs, the birds of the sky have nests, but the Son of Man has nowhere to lay His head." He tricks no one into following Him by making it sound rosy or romantic. He lays down the hard facts.

Another point Jesus makes is that the commitment should be a permanent one. "Whoever puts his hand to the plow but keeps looking back is unfit for the reign of God." Christ is telling us that we have a tendency to worry too much about our work, we are too much concerned about success. We become too easily engrossed in our work and recreation and forget our commitment to God and neighbor as true Christians.

Christian commitment is not a Sunday affair, or even a matter of prayer and daily Mass. It is much more. It means living our faith in action, at work, at recreation, in business, in politics, in all our contacts with our fellow men. It is not something we can turn off and on as we choose. It must be permanent, it must cover all the facets of our lives.

"O God, You are my God, You alone I seek. For you
my flesh pines, my soul thirsts. I will bless you while I
live. My soul clings fast to you" (Ps 63).

LIKE LAMBS AMONG WOLVES

Twenty-sixth Week of the Year, Thursday   Luke 10:1-12

Jesus assures His future missionaries that many souls await their
arrival: "The harvest is plentiful but the laborers are scarce." Much is
required of the Lord's laborers, if their work is to be effective. They
must be emptied of self and filled with Christ; their hearts must be
enlarged and deepened, that God's presence may fill them. Jesus
enjoins on Christians the duty to pray God for apostles of great zeal
and holiness: "Pray to the owner of the harvest to send out laborers to
reap it."

Though the harvest is great and plentiful, and the owner sends out
laborers to gather it, the enemies of man are always busy, and there is
continual danger to the good work of God's servants. Persecution,
disappointments, and even death may await the true disciple. Thus
Jesus reminds us, "Go then and remember, I am sending you like
lambs in the midst of wolves."

In these words, the Lord who is all wisdom spells out our
Christian vocation. It is one of both joy and sorrow, of success and
failure, of an abundant harvest and of wolves ever ready to devour the
unsuspecting lambs. Indeed, such has been the history of Christ's
Church, as prophesied by Himself.

We rejoice at the great courage and charity of the saints of God;
we are sad at the spectacle of ignorance, bad will, rejection, hatred
and cruelty on the part of their persecutors. We are glad at the spread
of Christ's kingdom on earth, for all the good things brought by faith
and the love of Christ. We sorrow at the many who remain blind and
cold at the news of their redemption.

These hard paradoxes are the mystery of Christianity, the mystery
of human freedom and human weakness, and the mystery of God's
way with man.

Jesus, King, and Mary, Queen of martyrs, help us not
to count the cost as we witness with our lives to the
Gospel.

THE LORD'S CURSES

Twenty-sixth Week of the Year, Friday   Luke 10:13-16

In the Gospel Jesus curses three towns of Galilee. Are we
surprised? Is it not the same Jesus who rebuked His disciples when
they sought to call down fire from heaven against a Samaritan town?
This Jesus told us to "love our enemies" and "pray for our
persecutors."

We realize, with Jesus and all the prophets, the dangers and the
tragedies born out of sin. We would give our lives, let us hope, to
"keep scandal from the little ones," the young, the pure, the innocent.
We would be angry, let us hope, on seeing evil done to innocent souls.
We would agree with Holy Scripture that the hatred of evil is the
beginning of wisdom.

Can we not see a paradox, then, in these curses of Jesus? They are
like a prophecy, warning sinners of the consequences of sins not
repented. They are a warning to us, who may "think ourselves just"
and fall into evils we have not the humility to recognize. And the
curses serve also to remind us how the infinite mercy of God brings
good out of evil. "All Scripture was written for our correction," writes
St. Paul. And so, we may add, the curses were also written for our
correction.

Though we do not wish literally that the sinner will perish, we can
surely wish that his worldly prosperity may perish, if that will save his
soul from worse evils. If we ourselves need punishment for our
correction, if suffering the consequences of our sins has enlightened
us and brought us wisdom and repentance, can we not desire the same
grace for those who anger us by their evil actions?

Here is the mystery, then, and the instruction contained in the
Lord's curses: not only the blessings of God, but the inspired curses
will save us, if we have the wisdom to heed them. May then the "curse

of sin" come upon the sinner now, while he has yet time to learn wisdom from it, and repent.

Lord Jesus Christ, Son of God, have mercy on me, a sinner.

PRAISE

Twenty-sixth Week of the Year, Saturday   Luke 10:17-24

Luke sums up the spirit of Jesus, man of praise, as His disciples come back from their mission preaching. Jesus shows them how to direct their joy to the praise of the Father. Then we get a glimpse at the style of Jesus' own prayer: it is joyful praise of the Father. "I offer you grateful praise, O Father, Lord of heaven and earth."

The truest prayer is praise; it is the most expanding form of communication. This is true in our relationships with one another. An attitude of praise, of appreciation, of outgoing love is the healthiest for both persons in the communication. All the more true in our attitude toward God. We communicate best when we know who the other person is, and who we are. Now God is everything great and wonderful. Jesus is simply the greatest! So praise is the most obvious and natural form of communication with Him. It expresses most accurately our right feelings in speaking with Him and in listening to Him. Let's not forget, listening is the better half of communication. Listening with praise and thanksgiving to the Lord.

Praise can take many forms, even silence or song. The song of praise opens us to God and the deepest feelings about Him. There are many prayers of praise in the Bible, God's prayerbook, and many of them are songs.

It is good to enjoy singing; it is a marvelous creation of God. But prayer-singing is communicating with the Lord, telling Him how we feel about Him, telling Him what it is that makes us love Him and thank Him and trust Him and make Him the center of our life. The song-prayer, when we enter in with this attitude, expands us and makes us grow spiritually. It saves us from the narrow and rather selfish "gimme-gimme" type of prayer, using God as a sugar-Daddy who has to give us what we whine for. With too much one-sided petition-prayer, we become "wheeler-dealers" with God. We make bargains and even threats. Prayer is much wiser when it is Praise. "Praise the Lord Anyway" is a great motto. It teaches you how to turn everything into a blessing for your life.

> **"Sing a new song to the Lord; sing His praise in the vast assembly!"** (Ps 96).

GOOD SAMARITAN

Twenty-seventh Week of the Year, Monday   **Luke 10:25-37**

Whatever his intentions may have been, thanks to the lawyer for questioning the Lord about our neighbor, because the answer came in a most touching and instructive parable, "The good Samaritan." The parable brings to our minds very vividly what real Christian charity is. It confronts us with the question whether we, too, are good Samaritans.

We know about the law of love. We know our sentence on the day of judgment will depend on our charity to neighbor. And so we ought to ask ourselves: Are we usually "good Samaritans" to our neighbor, the aged, the sick, the poor? Or do we pass by them quickly as though we didn't notice they need help, not necessarily out of malice, but with a poor excuse. Let someone else help them. I'm too busy right now—I have my own family to take care of—I'll be late for work, and other excuses.

Many so-called "good" Catholics, when listening to a sermon on Our Lord's Passion and Cross, feel compassion and say to Our Lord that they would do anything to relieve His suffering. Our Lord gives them the test of their sincerity when He says to us, "As long as you did not do it for one of these least ones, you did not do it for Me."

His "least" ones, His hungry, His poor are all around us within easy reach of any sincere Catholic today. It isn't the amount you give or the time you devote to the help and comfort of the afflicted that counts most. It's the sacrifice you make out of the blessings God gave you. Even the poorest and the busiest among us can find occasions when we can be of help to someone in need. We can and should all be good Samaritans.

What a joy, O Lord, it should be to be channels of Your love, to be the loving touch of Your hands!

MARTHA AND MARY

Twenty-seventh Week of the Year, Tuesday   Luke 10:38-42

Jesus and the apostles are invited to the home of Martha and Mary. Lazarus, their brother, takes the apostles out to look at the cattle and the crops, but Jesus is tired. He has been doing all the work, while the apostles are standing around learning. By their own word in the Gospels, they are poor learners, too.

In the house we have nervous, energetic Martha: rush, rush, get a big banquet on the table, blow at the fire, stir the soup, clank platters and plates, check the meat in the pan.

Is Mary lazy by not helping her sister? "Not at all," says Jesus. Mary lives by the Spirit, and Jesus declares this to be of first importance. He is not, however, condemning Martha's hospitality. It's genuine, it's good, and Jesus knows Martha's faith. But there is a greater kind of hospitality, and Mary has found it. It is "listening to the Lord," opening not only our house but our mind and heart to Jesus.

Most of us are, or have been, the Martha type. We rush around and work long hours, and often for motives less than Martha's. Martha at least was working overtime to please Jesus, to take care of His needs, to honor Him. And our motives? To make lots of money, with which to maintain a fine house and every comfort—so as to live on what? On rice and milk for our ulcers? How often we forget: "You can't take it with you."

What is our hurry all about? Is it a leap into distractions, to save us from thinking? How many blunders are made by people who won't take the time to think, to pray, to meditate, to consult the Lord and His wisdom.

In this Gospel, Martha forgot that not only had she invited Jesus: Jesus had invited her, and that is the more important invitation, the "better portion" of which Jesus speaks. And what kind of hospitality is it to leave the honored guest alone, while both hostesses rush around in the kitchen? If you want to get close to the Lord, you can't rush around in the kitchen while leaving God out there somewhere. You must take the time to go with Him, sit at His feet, and listen to Him. This is what Jesus wants.

Stop everything and say, "Jesus, I'm here. I'm happy to spend this time with You."

PRAYER OF FORGIVENESS

Twenty-seventh Week of the Year, Wednesday   Luke 11:1-4

The disciples ask Jesus, "Teach us to pray." In the prayer He teaches them, Jesus tells us to say to our heavenly Father, "Forgive us our sins, for we too forgive all who do us wrong." We know how often Jesus told us that everything we say must be real, must come from the heart, must be pure and free from hypocrisy. Then surely He is teaching us here to forgive from our hearts whenever we pray, and thus we shall be open and able to receive our heavenly Father's forgiveness for our own sins.

Unless we forgive, we really hurt inside and we block the way to God's forgiving love. A Christian simply cannot hold a grudge, for that is the flesh, not the spirit. The Spirit of Jesus is always a forgiving spirit. When Jesus warned us not to judge others, He meant that we are not to resurrect the buried bones of past hurts. Rather, we should ask God to flood those persons with His healing forgiveness.

If we find this hard to do, we need to ask God for that greatest gift: the gift of a healing, forgiving love. Jesus will not refuse that request; He knows better than anyone how essential that gift is to our spiritual life and health. Here is a prayer we can use as a start in asking Jesus for that precious healing spirit of forgiveness:

Lord Jesus, I believe in Your unlimited love for me. I thank You for Your faithfulness to me. I praise You for Your forgiving love for me. I thank You for Your faithfulness to me. I praise You for Your forgiving love. Lord, You know what sins have hurt me, and how it all happened. Jesus, I want to be set free, free of the chains of all my resentments. Fill me with Your Spirit, Jesus, Your powerful Spirit of forgiving love. Share Your perfect love with me, that I may forgive all who have ever hurt me. I want to forgive them in every way. Jesus, I ask Your special blessing on all those sons and daughters of Yours who have ever caused me pain or humiliation. I forgive every one of them from my heart. Give them a full measure of Your love, Jesus, that they may be healed of whatever wounds in their life have caused them to hurt others. I love you, forgiving Jesus, because You are bringing healing into my life. Heal me, Lord: keep me open to the power of Your love. Forgive those whom I now forgive, that we may be reunited in Your heart. I thank You and praise You forever.

ASK AND RECEIVE

Twenty-seventh Week of the Year, Thursday   Luke 11:5-13

When His disciples asked Jesus to teach them about prayer, Jesus gave them the words of the Our Father. Then He followed with the advice contained in this Gospel. What in effect Jesus told us was:

1) That prayer must be persistent, a constant habit, day to day. Prayer is a fire which we cannot let die. It must be fed and cared for daily. Prayer is life: the fuel of our soul's very life. Only habitual prayer can bring results.

2) That prayer is necessary: in order to give us wisdom, to make us think with Christ. That we must "seek in order to find." That families and communities and nations decline and corrupt and fall if there are not enough men who think with the heart, who pray well and seriously, who ask that they may receive.

3) That prayer is the necessary expression of our human nature

itself. It is natural to ask to receive, to seek and find, to knock and be admitted. You and I were created to the image of God. We are made in His likeness. What does this mean? Two things, expressed well by a nine-year old boy to his religion teacher, when he was asked how we are made to the likeness of God. He answered, "God always was and always will be; we always will be, too, but we weren't always was."

He saw the important likeness and the important difference. "We always will be," and so we need to grow into that eternal state of happiness. We need to become more and more like God daily. Real, honest-to-goodness prayer will do that for us.

We are also unlike God, because we "weren't always was." We are not divinely perfect from all eternity. We are God's work, yet we are given freedom to become what we choose. Therefore we must work to become like God. If we do not, we lose that divine image.

Prayer is our natural, human, habitual communication with God, the necessary way in which we grow in that image of God.

> **Lord, make our hands to open wide for all,**
> **Lord, make our ears attuned to hear Your call,**
> **Lord, light our eyes to see Your love in all!**

GATHERING OR SCATTERING

Twenty-seventh Week of the Year, Friday   **Luke 11:15-26**

Jesus tells us in today's Gospel, "He who is not with me is against me, and he who does not gather with me scatters." He might have added in explanation: "He who does not help me carry the cross, actually makes it heavier: he who does not walk with me and talk with me and work with me and live with me, he surely is following someone else besides me."

If you wonder whether you are a true follower of Christ or not, whether you are for Christ or against Christ, you can easily find out by asking yourself—and a Friday is certainly a good day to do this— am I helping Christ carry His cross? Am I denying myself to be of help to others when they are in need? Christ gave His life for all of us. Am I willing to carry the cross a bit out of love for the poor, the needy, the lonely? Can I sacrifice a bit of my time, my energy, my money so that others may live more decently and more happily?

Are we with Christ in our thoughts and words? Is our prayer life such that Christ is often with us and we with Him? Friends tend to be together a lot. If we are for Christ, if we consider Him our friend, our beloved, we will be with Him regularly in prayer.

Christ is still with us in His Church. He makes His will known to us through the Church in many areas. Are we with the Church? Do we live for Christ by living with and for the Church? Or do we perhaps knock the Church and so knock Christ, show that we are against Him?

Again listen to His Word, "He who is not with Me is against Me."

Jesus, You are the Way, the only way. Only if we die with You can we truly be with You.

PRAISE GOD

Twenty-seventh Week of the Year, Saturday   **Luke 11:27-28**

What Jesus says to the woman here is an echo of what He said earlier to the seventy-two disciples when they returned from their missionary journey (Lk 10:17). The whole life of Jesus is praise of God, and He directs others to that same goal.

When the disciples praised Him and themselves for the power they had over demons, Jesus redirected that praise: "Do not rejoice so much in the fact that the devils are subject to you, as that your names are inscribed in heaven." At once Jesus Himself rejoices in the Holy Spirit and praises the Father for what He has revealed to these disciples.

Now, when the woman praises Jesus and His mother, declaring her "blessed" for having borne such a great prophet, Jesus again redirects that praise to God, and to those whose lives praise Him: "Rather, blest are those who hear the word of God and keep it." Jesus could read the woman's thoughts, as He had read His disciples' thoughts. To the disciples Jesus had warned, "I saw Satan fall from heaven like lightning." In other words, don't take credit as if you did the work yourselves. It was God's work, so give the praise to Him.

To the woman Jesus has the same advice: "If your meaning is, 'too bad I couldn't be the Messiah's mother,' just remember, you can be close to God, too. You can hear the word of God and keep it, too. And that is what made Mary, my Mother, the great woman she is. Mary has always turned her privileges and honors, as well as her trials, her poverty and hardships into praise of God. You can do the same, and you will be blessed. Most happy and blessed are those who listen to God's message, and respond to it, obey it, keep faithful to it in their own lives. Neither my Mother nor I seek praise for ourselves. Our lives are meant to be praise of my heavenly Father, and we praise Him by holding to His word, by carrying out His plan for us."

Thank you, Jesus, for pointing out what direction my life is to take. Give me light to listen to Your word, God's word, and to keep it faithfully.

WHAT IS WRONG

Twenty-eighth Week of the Year, Monday   Luke 11:29-32

Jesus says, "At the judgment the citizens of Nineveh will rise along with the present generation, and they will condemn it. For at the preaching of Jonah they reformed, but you have a greater than Jonah here."

It has become trite to describe our present day writings, dramas and films as excessively preoccupied with sin. This is "realism," we are informed, "facing our problems." Authors seem like contestants in a race to shock readers and viewers with the evils people can do, with the horrible dangers to which we are exposed, with the blood-stirring traps into which betrayers lead their victims.

There is danger here that we will thus become "lovers of darkness rather than light." Those "artistic portraits of life" will lead us into a false delight in wickedness. The evils dramatized before our saturated imaginations will cause us to think "we're not so bad after all," simply because we avoid the grislier crimes.

God condemned the ever wayward hearts of His people, but not without telling them clearly of the ideals they were to attain. He had instructed them thoroughly on justice and mercy, on true worship and reverence, on hospitality and charity.

There is no need for us to bemoan the rejection of Christ by the very people to whom He had been given, by the very nation which was to hold up the divine ideal before the world. There is no need, because on us has fallen this responsibility. To all appearances we, too, have failed. We cry out against abuses, but what is corrected? We say it is high time for reform, for a return to solid Christian living, but time passes and the opportunity passes. What is really wrong, that we are not able to correct what we say is wrong?

"What is wrong," writes Chesterton, "is that we do not ask what is right."

> **Lord Jesus, make us open to Your Word. You have told us what is right, but we listen so little and so poorly that we remain confused. Lord, teach us again and again to "hear the Word of God and keep it."**

ENTRENCHED SIN

Twenty-eighth Week of the Year, Tuesday   **Luke 11:37-41**

"Be on guard against the yeast of the Pharisees, which is hypocrisy." "Your law is my delight," sang the psalmist, long years before the Pharisees had multiplied that law into trivia, so that one could easily strain out gnats and swallow a camel. Pharisees throughout the centuries since—Christian and pagan alike—have faithfully followed that pattern.

Reform has always been cried for, at times even died for, but how seldom really tried for!

Is this why literary prophets complained bitterly of the "damned human race," writing savagely and even cruelly of the endless human foibles and failures?

Surely this hypocrisy of the rich and powerful inspires rebellion. Yet each new generation of rebels soon becomes an old generation of hypocrites. Is it too easy to rebel, to condemn and destroy, and too nigh impossible to lead, to plan, to build and preserve?

We cannot deny value to the prophets of doom, nor pretend surprise at the depression and despair of the young, whose eyes are opened to the shock of entrenched sin. But who shall build the new city if the old one is torn down? Who shall make sure it is better? Who shall preserve it from its own time of decay? Where are the prophets to lay the plans, and the builders to raise the better structure?

Watch the meetings called to solve serious problems. Listen to each person saying exactly what must be done, and then voting by a different standard, the standard of unscrupulous self-interest.

Lord, make us honest, genuine and truthful. Make us aware of the dangers of hypocrisy everywhere, but don't let us forget our own hypocrisies. This reform like all others, must begin from within—and that means within our own minds and hearts.

NARROW RELIGION

Twenty-eighth Week of the Year, Wednesday   Luke 11:42-46

See in the Gospel the divine wisdom of Jesus. He can see through the protective covering of the gimmicks we use to convince ourselves that we're great stuff and everything is fine. The Pharisees had their fine little religious rituals, but theirs was a self-centered religion. It was not a matter of listening to God. It was listening to oneself, glorifying a smug, narrow, formalistic fussing.

God's great demands for a deep charity, a deep consciousness of our neighbors' needs—that was over their heads. They "neglected justice and the love of God." But lest we misunderstand, Jesus clarified: "These greater things you should have done, and not leave the smaller ones undone." Ritual worship is important, too. Although religion is empty without an active practice of justice and charity, a love of others does not excuse us from worship of God. Both are needed!

Again the Lord shows His balance of mind, His honesty and His integrity. He is not the kind of radical who emphasizes one need at the expense of others. Jesus is indeed radical in the sense that He demands all; that He is never satisfied with half-truths or with a half-hearted religion. He demands a response which is full, open, unhindered by narrowness. He knows how to aim at dead center. "You cannot fool God by putting on a show of giving tithes to the temple. The essentials come first," says Jesus, "Justice to fellow man and love of God. These are the things you should practice—but without omitting the others."

Is our religion one-sided? Are we smug in our practice of the Faith, because we do a few things? How about the essentials we may be missing? Are we making it hard for other people to be good Christians, because of our bad example, our narrow half-way piety?

Be my judge, O Lord my God! Let me walk in honesty.
In Your Name I trust, my God! Search my heart and challenge me:
May Your kindness and Your truth light my path that I may see!

OLD COMPLAINTS

Twenty-eighth Week of the Year, Thursday   Luke 11:47-54

Jesus accuses the Pharisees of "taking away the key of knowledge." He not only assured them that they themselves have not attained to any wisdom, but their teaching has prevented others from knowing the truth.

The young are quick to detect hypocrisy in their elders. You hear them say, "My parents keep tearing into me for doing things that I know they do. What sense does that make?" Another one: "The older generation just doesn't understand. But I'm sure they were no better when they were young enough to enjoy life."

"They should yell at us. Look at the mess they made of the world."

"They keep preaching to us about the evils of drinking, and we can smell it on their breath every time they come home."

Are these complaints as old as the world? We may wonder. Each new generation of youth rises to accuse its elders of hypocrisy, to blame society for the world's evils, to blame even the God of their fathers—but no generation ever seems to have done much about it. What have *we* done about it?

The Pharisees of all centuries tried to solve this thorny problem by a multiplication of laws, a heavy armor of righteousness to be invoked freely by the authorities, to be too eagerly obeyed by the scrupulous, and easily ignored by the free-wheelers.

Hypocrisy is a two-edged knife. We use it against others to cover up our own failures. Why is it always so easy to see hypocrisy in others, but not in ourselves? There is no way out of the vicious circle, but the way of open honesty.

"Lord, that I might see!" prayed the blind man. It's a prayer we all need. We need the honesty of Christ, to see ourselves as we are. Hypocrisy can never be conquered, unless each of us learns to overcome our own. No one else can do it for you.

Free me, Lord, from words of hate, let no falsehood blind my way,
Let no evil plot be mine: make me holy day by day.
Wash my hands in innocence, at Your dwelling let me stay.

WEARING MASKS

Twenty-eighth Week of the Year, Friday   **Luke 12:1-7**

Once again Jesus speaks first to His disciples before addressing Himself to the crowd. He warns them to be sure to avoid the hypocrisy of the Pharisees, which He has just spoken about. Evidently Jesus knows how easy it is to fall into this trap. And so He says, "Be on guard." Watch out that you do not deceive yourselves.

What is hypocrisy? The very meaning of the Greek word from which it is derived is "pretending." When you pretend to be something you aren't, when you show an exterior that doesn't fit the interior, you are a hypocrite. A hypocrite wears a mask. He covers up his true face. He may act busy to cover up laziness or failure; he may pretend to be extremely prayerful to cover up shallowness.

Jesus is saying that a mask is no protection. It cannot give you anything solid, no honor, no peace. There is always the danger of being exposed as we really are. Wearing a mask makes one anxious, afraid of being found out. As Jesus says, "There is nothing concealed that will not be revealed, nothing hidden that will not be made known."

We all wear masks of one kind or another at times. We are all inclined to try to cover up our true selves. Heavy make-up is not the only mask we wear. We try in all kinds of ways to look more beautiful than we are. We do everything we can to hide our ignorance and other limitations. We wear the mask of Mr. Calm, because we want to cover up anxieties and fears. We wear the mask of Mrs. Busybody to cover up the fear of not being accepted. We all have tendencies to wear masks because we are afraid of revealing our true selves.

But Jesus says, "I say to you who are my friends, 'Do not be afraid of those who kill the body and can do no more.' " As disciples I promise you final victory, Jesus is saying. Isn't that enough? Isn't that our peace?

Lord, to be Your disciple demands honesty and openness. Help me, Lord, to take off the masks I have been wearing.

TRUE DISCIPLESHIP

Twenty-eighth Week of the Year, Saturday   Luke 12:8-12

Jesus continues His short discourse to His disciples before addressing the crowd. He tells them to be strong in the face of trials. The cost of true discipleship is suffering and persecution, but the final victory is certain. He says plainly that if they acknowledge Him before men, He will acknowledge them before God. But if they disown Him, He will also disown them.

The martyrs of the early Church must have been keenly aware of these words. They knew and believed in the promise of Jesus. In no way would they disown Him and lose out on that promise.

We are all called to be disciples. There is no "crowd" in true Christianity. All of us are to be followers of Christ. That's what it must mean to be called "Christian." These words of Jesus are addressed to us as well. We may not become martyrs as so many of those early disciples. Yet we need to be strong to resist the spirit of the world, its evil ways and watered down values. We are to live the true Christian life with a joy and love which acknowledges Christ before men.

Jesus told His disciples to expect persecutions. He takes for granted that they will be called before the courts because of their faith in Him. He says, "Don't worry, I am with you. My Spirit will tell you what to say and do."

Maybe we won't be called into court because of our faith in Jesus. But there are times in the lives of every one of us when we must confront the evils of the world. Let us not hesitate, because Christ has promised to be with us, to give His Holy Spirit to direct and guide us in the battle against the power of evil.

Truly there is a reward for the just;
Truly there is a God who is judge on earth! (Ps 58:12)

MERCY AND INGRATITUDE

Twenty-ninth Week of the Year, Monday   **Luke 12:13-21**

Jesus says, "Avoid greed in all its forms. A man may be wealthy, but his possessions do not guarantee him life."

A generous soul, God-centered and responding to the gift of faith, would see the emptiness of the material gain for which our pride thirsts—and thirsts in vain. Even an intelligent pagan without the gift of faith would see the emptiness of mere material wealth. He would learn from experience how paltry and frustrating is the "happiness" of worshipping golden images, seeking satisfaction in material goods.

Clinging to matter has warped our imaginations, and we have

convinced ourselves that God is far away, that God is hardly real. The distant, unattainable material goals seem deceivingly near. "Come, soul, you have goods in plenty laid up for many years to come. Take your rest now, eat drink, and be merry!" (Lk 12:19).

Thus greed conquers us. God is really near, but our burdened imaginations hardly see Him from afar. Wealth and comfort become our reality and seem always within reach. "One more gain," we tell ourselves, "and I've got all I want."

If I am "lucky" enough to get it, the fire of greed is fanned all the more. "One more gain—" but there is no end. Each new success becomes more bitter than the last, until finally we are insane with greed.

While we continue to invite punishment and destruction upon ourselves for our ingratitude and greed, God's mercy continues; His infinite patience pursues us.

Lord Jesus, may Your mercy at last conquer our ingratitude, even if it requires some hard-learned lessons. We remember, Lord, that the starvation of the prodigal son was not exactly an easy experience, but it did bring him back to his Father's house.

PREPARED?

Twenty-ninth Week of the Year, Tuesday   Luke 12:35-38

"It will go well with those servants whom the Master finds wide awake. Should he happen to come at midnight or before sunrise and find them prepared, it will go well with them." Jesus warns us to be prepared, "wide awake" and ready for His coming.

If every true lover on earth has realized his unworthiness of the beloved, how much greater is that conviction in the saints! We think of the story told of St. Perpetua the martyr. Thrown to the ground by a wild beast in the arena, she stood up again, combed her hair, and straightened her clothing, because she "didn't want to go to glory unkempt and soiled."

The departed souls know that they have arrived before God with too much of this world still clinging to them. They are fully aware that they cannot yet remain in God's company without much purification. St. Catherine of Genoa explains how gladly the departed soul avails itself of the opportunity to be cleansed. The soul in Purgatory, she writes, is like a freshly cut diamond. It is truly one of God's most beautiful creatures, and being directed toward God, it has not lost its primeval beauty. But it is far from perfect. The Divine Artisan must bring it to its full potential by polishing it. This is the process of purification.

These are earthly figures, but we who use them are earthly. Our experience has not yet extended beyond this world. We do know that we ourselves would not come before a great earthly personage—king, prince, or president—unwashed, improperly dressed, soiled or bleeding. If by accident we arrive in such a condition, we would look for a place to wash and prepare ourselves for the occasion.

How then shall we prepare for the Lord, who knows every corner of the mind and heart? Where shall we go to burn away our blemishes? "How did you come in here without a wedding garment?" asked the Master of his guest in the parable. But death, "coming like a thief in the night," caught us unprepared.

Lord, if the best of saints had to suffer so many things to be worthy of You, how far we have yet to go! Lord, have mercy on us all along the way!

MUCH GIVEN, MUCH REQUIRED

Twenty-ninth Week of the Year, Wednesday   Luke 12:39-48

"When much has been given a man, much will be required of him. More will be asked of a man to whom more has been entrusted." So ends the Gospel passage today. The immediate application is to the responsibility of the religious leaders to whom Christ gives more graces, but also expects more from them than from others.

We can and should also apply these words to the many gifts of

God we all have received, especially in this prosperous country of ours. We have been blessed greatly in a material way. Christ wants us to use these good things, because God created them and they are good. However, a part of that good consists in the way we use them in a responsible way. The way we do use God's gifts is determined by our basic commitment and attitude to God and neighbor.

This basic attitude must be lived out in our daily lives. Otherwise it isn't real. It is not just a matter of prayer. The road to God is partly through the world, the world of work, family life, our neighborhood. For it is in all these areas that we use God's gifts and return them to Him as He requires.

Our riches, our talents, our energy and efforts are all gifts from God. And according to the degree in which we have been given we must give. Our fellow men need us. If we own more than we sensibly need, the poor have a right to our surplus. If we have talents for leadership, our community should benefit from these qualities. We should contribute to the development of the created world through energetic and enthusiastic work. It is part of God's plan.

We should put the spirit of today's Gospel into practice in the circumstances of our daily life. Let us respond to Christ's message and give according to the measure in which we have received.

You have filled us, Lord, with your bounty. All our works are for Your glory and praise, and for the building up of Your people.

A BAPTISM

Twenty-ninth Week of the Year, Thursday   **Luke 12:49-53**

The words of our Lord in today's gospel reading are strong ones. "I have come to light a fire on the earth. How I wish the blaze were ignited." He is saying that he came to fire us up, to stir us into living for God; that we are like a fire, like a flame that has nearly gone out. Our faith is burning very low, if at all. We are constantly occupied with things of this world, and have very little time to give fuel to that little flame of faith in us.

Jesus says, "Make no mistake. I didn't come just to sneak you into heaven, to make Sunday Christians out of you. I came to set you on fire with Christian love, with a desire to witness to Me, a willingness to die to self so that others, too, might live. Why don't you let that fire, that blaze be ignited? It is My desire for you."

That fire will purify us, if we let it. It will make us true disciples, true followers of Jesus, ready to go with Him wherever He leads.

Jesus also says, "I have a baptism to receive. What anguish I feel till it is over!" He speaks, of course, of His passion and death, His cross. Only through that suffering, through that crucible, could He come to the joy of the resurrection and glory.

We, too, must be baptised with Christ in His cross, in His suffering. We must die to self and rise to Christ Jesus. We must deny self and live for others. And we will be in anguish until we arrive there.

Many people want to be healed; they want to be free from the inner chains that bind them: fear, worries, anger, anxieties, some of which even cause physical, bodily, illness. But they are not willing to go through the crucible, the dying to self, that they must go through first. So they are in anguish, and they will be in anguish until they are willing to go through that baptism. As long as self is in control we will be in anguish, in constant trouble. Once we have died to self, let Jesus be really in control, our anguish is over and we experience the joy of love, the joy of living for God, for others.

As Jesus says, this fire, this anguish, this baptism, this purification doesn't necessarily establish earthly peace. It may well divide us from loved ones.

Loyalty to Christ will mean we need to put all other loyalties in life second. If that creates divisions, let it be so. Jesus must be first in our lives if we are to have any lasting peace. Better a true and genuine peace with divisions, than a false peace created by not giving first place to Christ in our lives.

Jesus, I want to go through the baptism of the cross with You.

SETTLE IT NOW

Twenty-ninth Week of the Year, Friday   Luke 12:54-59

Jesus advises that we settle our disputes with one another before going to court. The court, the judge, and the jailer are not going to be so merciful! They will demand strict justice. Jesus was referring immediately to the divine judgment that would come, because His people refused forgiveness, they refused to settle matters with the Messiah on their way to this divine judgment.

He means for each of us to abide by that same advice. The opportunities we are given must be used now! Day after day, He offers us forgiveness. He taught us to pray to our Father in heaven, asking Him to forgive us, just as we forgive those who offend us. It is this everyday forgiveness of one another that prepares our hearts to be forgiven by the Lord. We must "settle with him on the way," by a spirit of charity and forgiveness. If we do not, it is the Lord who then takes over as our judge, and it is then a matter of strict justice. Therefore Jesus warns us to seek God's mercy in time. For "you will not be released" from that just punishment "until you have paid the last penny."

Every day, in every person we meet, in every member of our family, all over our neighborhood, God gives us opportunities to settle matters of justice and charity, so that we will be ready to meet our own judgment. What Jesus meant to say in the Gospel was, "Don't pass these chances by. I hold out to you these many opportunities. But each one comes only once. I think it will be a lot better for you to settle your spiritual affairs now, before you come to that final court."

The Lord has said, "Return to Me, do not oppress the weak; Assist the poor in charity; no malice shall you speak. Then from the gloom your light shall dawn, and night shall be as day: New life from fountains shall be drawn; new strength will guide your way."

(Is 58:10-11)

PENANCE

Twenty-ninth Week of the Year, Saturday   **Luke 13:1-9**

Jesus keeps prodding us to think about personal renewal. So let's think about it.

A starting place might be at the hopeful note you hear in that stirring story, "Down in the Valley," when Brad, the murderer, says to his girl, "I'll make it all up to ya, Jennie, I'll make it all up to ya, I swear." And isn't that what a lover with a heart would say to an offended loved one? That's the heart of penance, I gather from Isaiah, from all the Scriptures, from literature, from common sense, from everyday experience. If the dear little wife complains about the leaking roof, there's only one thing to do: kiss her, speak softly, and promise to fix it. That's penance on the inside. Then you get up on the roof, look over the situation, and either go to work or call the roofing company. That's the outside—proof and expression and completion of the inside.

Where do the negative elements fit in—the denials that scare us? Not because they're hard or distasteful, we say, but because they're horribly outdated and too comforting to some people who are missing essentials. Either because they miss charity in action or they don't develop one's personality. An oversimplification! Love itself demands negative things. It demands cutting out things offensive to your dear ones, it demands giving of yourself for them, and hence a denial of anything that may harm your love. Denying one's self is a healthy process. A pruned tree, a clipped hedge, a snipped tomato plant—all are healthier for it. Penance is healthy. Pruning of personal comforts is wise, because being smug and complacent is also being stagnant, and stagnation kills. Our human goals are best reached by denial of any garbage that side-tracks us.

> **You, Lord, will unite us, Your teaching will light us,**
> **With You our old self will be nailed to the cross:**
> **May sin no more blight us, Your mercy delight us,**
> **Your love we count our gain, all else we count loss.**

SPIRIT OF PRAISE

Thirtieth Week of the Year, Monday   **Luke 13:10-17**

The Lord tells us through St. Luke that the spirit of praise is not to be stifled but encouraged and nourished. When Jesus saw the crippled woman who was bent over and could not stand up straight, "He laid His hand on her, and at once she stood up straight and praised God." And in spite of the objections of the Pharisees, Luke says, "the people rejoiced at the wonderful things Jesus did" (Lk 13:17).

The same spirit of praise is there when Jesus heals the blind beggar. The healed man "followed Jesus giving thanks to God, and when the crowd saw it, they all praised God" (Lk 18:43). When Jesus raised the widow's only son from the dead, the bystanders praised God and said, "God has come to save His people" (7:16).

On Palm Sunday, when the crowds joined in praising Jesus, the Pharisees naturally objected. And there Jesus pointed out the necessity of praising God!

Luke tells it like this: "The large crowd of His disciples began to thank and praise God in loud voices for all the great things they had seen. . . . Then some of the Pharisees in the crowd said to Jesus, "Teacher, command your disciples to be quiet." Jesus answered, "I tell you, if they keep quiet, the very stones will start shouting!"

The implication is, God must be praised! We, His children, should be praising Him. If we refuse or neglect the praise of God, God will raise up others for that praise. And if we do recognize the wonderful works of Jesus in our lives, our natural response will be that of praising and thanking Him.

> Sing to God a song of joy,
> Sing to God in every nation,
> Sing His praises day to day,
> Tell His glorious creation:
> "Great is God in every way,
> Over gods His might and sway."
> Gods of heathens fade away,
> For our God has made all heaven;
> Praise the Lord through endless day,

To us all His love is given.
"Earth and sea, your chorus raise,
All creation, sing His praise!" (Ps 96).

THE RIGHT SEEDS

Thirtieth Week of the Year, Tuesday **Luke 13:18-21**

In the two comparisons of today's Gospel, Jesus shows us that He knows how to think big—in the good sense of the word. He's not in the numbers game; He's not out merely to attract a big audience. In fact, He knows that in a short time, on a fateful Thursday night, the number of His followers will be cut down to almost the irreducible minimum.

Yet Jesus shows here that His heart is filled with confidence. From the tiny mustard seed a huge shrub will grow. From the tiny amount of yeast the whole mass of dough will rise. Such is the kingdom of God: it may grow slowly, but it will grow, because it is lined up correctly with the heavenly Father's will.

Jesus is not worried about seeing big results in numbers or political clout before He leaves this earth. He is simply concerned that the right seeds are planted. In fact, can't we say that the plan of God for His people points to the humility and the complete trust of Jesus in the Father and in the Holy Spirit?

Jesus plants the seeds, but He leaves the phenomenal growth of the kingdom to the work of His successor, the Holy Spirit. After the ascension of Jesus, on the tenth day, comes the mighty wind and the spreading flame of Pentecost. Jesus leaves the growth of the kingdom of God to the work of the Holy Spirit in the lives of His followers. As bringers of the Good News, as missionaries of the Lord, we need that confidence, that humility and trust of Jesus. We ask the Lord to guide, so that we may plant the right seeds, and then we depend on the mighty work of the Spirit to make the kingdom grow.

**Bless the Lord, young rain in springtime,
Praise the Lord, white frost and cold,**

Ice and snow, bless God forever,
Praise Him as seasons unfold.
Day by day, sunrise and darkness of night,
Praise Him, great storm clouds and flashes of light,
Bless Him, good earth, ceasing never,
Praise Him for ages untold (Dn 3).

THE NARROW GATE

Thirtieth Week of the Year, Wednesday   **Luke 13:22-30**

The theme of today's Gospel is the unpopular one of the narrow gate and the fact that not everyone is going to make it through. It sounds as if Jesus has some rather strict standards, for He says, "Many will try to enter and be unable . . . The last will be first and the first will be last."

In other words he's telling us, "After all, we people in heaven have our standards! We're an elite group, but not by your worldly standards! You people go by the size of someone's bankroll, but here we go by the size of your heart, your love, your generosity, the quality of your character. In heaven we don't have your lousy prejudices. We take anybody, any color, size, or shape—as long as you have produced! What you have done is important here."

Education, parents, means setting your children on that narrow road! Show them how to stay on the road, so that they'll get to the right place. Good education sets limits, and within these limits you let your children use their own talents and energy, and they grow up self-reliant. But beyond the limits set by wise rules, they cannot step. A group of youngsters were in the kitchen banging all the pots and pans and doors and walls, like a rock-band. Finally one of them said, "I wish Mom would come and stop us! This noise is killing me!" Lots of people realize that confusion and mere noise is killing, and that we need someone to bring order into the mess.

We learn a lot from the example of Jesus. He was very interested in His Father's rules. "I always do the will of my Father." Self-discipline is the way we develop the character to be able to fit through the narrow door that leads to the kingdom of God. Those that make themselves first by pride and pushiness and lack of control will be last, says the Lord. And the last—these will be the first in God's kingdom.

> **In the garden Jesus praying**
> **In His agony is saying,**
> **"Father, may Your will be done."**

UNLESS THE LORD—

Thirtieth Week of the Year, Thursday   **Luke 13:31-35**

Jesus weeps over His fallen city, fallen from God long before it fell to the Roman army. And Herod—if his tomb, if kings' and emperors' tombs could speak to us, what would they say? "You look upon us as antiques from a dim past," they would tell us, "but there is one quiet message we bear, and that should be no secret, for your own prophets and writers have told you: All is vain that is not of God; all is vanity but to serve Him."

If we may allow prophecy to speak to our secularized world, we may surely read this lament of Jesus as a note to the leaders of our confused society:

"You toil much, you great scientific builders, you great political advisers, you great intellectual speech-makers—but have you noticed lately that your toil is in vain? You have wasted untold hours, days, months, years, on 'disarmament.' You would save the world for 'freedom,' you who abuse that freedom. You have appointed committees and established investigations until I fear you may run out of personnel, but do you on this account feel safe? Have your problems approached solutions?"

"You are men of good will, you 'seek solutions,' but are you pleased with the results?"

"I am but an ancient message scribbled by an evangelist now long dead, written on parchment now long buried in the dust. I have no recognized claim to your 'modern' ear—unless you have been thinking lately. Have you? Do you really believe that your world is closer to perfect than the world of my day?

"Or do you remember the psalmist's warning, 'Unless the Lord build the house, they labor in vain who build it. Unless the Lord guard the city, in vain does the guard keep vigil' " (Ps 127).

> Help us, O Lord, for faithfulness is dying,
> A darkened earth for honest men is crying.
> False lips and double hearts delight in lying,
> All trust denying.
> "Because they rob the poor and cheat the needy,
> I shall arise," says God, "And strike the greedy.
> The poor who cries to me shall never perish,
> His life I cherish" (Ps 12).

AS JESUS LOVES

Thirtieth Week of the Year, Friday   Luke 14:1-6

We must always put God first in our lives, then our neighbor, and lastly ourselves if we want to practice true Christian Charity, as well as the humility Jesus teaches us in today's Gospel.

He teaches us to be humble enough to forgive those who are against us. I'm sure it was not very pleasant to go to eat with the Pharisees. Five times Jesus was invited to eat with the Pharisees. He never once refused. He put forgiveness of others before His own feelings. Do we?

He also risked the envy and hatred of the Pharisees in order to show love for the sick man. He knew He might be ridiculed for healing on the Sabbath. He knew the Pharisees would envy Him because of the favor He would find with the people for curing the sick. But love came first with Him. Are we always ready to love, even when it puts us into some risk, some difficulty?

Jesus makes it very clear how important it is to be truly humble in order to practice charity. Our pride is frequently the main obstacle to love.

There is also the need for true sympathy. Charity demands being disturbed that others are suffering. We try to help an animal that is in trouble, even if we are dressed in our better clothes. How much more ought we to be ready to help out our fellow men when they need help, even if it may mean delaying our fishing trip, cause us to be late at the theatre or go hungry for a few hours.

Where do I stand? Am I really sympathetic? Am I disturbed at all the suffering in the world? Do I find practical ways in which to show my true concern to those in need right around me?

How gracious is your love, O Lord, to all those who call upon You. Let me be an instrument of Your love.

JESUS LAUGHED

Thirtieth Week of the Year, Saturday   **Luke 14:1, 7:11**

Did Jesus ever laugh? Yes! Surely He laughed to see the Pharisees pulling rank, stepping on each other's toes and pulling sleeves and beards to get ahead of each other. Jesus laughed at this scramble for first places. Were they afraid they wouldn't get enough to eat, or afraid they wouldn't be top-dog in the lineup?

We read that often the Pharisees were watching Jesus to see what He would do. It seems that He took the last place—imagine, the all-powerful God took the foot end of the table—and then He explained why: "Those who push themselves will be envied and disliked for it; those who put others first will be respected and honored for it."

Everybody dislikes a person who is proud and pushy and looks down on others. Even in the town tavern you hear people say, "One thing I can't stand is a guy coming in here and pretending he knows everything, acting like he's almighty God!" And like most judgments made in the town tavern, that's a wrong judgment. A guy who acts arrogant and proud is *not* acting like almighty God, but like the devil, who wanted to be better than God. We see how God acts in the actions of Jesus. Does Jesus act like a well-to-do executive? No. Look at the choices He made: poor parents; not a palace with a gold cradle and silk pillows, but a manger and straw in a cave for sheep. Who are His friends? Governors and emperors? No. A king was His worst enemy: Herod tried to kill Him. His first friends were poor shepherds who smelled no better than their sheep.

Who hated Jesus? The rich and proud—people who couldn't stand being in last place. How about us? Can we be more like Jesus? Yes, we must, to belong to His kingdom! Jesus says, "Blessed are the poor, the meek, the lowly." To His disciples He says,

> **"The greatest among you will be the one who serves the rest. Whoever exalts himself shall be humbled, but whoever humbles himself shall be exalted"** (Mt 23:12).

LOVE THE UNLOVED

Thirty-first Week of the Year, Monday   Luke 14:12-14

We notice in Luke's Gospel his constant emphasis on the compassion of Jesus, how Jesus keeps insisting on love of the poor, love of the unloved.

In today's passage Jesus suggests that we do acts of kindness, like inviting people to dinner, not only to those who will probably reciprocate, invite us in return, but also, and even especially, those who can't do such a return act of kindness to us. He even adds, "You should be pleased that they cannot repay you." Wow! That's going against the grain, isn't it? It is certainly contrary to the world's standards.

Maybe some of us are already thinking about Christmas presents. Do we usually give them only to those who will return the sign of love? Some families decide at Christmas time to give gifts to the poor anonymously instead of to each other. A pastor and his associate had annually given Christmas gifts worth about twenty-five dollars to each other. One year they decided that instead of giving each other gifts which they didn't need at all they would send a combined check of fifty dollars to the Bishops' Overseas Relief.

Jesus says, "Be pleased that they cannot repay." He is promising us joy, peace and happiness deep down if we act that way.

The poor are not only those with little of this world's goods. They are also those will little knowledge, few talents, poor looks, poor personality. There are many ways in which people are poor, and all need our love.

Loneliness is real poverty. You find it everywhere. Why can't we pick out someone we know who is lonely and show them love, invite them into our lives, love them in the way they need to be loved, in ways that will make them happy. Not try to make them over into our image, our standards.

Then we are truly imitating Jesus in His compassion, because the emphasis is on the other, not on ourselves.

Lord, I want to love the unloved because by Your love You have made them all lovable.

BANQUET OF PRAYER

Thirty-first Week of the Year, Tuesday   **Luke 14:15-24**

"A man was giving a large dinner and he invited many. At dinner time he sent his servant to say to those invited: Come along, everything is made ready now." Although these words of Our Lord in the parable refer mainly to the call of the chosen people to the reign of God and to the Gentiles' call as well, when many of the Israelites refused the invitation, we can apply it to ourselves, too.

We, too, have been invited by the Lord Jesus to a banquet, to partake in an intimate friendship with Him. Right at this moment He is calling us to an encounter, a dialogue with Him in prayer. Have we taken this invitation seriously?

Some of those invited in the Gospel parable made excuses: "I have bought some land and must go see it." "I bought oxen and I have to try them out." "I'm newly married—goodness, don't expect me to come." The master was not very pleased with these excuses and immediately invited others instead.

Do we regularly accept the Lord's invitation to prayer? Or do we find excuses, and put off our quiet time with the Lord until time runs out? If we come to prayer, are we too burdened with worldly cares and concerns which shut out the Lord, keep Him from speaking to us, from feeding us with His word?

There is no way our personal relationship of love, of friendship with Jesus can grow unless we accept His invitation to spend daily time with Him alone.

No one is denied this banquet with the Lord. It is simply up to us to come, to put aside our worries and material interest for a short time daily, or put them in His hands, and let Him speak to us, love us, hear us, make us His own.

Lord, we thank You for your call to friendship with You in prayer. Speak, Lord. We are here to listen. Speak Your Word and make us whole.

THE DAILY DISCIPLINE

Thirty-first Week of the Year, Wednesday   Luke 14:25-33

In the Gospel, Jesus speaks of "taking up our cross." The great poet Chaucer observed that "he who wants a dear thing must give up a dear thing." That is to say, you cannot have real love without equally real self-discipline. Doctors, musicians, artists, scientists, authors, teachers, inventors—all have come to realize that greatness only comes with self-discipline. Honest work is a heavy cross, but it is accepted gladly for the love of the goal to which it leads. Spiritualize this truth, and you have the daily cross of which Jesus speaks. He gave up all else to pursue His great love, the Father's plan of redemption. "He emptied himself . . . accepting even death, death on a cross!"

The daily cross is the expression of love. A genuine love makes a person "deny himself" and follow Christ, for love makes him give up all that interferes with the pursuit of the beloved. Petty self-love considers every small annoyance or reversal a "daily cross," in which the mistaken "martyr" can indulge his or her self-pity. Really, most of the small troubles and dislikes which we consider great sacrifices are expressions of our selfishness. We exaggerate our tiny ill feelings into great artificial crosses. If we were truthful, we would see them as mere slivers, shavings, sawdust that fall here and there from the cross. But they are not the cross; they are the crude signs of our weakness.

The cross Jesus carried and asks us to carry is the life of Christian love itself, the great "baptism" toward which His whole life was directed. The cross is our state of life: our apostolate, our daily duties, our marriage, our family, our teaching, our nursing, our studies, our job—whatever work of unselfish love and devotion God has given us. The small daily vexations are only the shadows cast by that great cross, for the cross is the towering tree of overwhelming love. It is that great "dear thing" for which all other "dear things" are given up with joy.

Jesus, the triumph of Your cross is the triumph of Your perfect love.

JOY IN HEAVEN

Thirty-first Week of the Year, Thursday   **Luke 15:1-10**

The lesson Christ teaches us in this Gospel passage is clearly a lesson of hope and confidence in the great mercy of God. Are we not all sinners? Have we not all "gone astray" sometime or other as the lost sheep?

If we only had the justice of God to deal with we might well despair. There would seem to be no hope for us. But in the history of God's dealings with man in the Old Testament we see that His justice is always tempered with mercy.

The climax and crowning act of God's mercy was the Incarnation, the coming of His only Son, in human nature, to live on earth, to teach us God's mercy and love, to die on the cross in order to reopen heaven for us and lead us there. He left us His Church to teach us. He gave us the sacraments by which He still acts among us and reconciles us to the Father.

Think of the sinners Christ met during His lifetime: the robbers, the adulterers, the unjust tax collectors. Even among His chosen

Twelve, there was Peter who denied Him and Judas, the traitor. Yet never did He utter a harsh word against any of these sinners, except the hypocritical Pharisees.

No sinner was ever lost and no sinner ever will be lost only because of his sin. Sinners are lost because they will not turn to their merciful Father to ask His forgiveness. This kind Father constantly sends out a merciful call to sinners urging them to return to their Father's household.

All of us are sinners in some degree. We, too, must try to hear this call to ever greater repentance and more intimate love. That call is always there; in the Scriptures, in the sacraments, in this time of prayer.

Lord, You tell us that there is joy in heaven because of the repentance of one sinner. I thank you Lord for telling us that. I thank you for your mercy.

A CLEVER MANAGER

Thirty-first Week of the Year, Friday   **Luke 16:1-8**

The administrator cheated, making friends with money that wasn't his, and Jesus says, "The owner gave his devious employee credit for being enterprising." Do you think the Lord is advising us to be dishonest? If so, you are missing the point. For Jesus adds, "The worldly take more initiative than the other-worldly when it comes to dealing with their own kind." What He says is this, "Every one of you is an administrator, not an owner of the goods you have. Only the Lord God is the owner of your wealth. Why, then, aren't you like the administrator in my parable, who made friends by being generous with the owner's money?"

The point of Christ's parable is, "What we have is temporary, and it really isn't ours, it's God's. What we *are* is permanent. When our time runs out, it's what we are inside that will count.

Jesus, you see, saw life from all sides—inside and outside. He saw that the outside, the goods we accumulate, means nothing, but what happens inside of us will remain, and will grow in us, on and on into eternity.

If only we had the wisdom of Jesus! Too often we act as if that reality were turned around, as if our things were permanent, and what we are or become didn't matter very much. We look at our neighbors, too, for what they have rather than what they are. We look at what kind of worldly success they seem to enjoy, and we make that very unimportant external our standard of judgment. How foolish!

The real truth is deep inside, but it has many ways of expressing itself outside, too. It is the truth of putting God first in everything because we have everything on loan from Him, and He alone matters. It is the truth of self-giving rather than self-satisfying, because that is the lesson Jesus teaches us everywhere.

> O God, Your Name is Love itself:
>   I love You, Jesus Christ my Lord!
> Though all Your gifts have brought me joy,
>   to love You is my great reward.
> O Lord my God, You are all good:
>   what is not God is gloomy night;
> I seek Your love, as You seek mine;
>   then lead me on to Love's full light.

SPIRIT OF GIVING

Thirty-first Week of the Year, Saturday   **Luke 16:9-15**

"Make friends for yourselves through your use of this world's goods," says Jesus. Then He reminds us that we do not really own this world's goods, "If you cannot be trusted with elusive wealth, who will trust you with lasting wealth?

This is the Lord's teaching on the use of wealth, following the parable of the employee who was generous with his Master's money. What Jesus tells us in that parable is, "Your wealth is not your own to do with as you please. It belongs to God, and you merely are appointed to take care of it for Him. You will be held accountable by God for what you do with it."

That is why Jesus says, "You cannot serve both God and money." You cannot be a contradiction, living both a selfish and an unselfish life. You must make up your mind. What a warning to the very rich of our own day! Jesus says, "God holds you responsible for the misery of the poor, the victims of injustice, the low-income people who pay too much of the tax burdens which the rich have the power to evade."

Every honest person knows what Jesus is talking about: "You cannot serve both God and money." If you serve money, you grab all you can get, and this greed makes you more and more unscrupulous about how you get it: high wages without earning them; lust for pleasures at the expense of someone else who gets hurt by it; neglect of family and community duties in favor of selfish pursuits or sloth.

But if you serve God, you give of your best: your time, your talents, your loving concern, your earthly goods. You give out of love.

In the comparisons Jesus says, "By your actions, by what you do with the goods God gave you *on loan*, you are making a choice. And the choice you make will determine your eternity. It will also determine the kind of happiness you have on earth."

Lord Jesus, keep my soul awake and my spirit healthy. Remind me often of Your strong words, "You justify yourselves in the eyes of men, but God reads your hearts. What man thinks important, God holds in contempt."

NO MAN AN ISLAND

Thirty-second Week of the Year, Monday   **Luke 17:1-6**

"Scandals will inevitably arise, but woe to him through whom they come." With these words Christ warns His disciples about the greatest sin against charity.

The word scandal is often misunderstood to simply mean shock or astonishment. The true meaning of scandal is to lead someone into sin.

Scandal is given in various ways. We lead others to think or act sinfully, uncharitably, speaking against our neighbor, against the Church, by impure talk and by urging one to do something sinful. We give scandal by our actions in various possible ways: by offering opportunities or occasions of sin, giving someone too much to drink, by immodest actions or dress. We scandalize by omission. Parents give scandal to their children by neglecting their duties as Christians, missing Sunday Mass, not paying their debts, not correcting their children when they should.

Scandal is a very common sin. Many people are making their money through works of scandal; for example, by producing movies, publishing magazines, pictures or running places of amusement which are occasions of sin.

You see why Our Lord exclaimed: "Woe to the man through whom scandal comes!" What a great evil he perpetrates.

Scandal is an outrage against the Majesty of God. He calls His children to Himself. The scandal giver keeps God's people from answering that call. St. Bernard said that scandal givers are worse that the executioners of Christ. They counteract the effects of Christ's death.

No man is an island. We all influence each other. We will never go to heaven or to hell alone. Many others will follow us on account of our example, be it good or bad. Let ours be a good example, rather than scandal, and we shall bring many with us to a happy eternity.

Lord, I am my brother's keeper. May my life lead others closer to You.

TOTAL DEDICATION

Thirty-second Week of the Year, Tuesday   Luke 17:7-10

The words of Jesus here addressed to the apostles seem very hard, almost severe. Jesus is telling them that even when they have done all that He asks they should still consider themselves useless servants.

How can you explain these words of Jesus in light of His great love and understanding? We know that Luke's is the Gospel of total dedication. We are reminded here in this short parable that we must be unceasing in our labors for Christ. Who are we to judge or to criticize the Lord? It is His privilege to ask much of us, to make demands. We simply are to live out His Will, to do the work He asks of us. The emphasis of the short parable is dedication—work when the Lord asks it, rest when He so decides. We really can never stop and relax with the idea that we have done enough. That decision is up to God.

St. Paul understood this kind of total dedication well. He wasn't looking for any special praise or reward. In his first letter to the Corinthians he writes, "Yet preaching the Gospel is not the subject of a boast; I am under compulsion and have no choice. I am ruined if I do not preach it" (1 Cor 9:16).

These words of Jesus were addressed to His apostles. They had just told Him their need for an increase of faith, if they were to follow Him in all His demands. Jesus simply answers with His demand for total dedication as if to say, "If you trust in Me, do all I ask, your faith in Me will grow; it will be sufficient."

We are the present day apostles. Jesus expects total dedication from us, too. We cannot rest on our laurels. We have done nothing unusual in His service, even if we have done what He asks of each of us. We ought simply to work for the kingdom and put our trust in Him.

Jesus, we are useless servants. We have done no more than our duty. Yet we trust in You to increase our faith and our love.

GIVE THANKS

Thirty-second Week of the Year, Wednesday   Luke 17:11-19

Today's Gospel incident is a lesson in thanksgiving. It would seem that nine out of the ten lepers were not in the habit of thanking people. This surely had to be one of the greatest gifts any of them had ever received. Maybe we should excuse them by saying, "They were so excited over their healing that all they could think of was jumping on the nearest ox-cart for a ride home to show their families."

But strangely, Jesus didn't think of that excuse. He said, "Ten men were healed: where are the other nine? Is this foreigner the only one who came back to give thanks to God?"

How about us? Is the only time that we turn to God a time of trouble? Are the only words we speak with Him words of petition? Do we forget the Lord's love for us in everyday things like fresh air, sunlight, food, friends, life itself?

If we don't realize that what is great about our life is not what we do for God, but what God does for us, we will miss the whole joy of thanksgiving. Jesus really did not personally need the thanks of the other nine lepers. He would survive without it. So when He expressed sadness at their ingratitude, it wasn't a matter of Jesus feeling sorry for Himself "because nobody appreciates me." He was feeling sorry for *them. They* were the losers. The greatest joy of their healing would have been the opening of their hearts, the deepening of their love for God who had healed them.

This greater healing and deeper blessing they had missed. They had missed the deep inner peace and joy of thanksgiving.

Now give we thanks and praises sing,
All people of the Lord,
Rejoice we in the angels' King,
Praise God with one accord!
Awake we now, and loud our song
To God who made all things;
From high and low and wide and long
Each heart its worship brings.

KINGDOM TODAY

Thirty-second Week of the Year, Thursday   **Luke 17:20-25**

Jesus really wants us to know that He is the Lord. That His kingdom is here. That the Good News is now. He tells the sceptical and unbelieving Pharisees, "The reign of God is already in your midst."

The trouble with the Pharisees, and with us too, is that we don't recognize it, our eyes are blinded with too many other things. The Pharisees were blinded with their legalism. We are blinded by all kinds of earthly considerations.

Jesus says the kingdom of God is in your midst. It surely doesn't look that way, does it? There is so much suffering, so much oppression, so little love around us. Does God's kingdom coincide, is it compatible with, all the suffering, the hate, the anger, the violence, the lack of peace we see about us on all sides?

No, it doesn't. But it can be an answer, in fact the only answer, to all these ills. God's kingdom is not forced on anybody. Jesus as Lord is not a dictator, not a tyrant. He will not interfere with our freedom, a natural gift of our nature.

But if we let him be Lord, if we let his reign, his kingdom, rule in our lives, then his peace, his love, his joy and all those other fruits of the Holy Spirit will come to life in our lives.

If all peoples and all nations would accept the reign of God, accept the fact that Jesus is Lord of all, those evils that are so incompatible with God's kingdom—poverty, oppression, violence, lack of peace between nations, hatreds—all these would disappear. At least they would immediately be considerably lessened, and we would be able to recognize the reign of God in our midst.

So where shall we start. Well, we first must remember that nations are made up of people. So we must begin with ourselves. We must daily try to live with Jesus as Lord. His will must be the most important factor in all our decisions. Then we will be doing our part to make the reign of God visible.

Jesus, we do want You to be Lord in our lives, so that we may be a little sign of Your kingdom.

CONFIDENCE

Thirty-second Week of the Year, Friday   Luke 17:26-37

We all build walls to protect ourselves. We try to lay aside money for retirement, we plan for the future, we watch our health and try to develop our talents. But along comes a storm, and all of this can blow down.

Perhaps we think that Christ's awful account of terrible days to come is very depressing. To think about such a future spoils our happiness and shrouds everything with gloom and fear.

Quite the opposite. It was not for despair that Jesus so often talked about His second coming. It was to strengthen our hope and confidence, it was to build us a wall of trust and a bright future. The future He predicted, the picture of life He gave, is the one security that cannot tumble down. That wall of trust will be much higher when the storms of life are over. Jesus foretells days "of great distress," and we surely experience them. But He predicts them so that we will not run after false prophets. We mistake the meaning of His prophecy if we forget the final words of confidence and hope: "Heaven and earth may pass away, but My words will never pass." My promise is sure, He says, you can trust me completely.

> I will thank You, Lord, forever,
> All Your wondrous works I sing:
> In Your Name I glory ever,
> Joy of heart and peace You bring!
> Faithless foes turn back before You,
> Conquered by their rightful king!
> Lord our God, You reign forever,
> Justice guards Your royal throne;
> Humble folk You rescue ever,
> Poor and weak are called Your own:
> Happy those who love and trust You,
> Those who seek Your praise alone! (Ps 138).

PERSISTENT PRAYER

Thirty-second Week of the Year, Saturday   **Luke 18:1-8**

If prayer were not necessary, surely Jesus Himself would not have spent so much time at it. He really didn't need prayer for self-improvement. But it was His example that made the disciples ask, "Lord, teach us how to pray." They witnessed the power that prayer gave to the life of Jesus. St. Luke shows us Jesus regularly at prayer. He also gives us many of our Lord's teachings on prayer, as in today's Gospel.

In teaching prayer, Jesus stressed two points: 1) Be sincere, pray from your heart, make your prayer honest. He contrasted real prayer with the shallow lip-service of the Pharisees. 2) Stick with it, persevere, make it a constant habit. Thus He told the parable in today's Gospel to stress "the necessity of praying always and not losing heart" (18:1).

Prayer is the beginning of heaven. It means getting close to God, who is heaven. A good Christian teaches others how to pray; it is the greatest gift he can give them. Good parents teach prayer to their youngsters; they teach the young ones that they come to church to talk to God, not each other. They teach their children how to give God the best time of their day, because He deserves it.

Sister Laura Hesch, O.S.B., Indian missioner in Minnesota, used to read from a diary of notes kept by her grandfather, Anton Otremba, who as a young man had made a pilgrimage on foot to Rome from Germany. In his notes he wrote, "Every minute I am close to God. These are the happiest days of my life." Sister Laura used to say that her grandfather's diary of that pilgrimage was really a book of prayer. We can well believe it, since he writes, "Every minute I am close to God." That happens when we take our Lord's advice and form a daily habit of prayer: we come ever closer to God, and experience the deepest happiness.

Lord Jesus, open my heart to respond to Your teaching. Make me sincere and honest at prayer, open to Your word, and persevering in loving You at prayer.

FAITH SAVES

Thirty-third Week of the Year, Monday   **Luke 18:35-43**

"Receive your sight. Your faith has healed you." So often when healing a blind or crippled person, or curing a sick person, Jesus tells the person, "Your faith has saved you." Faith gives us the deep inner vision which is more important than the gift of eyesight itself. The person of faith has eyes open to see the finger of God tracing out the plan of his earthly life.

In everything he observes, the person of faith always sees God first. Perhaps we can illustrate it best by a contrast: the man of God aside of the man of nature—a good man, but a man of this world—let us call him a man of science. For there is a tendency in our present world to find a contradiction between God and science, as if God were not the master of science, or science the creature of God, as though science somehow could seal off the fountain of higher knowledge.

Basically such an assumption amounts to saying that since things are not persons, you cannot have persons; or if you accept the existence of persons, you cannot believe in things. Why can't we have both? Don't we have the evidence of both persons and things? Can't we know both creation and the Creator?

How does the man of science look upon this world? He studies things and the relations between things and the laws governing things. The world is made up of things—elements, combinations, and the laws governing them.

The man of prayer, looking at the same world, searches for a person: he studies the personal action, the purpose, the plan by which that Person moves the world.

Why should these be contradictory? The scientist searches the law, the man of faith speaks to the lawmaker. The scientist is after knowledge: he examines the observable, he classifies the material, he inquires after the secondary causes.

The person of prayer is after a personal relationship: he responds to the Person who has given the laws and the causes their meaning. He, too, is after knowledge, but for the sake of Love. This is the person Jesus praises when He says, "Your faith has saved you. You have gone beyond things to a trust in the Person from whom all things have come, and this trust, this faith, this love has worked powerfully in your life."

JESUS AND ZACCHAEUS

Thirty-third Week of the Year, Tuesday   **Luke 19:1-10**

"The Son of Man has come to search out and save what was lost." How had Zacchaeus been lost? Well, he had become rich by cheating people. So much he himself admitted. The corrupt Roman tax system made it too easy for him to get rich quick. Only these revenue men knew exactly how much tax money the empire was to get from each person. The collectors then pushed up the amount to as much as they wanted to take as their personal salary. The principle on which a tax collector based his own earnings was, how much can I get away with? How much can I squeeze out of each person before he rebels?

Now Zacchaeus is sorry. He wants to see Jesus. He wants to get close to this holy man who forgives sins. He says to Jesus, "Lord, I am honestly sorry. I'm giving half my belongings to the poor, and if I have defrauded anyone in the least, I'll pay him back fourfold." We know this man was telling the truth, because Jesus was never at any time afraid to call a liar's bluff. He had identified liars before, exposing deceit and hypocrisy.

Here is true penance, true repentance at its best. Zacchaeus makes his confession, but before Jesus absolves, Zacchaeus makes his very firm resolution. It does us little good to have God forgive us, if we have no intention to make good the harm we have done.

The remark has been made at times by people, "Confession doesn't do me any good." That may be. If so, it's because you ignored the third and most important part of the sacrament: reparation. Confession, contrition, reparation: all are needed! The sorrow is hardly real if there is no resolution that produces real fruit. Weakness of faith and weakness of resolution drain away the grace that should come.

"Not everyone who says to me, Lord, Lord, shall enter
the kingdom. Only those who do the will of my Father
shall enter."

ARE YOU IMPORTANT?

Thirty-third Week of the Year, Wednesday   Luke 19:11-28

If I were to walk up to you today and ask you, "Do you think of
yourself as a very important person in today's world?" what would
you answer?

Most people in the average audience would say, "No!" Many of
them would make it a very emphatic "No!"

Did you know that Jesus in today's Gospel says, "You're wrong,
Honey. You are definitely wrong." Did you know that everywhere in
the Bible, and especially in the Gospels, the Lord keeps telling each of
us just how important we are?

You see, that's the whole point of today's parable: the man who
buried the talent God gave him had too low an opinion of himself. He
was saying, "Everybody knows I'm not important, so what does it
matter what I do with the few talents I have? Let those other smart
guys run the world if they think they can. My talents don't count."

And Jesus says in the parable, "The Lord isn't fooled by that. He
knows very well what you can do and what you can't do. There is very
much you can do with the talents God gave you, and don't try to kid
yourself. You can't fool God, so why try to fool yourself? You know
that God is going to hold you responsible for how you use every gift
He gave you."

Maybe we think we're not important because we are not sure what
is really important. Let's go to the most important person in history,
then, to find out. Let's ask Him what we'd have to do to be a really
important person.

Jesus, that most important one, says, "The greatest among you
will be the one who serves the rest" (Mt 23:11). Jesus means, "What
you do out of love for God and neighbor, that's what is really
important."

Lord God, You have made us your children, brothers
and sisters of our Savior Jesus! What more than that
does anyone need to feel important? Lord, teach us to
live as Your true children, to recongize our importance
as members of Your family.

JESUS WEEPS

Thirty-third Week of the Year, Thursday   Luke 19:41-44

The evangelist Luke often uses strong contrasts in his narrative.
Think, for example, of the rich man and Lazarus, the Pharisee and
the Publican. This Gospel passage is preceded by joy and singing, the
Palm Sunday incident of Jesus entering Jerusalem and crowds of
disciples praising God. They loudly sing "Blessed is He who comes as
king in the name of the Lord! Peace in heaven and glory in the
highest." Now we immediately have Jesus, as He sees the city,
weeping over Jerusalem and saying, "If only you had known the path
to peace this day!" He goes on to predict the city's destruction.

Jerusalem could have become the principal center of Christianity,
the center from which the Christian message would go out to the
world. Because of its refusal to accept the Messiah, for only a very
short time was it the center from which Christianity spread. In the
year 70 the city was destroyed. Jesus foresaw all this.

So He wept over Jerusalem. He knew what would befall her
because she, that is, her inhabitants, refused to use God's grace. They
could have known what might happen. They wouldn't listen. They
rejected Christ.

What about us? Much of God's grace often comes to us in the
form of the teaching of the Church, preparing us for living the
Christian message, guiding us, giving us God's Holy Word. Are we
using God's guidance through the Church, getting a true sense of the
right and the wrong, growing in true values?

Or does Christ have to weep over us, too? Does He have to weep
over our families, over our communities, our cities? Does He have to
weep because of our weak faith, because we don't trust in Him or even

reject Him? Does He weep because we refuse to listen to His Word or to the guidance of His Church?

Lord Jesus, we do know the path to peace. It is in Your Word, in Your Church, Your Body here on earth.

GOD'S TEMPLE

Thirty-third Week of the Year, Friday   **Luke 19:45-48**

The prophets spoke of the Lord coming to cleanse His temple from all the impurities of the hypocritical and rebellious. The prophet Malachy observes (3:1-2): "The Lord will suddenly come to His temple.... But who will endure the day of His coming? For He is like the refiner's fire . . . and He will purify the sons of Levi."

In Luke's Gospel, Jesus enters the temple on Palm Sunday to purify it of all its corruption. The temple, God's relationship with His people, has been abused and polluted. The sad state of the Lord's house indicates why Jesus is rejected by the religious leaders.

Luke tells us that Jesus takes over the temple, so to speak, from the religious leaders of His day, who fail to give the temple its rightful use as a place of quiet for prayer and for godly teaching. Jesus tells the leaders they have made God's house a "den of thieves." The traders have cheated people by high-handed money changing. They have also robbed the people of a much more valuable possession—their place of prayer, a place where they can listen to the Lord, learn to know the true God and respond to Him with love.

So Jesus cleanses the temple for a place where He, the Lord, can teach His people. He chooses the temple because it has been the scriptural place where God meets His chosen people and lives among them. Jesus, the living temple of the unseen God, is fittingly present here in His Father's "earthly house," the God-man present among His loved ones.

From this time on, the living Body of Jesus is the new temple of God. So John tells us that when Jesus told the Pharisees, "Destroy this temple of God, and in three days I will rebuild it," He was referring to the temple of His own body. And that glorious, new, divine temple will be available to true worshippers everywhere. Thus Jesus tells the Samaritan woman, "An hour is coming when you will worship the Father neither on this mountain nor in Jerusalem." He indicates that worshipping the Father "in Spirit and in truth" will be done in the temple of Jesus Himself. Yes, God has come to His temple, the all-holy human nature of Jesus.

HAPPY ENDING

Thirty-third Week of the Year, Saturday   Luke 20:27-40

Are you the type of person who picks up a good book-length story and reads the last chapter first? Are you the kind of reader who says, "I never read a whole book unless I like the ending?" If so, some people will criticize you for it, but you may be wise after all.

Jesus tells us, "Don't lay out the book of your life without planning the end of it first. Never choose a way of life unless you like the ending."

Notice how Jesus answers the liberal, unbelieving Sadducees in today's Gospel. They say, "Sir, we're going to stump you on this one. You believers talk of a resurrection. All right, what about the old tradition of getting remarried after your husband dies? Suppose a woman did so seven times: which one is her husband in the general resurrection?"

Jesus answers, "Your trouble is, you never got the ending of the book straight. You don't believe in the happy ending of life, because you have never been clear on what life is. But I assure you, whether you understand it or not, the resurrection is real. In fact, that glorious ending of the book is what gives meaning to all the rest. Without that victory, the glory of resurrection, what good is there in the suffering and death? Is not the final ending the most important part of your life story? Does it not make all the difference as to how you live the rest of the story?

We join Jesus in the resurrection only if we join Jesus in everything else He does. And if we do, then all the sufferings and sorrows and hardships of life make sense. Not only that; they have a great and glorious and victorious meaning. A Christian who knows well the ending of the book can live the victory of Jesus over Satan, and live it every day.

Lord Jesus, remind me often of how things look at the end of the book, so that I will plan the rest of my life accordingly.

POVERTY

Thirty-fourth Week of the Year, Monday   **Luke 21:1-11**

In this Gospel incident, we see again the blessing of poverty and the curse of wealth. The poor widow truly loves God, for she gives Him all that she has. But the rich Pharisees, tossing in some of their great surplus, have no understanding of love.

Any persons dealing with voluntary offerings to charitable causes can tell you about the strange paradox involved in free will giving. It is not the rich who give most to the church or to other charitable causes; it is the poor. The poor carry a much greater share of the burden. There are exceptions to the rule, of course, buy anyone with experience here can tell you the poor and the needy are the ones who give generously. This has not changed since the day Christ observed the generosity of the poor widow in the temple. Is not this the obvious reason for the great inequalities between rich and poor the world over? If the rich had a charity in proportion to the genrosity of so many of their poor brethren, how much human suffering we would be able to alleviate.

No wonder, then, that Jesus spoke so often and in such strong words about the danger of riches. And no wonder that He always showed a preference for the poor. Nor was this something new. Throughout the Old Testament, God showed His special love for the poor, the abandoned, the suffering, the needy. The great story of the Passover of Israel from slavery in Egypt, is the story of God's mercy and kindness to the downtrodden and enslaved. The Book of Psalms is a ringing testimony to God's love for the poor, the forsaken, the man whom no one else cares for.

Jesus Himself chose strict poverty. God chose Mary in her poverty and humility to be His Mother. Jesus chose His apostles and disciples from among the poor. The majority of His friends and followers were the poor, and many of His richer disciples made themselves poor, to imitate their Master.

Father of the poor, come near!
Gracious Giver, quench our fear!
Light of human hearts, appear!

THIS PASSING WORLD

Thirty-fourth Week of the Year, Tuesday   Luke 21:5-11

In Jesus' day the temple of Jerusalem was an imposing and beautiful structure. Herod had just rebuilt it, from the years 19 to 9 B.C. It was twice the size of the former temple and more ornate. At this time it was still being furnished and decorated.

No wonder, then, that as Jesus was in the temple preaching, there were many people on hand, admiring the structure and talking about its beauty and imposing size. As a people they were extremely proud of it.

So they must have been shocked when Jesus predicted the destruction of this new temple, a destruction so great that "not a stone would be left on another." Immediately they wanted details. When? What signs would point to the end?

We can compare ourselves to these people of Jesus' time. Just as they were proud of their temple and its glory, so we are very proud of our achievements, our buildings, our technology.

"Be careful," Jesus says, "Don't be misled. All these things are merely passing. Yes, I want you to improve the earth, to use all the resources I gave you. But you are to use them for good, for my poor, to bring a better life to my least brethren."

What are we in the developed countries doing with our resources, our wealth? Is it mostly for instruments of destruction? Certainly we haven't found peaceful ways to help the underdeveloped and the undernourished.

As individuals, what are we to do? Can we have any effect on worldwide hunger and oppression? Surely we can. We might not see any visible effects, but if we use our wealth sparingly, live simple lives, and give our surplus to reliable charities, we will have made a dent in the problem of poverty and suffering in the world. Take care not to be misled by our American worldly values.

Teach me, Lord, the passing nature of this world and its glory. Give me a hunger for the glory that is to come.

PATIENCE IS LOVE

Thirty-fourth Week of the Year, Wednesday   Luke 21:12-19

"By patient endurance you will save your lives." Good advice Jesus gives here.

I don't think any of us have to think back very far to recall the last thing that tried our patience. Perhaps some driver cutting in front of us, or some member of the family holding up everybody else, so you came late to a Sunday Mass. How often children without thinking try their parents' patience.

Another area that puts our patience to the test is that of our own weaknesses and failures. We may never seem to say the right thing at the right time. We always have our foot in our mouths, so to speak. Or after getting to bed we can never remember whether we set the alarm or not. We may have resolved again and again to be more kind to someone, but again and again we have to confess our failure. The same old sins over and over.

A very severe test of our patience, one over which we have no control, is sickness. How do we accept such a trial from God or other tragedies, deaths, various disappointments? We've worked hard without realizing any fruits of our labor. We planted the crops, but there was too little or too much rain. We worked hard at our job and hoped for a promotion, but because of circumstances we got laid off. These are all real tests of our patience. It may not be a serious sin. But it can lead us to such faults as anger, bitterness, murmuring against God.

We also have to remember that to be patient means more than just bearing something, just being passive about it. Patience is love. And love must act. It means greeting others with a sincere "Good morning," or "Glad to see you," even though we feel disappointed about something, a bit down in the mouth.

How often differences in a family could be resolved with a little loving patience! How much more happily people could work together if all were a bit more patient with each other! How much more unity the virtue of patience would create in families, parishes and communities!

Our next test of patience is not far off. Are we ready for it?

Lord, we need not worry. Our lives are completely in your hands.

HOLD YOUR HEADS HIGH

Thirty-fourth Week of the Year, Thursday   **Luke 21:20-28**

Our passage today from Luke has two parts. The first tells us about the siege and fall of Jerusalem in 70 A.D. The second predicts the coming of the Son of Man at the end of the world.

Luke wrote his Gospel about the year 75 A.D. The destruction of Jerusalem had happened and Luke tells it as it happened. But the Parousia, the Second Coming of the Lord, had not taken place. Luke describes this in profoundly prophetic language. It is also clear from this passage that the second coming of Jesus and the end of the world were not to be very soon. Christians are told that they must wait, and while they wait, suffer persecutions. After all, Jesus had to make the Way of the Cross to arrive at His glory. Certainly His disciples should not expect less.

Faith in Jesus' Second Coming, in His final victory at the end of time, gave strong support to the early Christians, even though this victory might be long in coming. The same faith should support us, too. Hope in this final victory is the whole reason for living the Christian life, for being faithful to the call of Jesus.

Jesus says, "Stand erect and hold your heads high, for your deliverance is near at hand." The Greek word used here is apolytrosis, which means, a 'buying back.' God in His love has bought us back, His people.

The prophecy is for us, too. The promise of Jesus to come back holds for us, too. We have been delivered, redeemed, bought back. Forgiveness, healing, wholeness and new life can be ours in the sacraments of God's redeeming love. The final proof and sign of this redemption will be Jesus' coming in glory.

Let's hold our heads high. We are God's redeemed children. He has adopted us. We simply must remain faithful.

Lord Jesus, as we await Your Second Coming, we praise You for the redemption which You already bring to us in the Sacraments of Your Church.

LOOK AHEAD

Thirty-fourth Week of the Year, Friday   **Luke 21:29-33**

"The heavens and the earth will pass away, but my words will not pass." Jesus often speaks about "the end," His second coming. That "return of the Son of Man" is a personal time in the life of each of us, a future that inspires both hope and fear. How eagerly we try to forget that future, certain as it is.

King Louis IX of France, a great saint and a much loved king, was known to have revealed the secret of his success as a ruler and as a Christian. In the center of his palace garden, in full view of his bedrooms and staterooms, he had built a chapel, in which he had the bodies of his ancestors buried. And so at any time during the day, he could look out upon the place where he would be buried. Thus daily he could look death in the face.

One of his descendants, Louis XIV, asked why that awful reminder was built so close to the palace. His advisors said, "Your father and your saintly great-grandfather used to meditate on that place, their burial place. There *you* will be one day!"

This king replied, "Have it torn down! I don't want to die! Get it out of my sight!"

But all workmen refused; they were terrified at the thought of removing that burial chapel. It was sacred to a saint, and he was buried in that chapel. To remove it would be sacrilegious.

This even frightened the king. So instead, he built a new palace in a different location to escape the thought of his death. His life was accordingly: selfish, miserable, worldly.

By contrast, this reminder of death had made Louis IX a holy man loved by all, a man of prayer, a wise and charitable ruler. St. Ignatius advised, "Choose your vocation from the viewpoint of your death." Live for the next world, and you will be much happier in this world, too.

Lord Jesus, may we await Your second coming with faith, hope and love.

THE RIDDLE OF DEATH

Thirty-fourth Week of the Year, Saturday   **Luke 21:34-36**

"Pray for the strength to stand secure before the Son of Man." When we sorrow over the death of a loved one, we are confronted by the most important fact of human life: this life can in no way explain itself. Poets who have pondered and perceived the mystery of life, have surely suspected that we have here on earth no lasting home, but are created for another. "What is life," they ask, "but the prelude to an unknown song?" Yet they fear, as Hamlet did, that unknown song. The fear of death stands over them. Who, asks Hamlet, would

". . . grunt and sweat under a weary life,
But that the dread of something after death,

The undiscovered country, from whose bourn
No traveller returns, puzzles the will,
And makes us rather bear those ills we have
Than fly to others that we know not of?" *(Hamlet,* III, i)

What is more consoling, then, amid the darkness and confusion, the fears of human life, its sorrows and despairs, than the ever-calm and grave voice of the Church, the ever-living assurance of Christ: "I am the resurrection and the life; he who believes in Me, though he be dead, shall live."

In the face of death we can make one of three choices: 1) we can despair, seeing death as the end of all things for us; 2) we can doubt: we can wonder merely, and stand confused before the great mystery of life and death; we can miss the divine order and beauty of life and death; 3) we can open the flood-gates of hope and strength and truth and grace; we can see life, even in its sorrows, as the sure road to joy; we can see with St. Paul that if we suffer and die with Christ, we will surely rise with Him.

"The life of those who are faithful to You, Lord, is but changed, not ended; and when their earthly dwelling place decays, an everlasting mansion stands prepared for them in heaven."

SOLEMNITY OF ST. JOSEPH

March 19   Matthew 1:16-24 or Luke 2:41-51

There are millions of Saints that we paint in royal red because they shed their blood as martyrs of Christ, witnesses to His own gift of His life.

There are thousands of Saints painted in shining gold because they were brilliant with miracles, eloquent as preachers, or attractive as missionaries.

Thousands of Saints are pictured with pen, scroll, ruler or book, because they were great teachers, scientists, founders of schools or monasteries or convents or hospitals. Many saints were authors of great books that are still read by thousands today.

Numerous other Saints are painted in bright colors because they were great leaders: kings, queens, emperors, knights in shining armor, even generals of armies like the famous young girl, Joan of Arc; or brightly robed bishops, popes, abbots, mother superiors and father superiors.

Take just one long look at the choirs of Saints in heaven, and you are dazzled by all the color, all the talent, all the most tremendous of human accomplishments. Then we come to today's Saint. What dazzling colors do we find for him? Not the red of martyrs nor the gold of a world leader nor the pulpit of a great preacher nor the scroll of a great author.

No—just a small workshop, a little hut with a battered shingle over the door. It says: "Joseph and Son, Carpenters."

But—oh! Which of all the Saints in heaven has the last laugh when those great millions start telling stories of their earthly accomplishments? Isn't it the humble carpenter, St. Joseph? Which of the other Saints, except Blessed Mother Mary, can say, "Every day for almost thirty years, I sat at table with the growing boy who was the Son of God. Daily I watched Him develop into manhood; I taught Him His prayers; I showed Him how to make chairs and tables. I couldn't count the times I held Him in my arms when He was little; the times He hugged me and kissed me; the meals we ate together, the miles we travelled together, the joy we had in working together.

But, Joseph, you are and always were a humble man, a good and holy man. As you reflect on your memories of the boy Jesus, you thank those millions of saints for "the great honors you pay to the Boy that we raised, Mary and I."

FEAST OF THE ANNUNCIATION OF THE LORD

March 25 **Luke 1:26-38**

The Annunciation tells us of the wonders of God's promise and plan of salvation for us. That mystery is written on the earliest pages of Holy Scripture and repeated and enlarged through the years by the prophets. It is unfolded in a great wealth of prophetic images and symbols throughout the books of Moses and great prophets like Isaiah and Daniel. It is foreshadowed in every promise of deliverance which God gave to His people.

The Gospel tells us that God chose Mary of Nazareth to be the Mother of His divine Son. God chose Mary to be the very first Christian, the first and best of God's children to believe in the message of salvation in Jesus. The angel says to Mary, "The Holy Spirit will come upon you, and the power of the Most High will overshadow you; and so the holy One to be born of you will be called Son of God."

We rejoice today in what God has done for Mary. But we also rejoice in what Mary has done for us. She has given us the perfect example of how to be a true Christian. Mary's response to God's messenger is the key to her whole success, her greatness, her perfect womanhood. Mary says, "I am the maid-servant of the Lord. Let it be done to me as you say." There is her secret: "I have complete trust in the Lord; I want to be His servant; I want Him to rule my life. Whatever comes, I will never lose faith in my Lord; I will trust in His word—always."

Thus Mary is the ideal Christian, the model Mother, the perfect daughter of God. And she opens up the way of faith for each of us.

"My soul praises God my Savior, joy in Him exalts my heart,
For the Lord my God regarded His poor maiden's humble part.
Henceforth all shall call me blessed, for the Lord has honored me;
To His people who revere Him comes His mercy endlessly.
Lo, the proud like wind He scatters;
 they shall fear His mighty arm;
From their thrones the great ones tumble,
 but the humble fear no harm.

With good things He fills the hungry, leaves the rich in poverty,
Grants to Israel His mercy, promised through eternity"
(Lk 1:46-55).

THE HAND OF GOD

Birth of John the Baptist, June 24   **Luke 1:57-66, 80**

We can see in Luke's Gospel account of John the Baptist's birth
that he was destined for unusual things right from the beginning. He
was born of an older barren woman. His name came directly from
God through the Angel who announced his birth (Lk 1:13). Elizabeth
and Zachary were faithful. In spite of opposition from friends and
relatives they insisted on calling him John, and Zachary recovered his
speech because he was faithful.

"What will this child be?" and "Was not the hand of the Lord
upon him?" were some of the comments made by the neighbors. They
saw God's hand here in a special way.

Luke says John grew up and matured in Spirit. For a long time he
lived in the desert preparing himself for his mission.

So many times the Lord makes it quite clear to us what He wants.
Even though strongly opposed by relatives, Elizabeth and Zachary
knew God's will regarding John's name and they were faithful. Oh,
yes, we are faithful to God's will when it is easy. Are we as faithful
when we meet opposition, especially from those close to us? The Lord
is generous. He blesses His servants. Zachary was given back his
speech for being a faithful servant. We, too, are blessed so much by
the Lord. He appreciates all the good we do, all the praise we give
Him.

The common folk took notice of the hand of the Lord working in
the life of this young boy, John. Are we humble enough to see God's
hand in many things that happen in our lives and in the lives of those
around us? Or do we take everything for granted, ascribe it all to our
own efforts? Have we lost the sense of wonder at the mighty, and
sometimes very quiet, work of God?

The Lord's hand is in everything around us and in us. We see his
power in nature and the power of His spirit working within us.

"Not to us, O Lord, not to us but to Your name give glory because of Your kindness, because of Your truth" (Ps 115:1).

PETER AND PAUL, APOSTLES

June 29   Matthew 16:13-19

Some people would say that in today's Gospel Jesus made a very unpopular move: He established an authority. He established a Church to make laws in His name, and He placed a man, Peter, at the head of that Church.

Both St. Peter and St. Paul in their letters stress obedience to authority. They say, "Honor authority as given by God," and "Children, obey your parents," and so on. This should not surprise us. Jesus Himself gave a clear example of lifelong obedience to authority. In His early years it was to His parents and Mosaic law. In His mature years, it was obedience to God His Father. Jesus obeys His Father in the face of every hardship, opposition, and even death on the cross.

Obedience is the oustanding virtue of Jesus. But it's a bad word in our time, an "unmentionable." We say, "It destroys freedom; it cramps my style." Does it really? Or does it rather preserve freedom? What does obedience to law mean? Call it a new name and you see the point. Obedience is the same as cooperation and unity. To reach a decision and do something, you need authority, law, and obedience to do it. Otherwise you can argue forever. Fifty people have fifty different ideas. Unity is found in the authority, and unified decisions become law.

Laws are needed for learning arts and sciences. Here the experts are the authority, and require obedience for learning, in whatever field. To be a Christian you can't follow pagan rules. Only Christ's rules will do. So He had to establish an authority to develop, explain and apply the rules.

The law of love requires obedience. Ultimately, to love is to conform, to obey the wishes of the one you love. Only phony love insists on loving God my way rather than God's way. Phony love is really love of myself, not of God.

When we try to run our own life—alone—and when we shut out obedience to God, we have only our own power to draw on, and that's always too little. But by that love which prompts us to listen to the Lord, His power comes into us. Then we are sure to win.

Jesus, if I follow You faithfully, I cannot fail.

HIS PRESENCE AMONG US

Transfiguration, August 6   Mt 17:1-9, Mk 9:2-10, Lk 9:28-36

The Transfiguration story is recorded in all three synoptic Gospels almost word for word. Jesus takes his three favorite Apostles up a high mountain. He is transfigured—glorified—before their eyes. Moses and Elijah appear; Peter speaks; a cloud overshadows them and a voice from heaven: "This is my beloved Son; listen to Him." It's all over. Jesus is there alone with them.

A very short interval, yet the three Apostles become aware of Jesus' divinity. He is God. Just look at His glory. It was terrific. They wanted to stay in that situation.

We also would like to experience such a sight, become aware of the Presence of Jesus in our midst in all His glory. But Jesus seems to prefer that we usually just take Him at His word. He lived like any other human being and except for this incident with the three Apostles, He always looked just like any other human being. He was very ordinary, very human.

Today Jesus also lives in our midst in very ordinary ways, ways in which we can only recognize Him as God through faith. In the Gospel, the Word of God, we can recognize Jesus in His Divinity speaking to us, but only if we have faith. In the Sacraments He works among us, but to see Him there we need faith.

Jesus lives among us in a very ordinary way in our fellow men, in people. In our Christlike attitudes towards one another we feel His Presence in our lives.

Truly we "reveal Jesus" to one another by the way we think, act and speak in our daily lives as we live with and encounter each other. If you are kind, you let Jesus act through you; if you see kindness in another, recognize there the love of Jesus for you.

In this way we let Jesus continue His transfiguration, His revelation of Himself, through our own lives, revealing His presence, His glory and especially His love.

O Lord, it is good for us to be here at prayer with You.

TRIUMPH OF THE CROSS

September 14   **John 3:13-17**

St. Augustine, observing the paradox in God's plan of salvation, writes, "That Cross which was the derision of His enemies is now displayed on the foreheads of kings. The effect has proved His power; He conquered the world, not by the sword, but by the wood. The wood of the Cross was thought a thing of scorn by His enemies, who stood before it and wagged their heads shouting, 'If He is the Son of God, let Him come down from that Cross.' "

That wood scorned by men has been exalted to the heavens. The personification of the life-giving wood was taken up by an eighth century Anglo-Saxon poet, who made of it a beautiful masterpiece of Christian literature. The Cross itself speaks:

"Well I remember, a day in the woodland,
How I was hewed, hacked from my trunk,
Fierce fiends snatched and shaped me
For a spectacle of shame to men;
On their backs they bore me, bade me stand,
Made me bear their beaten criminals.
Standing I saw the Lord of love,
Maker of man, hasten Himself,
Come to the hill with courage high,
Me He ascended, mighty and strong.

"The young Hero stripped Himself, He who was mighty God,
Strong and stout-hearted, He climbed the towering Cross,
With spirit manly, for man He would save.
I trembled as He touched me, cowered as He clasped me;
Break down I dared not, nor fall with fear.
"Stand fast," my Lord commanded;
A rood I was raised; aloft I lifted the Lord,
King of high heaven; nor bend nor bow. . . .
"Hear and believe, my hero beloved,
That bitter woes had I to bear;
Hate and horror have happiness brought,
Far and wide men pray, as they ought,
By this saving sign; redemption bought
By the Lord of heroes, on me was wrought.
"For that am I splendid, high under heaven,
That I may heal my worshippers all.
The cruelest of gibbets I once was judged,
Hateful to men. But He, the Hero,
Opened by me the doors of life."

**Lord Jesus, we are redeemed because You were
unjustly condemned. You have won the everlasting
victory because You were defeated. "We are rescued
from the power of that lower darkness," because You
voluntarily steeped Yourself in unutterable darkness.
"So must the Son of Man be lifted up, that all who
believe may have eternal life in Him."**